The Church of Our Fathers as Seen in St. Osmund's Rite for the Cathedral of Salisbury

THE CHURCH OF OUR FATHERS

TOMB OF THOMAS, EARL OF ARUNDEL (*ob.* 1415), AND BEATRIX (DAUGHTER OF THE KING OF PORTUGAL) HIS WIFE

THE
CHURCH OF OUR FATHER

AS SEEN IN ST. OSMUND'S RITE FOR
THE CATHEDRAL OF SALISBURY

WITH DISSERTATIONS ON THE BELIEF AND RITE
IN ENGLAND BEFORE AND AFTER THE
COMING OF THE NORMANS

By DANIEL ROCK, D.D.

A NEW EDITION IN FOUR VOLUMES

EDITED BY G. W. HART AND W. H. FRERE
OF THE COMMUNITY OF THE RESURRECTION

LONDON
JOHN MURRAY, ALBEMARLE STREET
1905

THE
CHURCH OF OUR FATHERS

AS SEEN IN ST. OSMUND'S RITE FOR
THE CATHEDRAL OF SALISBURY

WITH DISSERTATIONS ON THE BELIEF AND RITUAL
IN ENGLAND BEFORE AND AFTER THE
COMING OF THE NORMANS

By DANIEL ROCK, D.D.
CANON OF THE ENGLISH CHAPTER

A NEW EDITION IN FOUR VOLUMES

EDITED BY G. W. HART AND W H. FRERE
OF THE COMMUNITY OF THE RESURRECTION

LONDON
JOHN MURRAY, ALBEMARLE STREET
1905

TO

BERTRAM ARTHUR

EIGHTEENTH EARL OF SHREWSBURY

EARL OF WATERFORD AND WEXFORD

Hereditary Lord High Steward of Ireland

ETC ETC

IN THE WELL-GROUNDED HOPE THAT, LIKE HIS EXEMPLARY KINSMAN THE
LATE GOOD EARL, WHOSE LOSS THE CATHOLICS OF ENGLAND ARE STILL
MOURNING, HE, IN HIS DAY, WILL BE ONE OF THOSE WHO WITH ALL THEIR
HEART FOLLOW THE TEACHINGS WHILE THEY LOVE THE BEAUTY OF THE
TRUE OLD BELIEF, AND WITH ALL HIS STRENGTH UPHOLD, IN THIS
LAND OF HIS SIRES, "THE CHURCH OF OUR FATHERS,"
THESE VOLUMES ARE DEDICATED BY
HIS FRIEND

DANIEL ROCK.

PREFATORY NOTE TO VOL. IV

IT has been found necessary to handle this volume more severely than the earlier ones, in order to bring it into line with them; for in the former edition it differed from the rest not only in type but also in arrangement; the clear line between text and notes was transgressed: Latin and English were mingled in the text in a confusing way, which was foreign to the other volumes. It seemed best, therefore, to bring this volume to better conformity by relegating Latin quotations to the footnotes, giving an abstract or summary in English, where it was necessary, in the place which they had occupied in the text. It has not been thought necessary, however, to bracket the additions which this handling has involved, or otherwise indicate the changes, since they are only changes in arrangement.

In the course of the four volumes there are a few of Dr. Rock's references which have baffled the editors: the citations have not as a rule been verified for verification's sake but where it seemed desirable to quote an improved or more accessible text. Thus new references have been supplied to the writers included in Migne's Patrology for the sake of uniformity and convenience: or again to those included in the Rolls Series for the sake of greater accuracy as well as accessibility: and the greater part of the baffling has been with texts of this sort, where the more critical editions have rejected passages which were allowed to have a place in older editions. Such alteration or verification has, however, not generally been made where Dr. Rock referred to a standard authority such as the *Acta Sanctorum :* and in many cases where better editions than those of Migne were readily accessible — such as Plummer's Bede, to quote one example—they have been given the preference.

The index has been made afresh, and since it now includes all the authors referred to, it does away with the necessity for a separate list of the authorities cited.

Our best thanks are due to several helpers, especially to Mr. Bedford Pim for much help in the matter of illustrations, and to Mr. Christopher Wordsworth for such valuable suggestions and criticisms as can only be had from one who has carried on Dr. Rock's work, as he has, both in popular writings such as his valuable *Medieval Services*, and also in his numerous scientific editions of liturgical works.

CONTENTS OF VOLUME IV

PART THE SECOND

CHAPTER XI

The canonical hours were kept by the Anglo-Saxons, 1. The people often joined in the canonical hours, 16. The service-books for the liturgy among the Anglo-Saxons, 18 The troper, 22 The missal rites, 31 The lower and higher orders in the Anglo-Saxon hierarchy, 53 The festivals of the year, 64 Public penance, 72 Ash Wednesday, 73 The way of keeping Lent, 75 Palm Sunday, 78 Holy week, Tenebræ, 82. Maundy Thursday, 85. Reservation of the Eucharist, 88. Hallowing of the holy oils, 89. Blessing of milk and honey, 95 Washing of feet, 95 The still days, 98. Good Friday, 99. Kissing the Cross, 99. The burial of the rood, 103 Mass of the presanctified, 105. Holy Saturday, 106 The Paschal, or Easter Fire, 107 The Paschal candle, 111 Easter Sunday, 116 Visit to the sepulchre, 116 Meats blessed, 118. Procession to the fonts, 119 The gang-days, 120. Use of lights, 121 Holy water, sign of the cross, 126. "Standing in the cross," 129. Deeds signed with the cross, 130.

CHAPTER XII

In what did the Sarum ritual vary from that of Rome, and of the Anglo-Saxons, 137. Choir Service, 138. The Wax-brede, 147 The Rulers of the Choir, 156. Bridal Mass, 200. The Mass for the Dead, 204 The blessing of Holy Water, 208 The Procession, 210. High Mass, according to the Sarum Rite, 214. The Fan, 229 The Eucharist used to

be kept hanging up over the High Altar, 234   A new way
of building the Altar and Choir, 242.   The Service-books
after Sarum Use, 245   Christmas Day, 248   St. Stephen's
Day, 249.   St. John the Evangelist's Day, 249   Holy Inno-
cents, or Childermas, 250.   The Boy-Bishop, 250.   The
Epiphany, or Twelfthtide, 256   Lent, 257   The Lenten
Curtain, 257.   The Processional Cross carried about in Lent,
was always of Wood painted red, 263   Palm Sunday, 264.
The Church-yard Cross, 266.   Tenebræ, 270.   Maundy
Thursday, 272.   Sheer Thursday, 272   The washing of
all the Altars, 273   The Maundy or washing of Feet, 274
Good Friday, 278   The Sepulchre, 278   The Kissing of the
Cross on Good Friday, 279   The Creeping to the Cross, 279
Holy Saturday, 281.   Paschal Candle, 283   Easter Morn-
ing, 287.   A Cross of Crystal, 290   Ascension Day, 292.
Whitsunday, 293.   All Hallows, 294.

POSTSCRIPT

The sources available since the first edition, 298   The
old English use in Anglican churches, 300   The illumination of the opening of the Canon, 305   Corrigenda et
emendanda, 308

INDEX   .   314

LIST OF ILLUSTRATIONS

The plates marked with an asterisk (18) appear now for the first time in the book ; those marked with a dagger (4) were in the previous edition, but have been more accurately made for this edition.

*The Fitz Alan Chapel at Arundel   *Frontispiece*

PAGE

*Corona, from a Scene representing St Clement saying Mass .   .   .   33

     A fresco in San Clemente, Rome   See Mullooly, *St Clement and his Basilica*, p 159, or Marucchi, *Éléments d'Archéologie Chrétienne*, p 297

*Crucifix   104

     From British Museum, Cotton MS Titus D xxvii , f 65ᵛ.

*The Deacon singing the *Exultet* .   .   112

     From an Italian *Exultet* Roll at the British Museum, MS Add 30,337.

*Monks in Choir .   .   .   157

     From British Museum, Cotton MS Domitian A xvii , f 121ᵛ , cp. the Frontispiece of vol ii

*Interior of a Friars' Church   .   161

     From British Museum MS. Add. 28,962, f 263

The Liturgical Fan   175

     Formerly the Frontispiece of this volume

*The Sacring Bell   .   .   178

     From British Museum, Royal MS 10, E 4, f 257

An old English Pax-brede, bronze gilt   187

PAGE

†The giving of the Pax . 188

This and the three following pictures are taken from *Dat Boexken vander Missen* See the illustrations in vol 1 See also the reproduction of the book in *Alcuin Club Collections*, No ▼ (ed Dearmer)

†The Pax-Brede standing on the Altar 189

†Draining the Chalice on the Paten 194

†Giving the last Blessing with the Paten 196

Liturgical Fans still in use (1853) 230

Dove and Canopy for the Eucharist 237

Cup and Canopy for the Eucharist . 239

Compare *Alcuin Club Collections*, No 1 Hope's *English Altars*, pl x fig 1

Modern Dove and Canopy . 241

The Inside of a Church during Lent 261

*Easter Sepulchre at Hawton Church . 279

Triangular Light for Holy Saturday 283

Compare the Sarum *Processionale*, ed Henderson, p. 80, or Wordsworth, *Salisbury Ceremonies*, p 84

Processional Banners; the Lion and Dragon . 292

Cp *ibid*, 122, or *ibid*, 93

*Modern English Chasuble . 300

The Community of S Mary the Virgin, Wantage

*Modern English Altar Cloth 300

Work of the same Community at S Paul's, Newton Abbot

*Modern English Cope 301

From S. Katherine's Convent, Queen Square, London

*Mitre of the Bishop of St Andrews . . 302

Work of Mrs Oliphant

PAGE

*Pastoral Staff of the Diocese of Albany, U.S A 302

*High Altar in Lent Array . 303
 St Mary the Virgin, Primrose Hill, London

*Egmanton Church 303

*The Beginning of the Canon in an Early Sacra-
 mentary . 307
 From Bodleian MS Auct D , i 20

*The Beginning of the Canon, Fourteenth Century 307
 From a York Missal, Fitzwilliam Museum, Cambridge, MS
  34, p 288

*The Opening of the Gradual 312
 From Trinity College, Cambridge, MS B xi 3, f 9

PART THE SECOND

CHAPTER XI

FROM having listened to our forefathers while they said, as it were, their belief aloud, let us now look at them going through the several public services of the Church; and, in the first place, we will see how

THE CANONICAL HOURS WERE KEPT BY THE ANGLO-SAXONS.

Together with their faith, from Rome was it that the Anglo-Saxons drew their liturgy also, and those books in which its rites were set forth.[1]

---

[1] Tertio decimo definitur decreto ut uno eodemque modo dominicæ dispensationis in carne sacrosanctæ festivitates, in omnibus ad eas rite competentibus rebus, id est, in baptismi officio, in missarum celebratione, in cantilenæ modo, celebrentur, juxta exemplar videlicet quod scriptum de Romana habemus ecclesia (*Concil Cloveshov*, A D. 747, can xiii, in Wilkins, *Conc*, i 96) Speaking of the ember-days' fast, Egbert, archbishop of York, says —Nos autem in ecclesia Anglorum idem primi mensis jejunium, ut noster didascalus beatus Gregorius, in suo antiphonario et missali libro, per pedagogum nostrum beatum Augustinum transmisit ordinatum et rescriptum . . servamus—*Dialogus Egberti*, in Thorpe, *Ancient Laws*, ii. 95 Quinto decimo definierunt capitulo ut septem canonicæ orationum diei et noctis horæ diligenti cura, cum psalmodia et cantilena sibimet convenienti

Like the rest of (2) Christendom then, seven
times within the day did each church-bell ring
and bid its clerks—from the subdeacon upwards
—to come thither and sing God's praises, morning, noon, and night;[2] and the parish priest
who forgot either of these duties was liable to
be punished by a fine.[3] Among those most conspicuous for their learning, or high position in
the Church at that period, we find such men
as Beda, Egbert, and Ælfric telling this country,
each in his own time, of this ritual usage, and
how it ought to be followed. Beda's notice of
the "hours" in general, or of some particular
part in them, is curious;[4] while the archbishop
of York, and the abbot who was afterwards called
to the primatial chair of Canterbury, both lay
down the canon-law upon this matter. So
thoroughly do those prelates' opinions agree, that
Egbert's Latin ordinance[5] seems to (3) have

---

observentur, et ut eandem monasterialis psalmodiæ parilitatem
ubique sectentur, nihilque quod communis usus non admittit,
præsumant cantare aut legere, sed tantum quod ex sacrarum
scripturarum auctoritate descendit, et quod Romanæ ecclesiæ
consuetudo permittit, cantent vel legant, quatenus unanimes,
uno ore laudent Deum.—*Concil Cloveshoi*, A D 747, in Wilkins,
Conc, i 97

[2] Ut omnes sacerdotes, horis compitentibus diei ac noctis
suarum sonent ecclesiarum signa, et sacra tunc Deo celebrent
officia —*Excerpt Egberti*, in Thorpe, ii 98

[3] If a priest, at the appointed time, do not ring the hours, or
sing the hours, let him make "bōt" for it —*Law of the Northumbrian Priests*, § 36, in Thorpe, ii 297.

[4] See notes 42, &c, further on

[5] Septem igitur sinaxes sancti patres canendas constituerunt
quas omni die clerus singulis horis canere debet, quarum prima

been put into Anglo-Saxon by Ælfric, who says :
—"Seven canonical hours they (the first four
general councils) appointed for us to sing daily
to the praise of our Lord ; as the prophet David
said in his prophecy : 'Septies in die, &c.' 'Seven
times, my Lord,' said he, 'I have said my praise
in one day, for the righteousness of Thy judg-
ments.' The first canonical hour is uht-song (or
matins), with the after-song (lauds) thereunto
belonging ; prime-song, undern (tierce) song, midday (sext) song, none-song, even-song, night-song
(complin). These seven canonical hours ye should
sing with great attention, to the praise of your
Lord, daily in church, always at the hour appointed ; and, in like manner, celebrate Mass at
the appointed time."[6]

That in their general construction and the
distribution of their component parts, the canonical hours were the same then that they are
now, we gather from a variety of documents. As
the ritual of Rome became the ritual for the whole
of Anglo-Saxondom, the comments written on
the first by such a man as our Alcuin's scholar

---

est nocturnalis sinaxis; secunda prima hora diei, tertia ipsa
hora est quam tertiam vocamus, quarta vero sexta hora est,
quinta nona hora est ; sexta autem sinaxis vespera hora est;
septimam namque sinaxim completorium vocitamus Has ergo
septem sinaxes omni die debemus sollicite reddere Deo pro nobis
et pro omni populo Christiano, sicut psalmista testatur dicens·
"Septies in die laudem dixi tibi super judicia justiciæ tuæ."—
Excerpt. Egberti, xxviii , in Thorpe, *Ancient Laws*, ii. 101.

[6] *Ib*, ii. 376 Uht-tide was the space of time between three
and six o'clock in the morning.

Amalarius, will show us most, if not all, of the most striking features in the other. From this great liturgical writer we learn that the first canonical hour began with those words of Psalm l. 17 [li. 15], "*Domine, labia mea aperies*—O Lord, Thou wilt open my lips, and my mouth shall declare Thy (4) praise": to them was added the "Glory be to the Father, &c." Then was sung that quickening call of the royal prophet, "*Venite, exultemus Domino*—Come, let us praise the Lord with joy, &c.,"[7] known in those times, as now, by the name of the "invitatory." After this, twelve psalms were chanted without any anthems, and the "Glory be to the Father, &c." only thrice repeated, once after every four psalms. Before the three lessons out of Holy Writ which, with their respective responses and versicles, were then recited, a blessing[8] was asked and given at each lesson, and but one short verse, followed by a prayer, was said.[9] Such was the substance of the first nocturn or service for the first watch of night on Sundays: for other days, six instead of twelve psalms were sung in the first nocturn.[10] The second nocturn consisted of three other psalms, each of which had attached to it its own anthem; the second verse was said before the three lessons were begun, with their proper re-

---

[7] Psalm xciv. [xcv]
[8] Amalarius, *De Ecc Offic*, iv. 3, Hittorp, 449
[9] *Ibid*, 501.
[10] Amalarius, *De Ordine Antiphonarii*, iii , Hittorp, 509

sponses. The third nocturn was just like the second, with the exception that instead of an anthem at each of its three psalms, *Alleluia* was recited.[11] As, by St. Benet's rule,[12] there were on Sundays and holydays twelve lessons, besides a lesson from the Gospel after the *Te Deum*, it is likely that the lessons at the second nocturn were drawn from the life of that saint whose feast happened to be kept; for we know that the (5) acts of a saint used, on his festival, to be read in church from the ambo or pulpit.[13] At the end of the third nocturn, on Sundays and saints' days, was chanted the Ambrosian hymn *Te Deum*.[14] While the psalms were sung, all stood; during the time of the lessons, every one, the reader only excepted, sat down.[15] Taken together, these three nocturns made what the Anglo-Saxons called "uht-song," but we "matins." On high days all the bells were rung for this service, and during the singing of it one wax taper at the least was lighted, and just as the office was drawn to an end the altar was fumed with incense.[16] If not

[11] Amal., *De Ecc Off*, iv. 9, in Hittorp, 460, 461 ; *De Ord. Antiph.*, I, Hittorp, 507

[12] Caps. xi, xiv, Holsten, *Codex Regularum*, ed Brockie, i. 121, 122 [see *P.L.* lxvi 435, 436, 449, 450]

[13] Sanctarum virginum Anatholiæ et Victoriæ præconia . schedarum apicibus quando rotante anni circulo natalitia earumdem catholici celebrant, in pulpito ecclesiæ recitantur.—St. Aldhelm, *Lib de Laud. Virginitatis*, lii [*P L* lxxxix 151].

[14] Amalarius, *Prolog in Ordin. Antiph.*, Hittorp, 505.

[15] *Ibid*, *De Ecc. Off.*, iv. 9, Hitt, 460.

[16] His diebus inter Innocentium festivitatem et octavas Domini

earlier, at least from St. Dunstan's times, in every minster-church, after matins and each of the other hours, psalms and a collect were said for the king and queen, as also for that house's benefactors, who, from having their names enrolled among its especial friends, were called familiars.[17] The Church's wish was, that in all collegiate (6) and monastic bodies, these nocturns should begin at such a time as to be ended just as morning's twilight broke, so that the next of her services, the "lauds" (or *matutinæ laudes*) might come on immediately after, like gladsome thankfulness for a new day then dawning, an emblem of Christ's second coming.[18] hence these "lauds," though forming by themselves a distinct canonical hour, were named by the Anglo-Saxons "after-song."[19] This service consisted of the same

---

. ad matutinas, licet, *Te Deum laudamus* non canatur et Evangelium minime festivo more legatur, cereus tamen accendatur et signa pulsentur omnia et thuribulum turificando deportetur (*Regularis Concordia*, in Reyner, *Apost Benedict*, Appendix, 85) This very valuable rule is the work of St Dunstan, and may be seen in the Cotton MS, *Tiberius A III*, with an interlinear Anglo-Saxon translation [*Anglia*, xiii, N F I iv]

[17] Peractis nocturnis, dicant duos psalmos, *Domine, ne in furore tuo*, et *Exaudiat te Deus*, unum videlicet pro rege specialiter, alterum pro rege et regina, ac familiaribus, cum collectis, *Quæsumus omnipotens Deus ut famulus tuus rex noster N , qui tua miseratione suscepit regni gubernacula*, &c . . et sic finitis omnibus regularibus horis semper agatur —*Regularis Concordia*, 80, 81 Of these especial friends we have before spoken (vol ii p 271)

[18] Amal , *De Ecc. Off* , iv , 9, Hittorp, 461. St Dunstan's *Regularis Concordia* says Quod si luce diei, ut oportet, finitum fuerit officium (laudes, &c) incipiunt primam —*Ut sup.* 81

[19] Ælfric says "And ye should sing sunrise, uhtan, and mass-uhton, always nine intervals with nine readings " Thorpe, *Ancient*

psalms as now; at the end of them was read a short lesson or little chapter: then was chanted the *Benedictus Dominus Deus Israel*, before which canticle of Zachary went a versicle; a prayer or collect said by the priest came next, and the whole ended with the blessing *Benedicamus Domino. Deo gratias.*[20] From the tenth century, perhaps sooner, the custom was to pray here for the king, the queen, and that particular minster's benefactors: then were sung different anthems —one of the Cross, another of our Blessed Lady, a third of that saint whose name the church bore. Afterwards a procession was made, first round the inside of the hallowed building, while an anthem was sung in praise of the saint whose (7) altar they were about to stop at for the collect.[21] The procession did not end at that spot, but after a very olden usage spoken of by Beda, as we said before, went unto the burial ground, where prayers and psalms were sung in behoof of such souls of the dead as had their graves there.[22]

Laws, ii 385; clearly marking the difference of the two parts of early daily service of the church, and separating them, as we still do, into matins and lauds

[20] Amal, *De Ordin Antiph.*, v, Hittorp, 510, 511, &c

[21] Post hoc, sequantur diei laudes. post *Miserere mei Deus*, &c, addant duos psalmos pro rege, reginaque, et familiaribus, *Beati quorum*, &c, *Inclina Domine*, &c Quibus finitis cantent antiphonam de cruce Inde, antiphonam de Sancta Maria, et de sancto cuius veneratio in præsenti colitur ecclesia, aut si minus fuerit, de ipsius loci consecratione Post quos, eundum est ad matutinales laudes de omnibus sanctis, decantando antiphonam, ad venerationem sancti, cui porticus, ad quam itur, dedicata est —*Reg. Conc.*, 81   [22] Vol ii., 272.

Prime-song began with *Deus in adjutorium meum intende,*—O God, make speed, &c.,—*Gloria Patri,* &c.,[23] at the end of which, from Septuagesima till Easter, *Alleluia* was dropped, and in its stead *Laus tibi, Domine, rex æternæ gloriæ*— Praise to thee, O Lord, King of eternal glory.[24] Then was chanted the psalm *Confitemini Domino quoniam bonus,*[25] &c. ; and after this the first part of the next psalm, *Beati immaculati,* &c No little chapter was read, but there was recited the versicle *Exurge Domine*—O Lord, arise, &c [26] The *Kyrie eleison,* &c., with the *Pater noster,* the *Credo in Deum,* and the *Miserere mei Deus,* Ps. l. [li.], &c., followed. At the end of this psalm, the priest said the versicle *Respice in servos tuos*—Look upon Thy servants, &c.,—and was answered by the choir with *Et sit splendor Domini*—And the glorious majesty, &c. ;—and then he recited the collect *Dirigere,* &c. In many of the stricter minsters, the brethren, (8) at this part of prime-song, went from church into their chapter-house to hear ghostly reading.[27]

Undern-song, or tierce, was begun by the officiating priest intoning *Deus in adjutorium,* &c. :[28] a versicle was then given out before each of the three psalms,[29] or rather parts of the same CXVIII.

---

[23] Amal , *De Ecc. Off* , iv. 2, Hittorp, 445   [24] *Ibid.*

[25] Ps. cxvii [cxviii].

[26] Amal , *De Ecc Off* , iv 2, *ibid* , 445.

[27] *Ibid* , 446, 447, 450

[CXIX.] psalm. A short lesson out of Holy Writ was read, the *Kyrie*, &c. repeated, and the collect said by the head-priest, who, for singing this last prayer both at undern-song and all other " hours," arose, alone of all theie, from the kneeling position[30] in which he had said, along with the choir, the *Kyrie*, &c. Having finished the collect, the priest called upon all to bless the Lord ; and thus ended undern-song.[31] In like manner, mid-day-song (or sext) and none-song, were gone through, the first having another portion of the CXVIII. [CXIX.] psalm, the other the rest of it, for their respective psalmody.[32]

After, however, undern-song or tierce, the first mass of the day, or the " morrow mass," was sung. This being over, all walked processionally to the chapter-house, where having bowed to the crucifix that always hung on the (9) eastern wall, and then to their brethren, each took his allotted seat. First came the reading of the martyrology, followed by

---

[28] *Ibid* , 448.

[29] *Ibid.*, 448, 450.

[30] Postremo surgit sacerdos vice illius sacerdotis qui in cœlo est, et quotidie interpellat pro nobis, et dicit stando orationem ... ut resurrectionem recolat ejus sacerdotis, cujus vicem tenet, surgit ab accubitu et stando dicit hanc orationem. Qui tamen prius jacendo orat cum cœteris, quoniam peccator est, cum peccatoribus prostratus est , et quia vicem tenet Christi, stando dicit specialem orationem —*Ibid* , 452. This same ritual custom is still followed in the Catholic Church, and the same beautiful symbolism expresses its meaning See also Amalarius again, *ut supra*, 457.

[31] *Ibid* , 452

[32] Amal , *De Oidin. Antiph* , vi. Hittorp, 513.

some prayers ; then, a chapter out of the rules, or were it a holyday, the gospel for the feast, upon which a sermon was preached. Those who had done any thing wrong, stood forth, and meekly acknowledging it, craved forgiveness ; all dead brethren were next prayed for, and immediately afterwards, in the same manner as they came to the chapter-house, so they left it.[33]

(10) At even-song, five psalms were sung ;[34] next to them came the lesson or little chapter, and after it, a versicle.[35] Then followed the canticle sung by our Blessed Lady, the *Magnificat ;* and,

---

[33] Incipiant horam tertiam, post cuius terminum dicat pro rege atque regina et benefactoribus suis psalmos, *Usquequo Domine,* et *Miserere mei,* subsequentibus collectis, deinde missam matutinalem celebrent . hoc expleto, facto signo a priore convenientes ad capitulum, ipso præcedente, versa facie ad orientem salutent crucem, et cæteris undique fratribus se vultu inclinato humilient. Tunc residentibus cunctis, legatur martyrologium Quo dicto surgentes omnes, dicant versum, *Preciosa in conspectu Domini,* &c, cum oratione ac versu, *Deus in adiutorium meum intende,* qui versus tertio repetatur ab omnibus priore incipiente, subiungentes, *Gloria,* humiliato capite. Sequitur oratio, *Dirigere et sanctificare,* &c . . Iterum autem residentibus legatur regula, vel si dies festus fuerit, Evangelium ipsius diei, de qua lectione a priore prout Dominus dederit, dicatur Post hoc quicunque se rerum alicuius culpæ agnoscit, veniam humiliter postulans, petat indulgentiam —*Reg. Conc,* 81 Finito hoc spiritualis purgaminis negotio, quinque psalmos, pro defunctis fratribus, decantent Ista vero omnia quæ diximus, post tertiam his temporibus agenda, Dominicis diebus omni tempore ante tertiam —*Ibid,* 82. In diebus autem festis . . ita protendatur Prima, ut capitulo facto, matutinalique missa celebrata, quæ die Dominica, de Trinitate celebranda est nisi alia festiva dies fuerit, si dies Dominica fuerit, mox accedant ad consecrationem conspersionis, si alia quælibet solemnitas, mox ad Tertiam.—*Ibid.,* 82.

[34] Amal, *De Ecc. Off,* iv. 7, Hittorp, 454

[35] *Ibid.,* 455.

to give full meaning to the versicle, *Dirigatur, Domine, oratio mea sicut incensum in conspectu tuo*—Let my prayer be set forth in Thy sight, O Lord, as the incense [36]—chanted on week days, incense was burned, then as now, at this part of the office : [37] a collect being afterwards said, this last of the canonical hours ended. For the matins, lauds, and even-song, the psalmody on each day of the week was so varied, that all the CL. psalms of the whole psalter might be gone through in the canonical hours within that space of time.

For complin or night-song, which is rather a complement to, than a distinct hour by itself of the divine office, four psalms, always the same, were sung ; [38] and, after them, the versicle *Custodi me, Domine, ut pupillam oculi sub umbra alarum tuarum protege me,*—Keep me, O Lord, as the apple of an eye, hide me under the shadow of Thy wings. [39] Then came Simeon's canticle, *Nunc dimittis.* [40] Like as at prime, so at complin, there was then no lesson. [41]

Such is the outline we have been able to draw from the larger and more detailed sketch left us by Amalarius of the Church's canonical hours according to the Roman usage—the usage too of Anglo-Saxondom—at the beginning of the ninth

---

[36] *Ibid*, 455

[37] *Ibid*, 456

[38] *Ibid.*, 457 ; and *De Ordin Antiph*, 515

[39] *Ibid*, 458

[40] *Ibid*, 458

[41] *De Ordin Antiph.*, 516

century. That these canonical hours were, in the main, the same when Beda lived, we may gather from those notices made on them by chance, and which lie scattered through the writings of our learned and sainted countryman. While Beda speaks of the (11) canonical course followed day and night, as a practice a very long time adopted by the Church when he wrote, he tells us that the custom of reading a lesson out of the Old or the New Testament, at each of those " hours," was borrowed from the Jews.[42] To the " invitatory" at the beginning of uht-song (or matins) he makes an especial reference ;[43] and in leading us to

---

[42] Commenting on those words, "they read in the book of the law of the Lord their God four times in the day,"—from Nehemias, or the second book of Esdras, ix 3,—Beda says. Quis enim non miretur populum tam eximiam habuisse curam pietatis, ut quater in die, hoc est primo mane, tertia hora, sexta et nona, quibus orationi sive psalmodiæ vacandum erat, auditui se legis divinæ contraderent . sed et in nocte quater, excusso torpore somni, ad confitenda peccata sua et postulandam veniam exsurgerent Quo exemplo reor in Ecclesia morem inoluisse, ut per singulas diurnæ psalmodiæ horas lectio una de Veteri sive Novo Testamento cunctis audientibus ex corde dicatur , et sic apostolicis sive propheticis confirmati verbis, ad instantiam orationis genua flectant. Sed et horis nocturnis, cum a laboribus cessatur operum, liberas auditui lectionum divinarum aures accommodantur —Beda, *Expos in Esdram et Nehemiam Prophetas,* iii 28 [*P.L*, xci 908]

[43] In his exposition on St Luke ii. 24, St. Beda says · Item cum intrans cubiculum clauso ostio oro Patrem in abscondito, turturem offero At cum ejusdem operis compares quæro, canendo cum Propheta *Venite, adoremus, et procidamus ante Deum, ploremus coram Domino qui fecit nos* · columbas ad altare deporto [*P L*, xcii 343] That this holy doctor of the Anglo-Saxon church had the " invitatorium" here before his eyes, Amalarius, Alcuin's scholar, tells us in *Liber de Antiphonarii Ordine,* i [Hittorp, 506] Another writer, who was most likely an Anglo-Saxon, thus glances at it also Sicut enim invitatorium dicitur ab invitando cum inchoatur officium noc-

understand why it is that (12) the Chuich has wished the third, sixth, and ninth, rather than the other hours of the day, to be more immediately hallowed by her public prayers, this same holy father lets us know the existence, at the period, of such a rite.[44] Through another observation which Beda drops by happy chance, we find that the canticle sung by Moses (*Deut.* xxxii.) took its place then, as it does now, among the psalms for lauds in Saturday's ferial office.[45]

The utter absence, in Beda's and Amalaiius's works, of the smallest mention about those metres known to us as hymns, would lead us to think that, at first, no such rhythmical compositions were embodied, as they are now, into the liturgy for the canonical hours, either in this island, or at Rome, at least up to the beginning of the ninth century.[46] That after that period hymns, as we

tui num, quando dicitur *Venite*, ita introitum ab introeundo cum initiatur diurnum Antiphonam autem ad Introitum Cœlestinus natione Campanus, pontifex Romæ constituit.—*De Ordine Missæ* Biblioth Bodl, MS Hatton 93, fol 1ˈ

[44] Tria enim tempora quibus Daniel in die flectere genua sua, et adorare legitur, tertia, sexta, et nona hora, ab Ecclesia intelligitur Quia et Dominus tertia hora Spiritum sanctum mittens, sexta ipse crucem ascendens, nona animam ponens, easdem horas nobis cæteris excellentius intimare et sanctificare dignatus est — S Beda, *In Acta Apost*, ii [*P L*, xcii 948]

[45] Confluebant autem die Sabbati in synagogis Cujus eo die devotionis agendæ hactenus in Ecclesia perdurat indicium, quæ ad memoriam priscæ religionis canticum Deuteronomii, in quo universus veteris populi status, quid videlicet offenso, quid propitio Deo meruerit, continetur, nonnullis in locis Sabbato dicere consuevit —*In Lucæ Evang*, iv [*P L*, xcii 373]

[46] Had hymns been a part of the canonical hours in Beda's days, hardly could he have helped telling us so while writing to his

now (13) understand the word, were sung in church
at the different hours, as well as just before the
gospel at mass, we learn from more than one
quarter. Many years before then, these poetical
productions came to be recited in the "hours,"
at the will and by the free devotion of individual bishops and abbots; thus what began with
certain cathedrals and minsters, grew at last into
the universal practice of Latin Christendom.
Some localities were not so quick as others in
following this liturgical usage, for while the monks
of Subiaco sang hymns at the canonical hours,
from St. Benet's time, it was not before the
twelfth [47] century that the clergy at Rome itself
began to use them; and until the last century,
perhaps even now, some few churches, like those
of Lyons and Vienne in France, admitted into
their breviary no other hymns than the one at
complin. [48] That our Anglo-Saxon brethren were

---

friend Cuthbert, for whom he had drawn up his little book, *De
Arte Metrica*, at the end of which he says. Hæc . . tibi collecta
obtuli, ut quemadmodum in divinis litteris statutisque ecclesiasticis imbuere studui, ita etiam metrica arte, quæ divinis non est
incognita libris, te solerter instruerem [*P L*, xc. 174] Of the
metrical compositions to be found in Holy Writ, Beda so speaks
as to let us know he did not understand them to be what we now
call hymns. Hujus modulatio carminis miserorum querimoniæ
congruit, ubi prior versus est hexameter, sequens pentameter
Quo genere metri ferunt canticum Deuteronomii apud Hebræos
et Psalmos cxviii et cxliv. esse descriptos   Nam librum Beati
Job simplici hexametro scriptum esse asseverant. [*Ibid*, 163]
[47] Grancolas, *Comment Hist in Breviarium Romanum*, 83
[48] *Ibid*, 84, and *Voyages Liturgiques de France*, 10

not slow in adopting these beautiful outpourings of the Christian poet, we know from one of Ælfric's enactments requiring each clerk to have, along with other volumes, a hymnar.[49] (14) Of such codices several early copies still exist in this country, showing us the Latin hymns overlined with an Anglo-Saxon translation;[50] and in these precious manuscripts we find not only each of the canonical hours had its own hymn, but that many of these hymns changed with the occurring festival.[51]

For chanting the canonical hours, the practice followed by the Anglo-Saxons was the same yet kept in all collegiate churches. Divided into two bodies sitting opposite, face to face, in the choir, the clergy on one side sang the verses of the psalms alternately with those seated over against them.[52]

If wayfaring, or something unforeseen, had hindered him from being with his brethren at public song-tide in the house of God, the devout Anglo-Saxon clergyman would halt before the first church upon his road, and, though its

---

[49] See note 58, further on.

[50] *The Latin Hymns of the Anglo-Saxon Church*, founded upon three of our best manuscripts, have been printed by the Surtees Society. [51] See the above work, *passim*.

[52]   Dulcibus antiphonæ pulsent accentibus aures,
        Classibus et geminis psalmorum concrepat oda,
        Hymnistæ crebro vox articulata resultet,
        Et celsum quatiat clamoso carmine culmen
        —St Aldhelm, *De Basilica ædif. a Bugga* [*P L*, lxxxix. 290]

Of Benet Biscop, as he lay in his last sickness, Beda tells us

(15) doors were locked, go through the unsaid canonical hour at its threshold.[53] Often, too, did the bishop, as he rode about the country to see his flock, say the psalter aloud with his clerks, on horseback.[54] But

THE PEOPLE OFTEN JOINED IN THE CANONICAL HOURS.

If the church-bells rang, by night as well as day, to bid priests and clerks to come and sing their Maker's praises, many, too, among the Anglo-Saxon lay-folk, heard and answered that same call to prayer, and, going to the house of God, joined themselves in heart and word with the chanting

---

Et quia nullatenus ad orandum surgere, non facile ad explendum solitæ psalmodiæ cursum linguam uocemue poterat leuare, didicit uir prudens, affectu religionis dictante, per singulas diurnæ sive nocturnæ orationis horas aliquos ad se fratrum uocare, quibus psalmos consuetos duobus in choris resonantibus, et ipse cum eis quatenus poterat psallendo, quod per se solum nequiuerat, eorum juuamine suppleret —*Hist. Abbat.*, 12 [Plummer, 1. 376]

[53] Venerunt incedentes per viam ad æcclesiam beato Papæ Gregorio consecratam. Ibique subsistens episcopus dixit beato Dunstano, "Compleamus hic apud oratorium sancti Patris nostri Gregorii nostram completorii horam " (*Vita S. Dunstani*, ab auctore coævo, *AA. SS Maji*, iv 349) [*R S*, lxiii. 15] Contigit ergo his impedientibus curis, ipsum horis vespertinalibus abesse, et cum psallentibus more solito non fuisse catervis . ipso tamen finiti diei crepusculo, cum se sequentibus scolasticis, ibat ad jam obseratam ecclesiam ut tardatum compleret officium Et dum foris ante ostium ecclesiæ psallendi gratia staret, vidit, etc —*Ibid.*, 350 [*R S.*, 18, 19]

[54] Such was St Wulstan's wont · Equo quocumque vadens psalterium frequentabat, orationales versus qui occurrissent ad fastidium concantantis crebro repetens. — Wil. Malmesb , *Gesta Pontif Anglor.*, iv. 140 [*R.S.*, lii. 282]

choir. Always did our great and glorious king Alfred carry about him his book of hours, hidden beneath the folds of his garments, on his bosom; and, while his daily wont was to hear holy mass, often likewise did he steal by night away from his household and bed, and went unknown to church to say his prayers, and sing uht-song or matins, with the clergy.[55]

(16) Though the going to hear the canonical hours at church on week days was left to each one's own devotion, the doing so upon Saturday evenings and Sunday mornings amounted to a religious obligation. Among our Anglo-Saxons the hallowing of the Sunday began with Saturday afternoon's service,[56] hence all were taught how " It is very highly fitting, that every Christian man very reverently honour that day; and it is fitting that every Christian man, who can accomplish it, come to church on Saturday, and bring light with him, and there hear even-song,

---

[55] Cursum diurnum, id est, celebrationes horarum, ac deinde psalmos quosdam, et orationes multas quos in uno libro congregatos in sinu suo die noctuque (sicut ipsi vidimus) secum inseparabiliter orationis gratia inter omnia præsentis vitæ curricula ubique circumducebat.—Asser, *De Rebus gest Ælfredi*, ed Wise, 16. Divina quoque ministeria et missam scilicet, quotidie audire psalmos quosdam et orationes, et horas diurnas, et nocturnas celebrare, et ecclesias nocturno tempore, ut diximus (*ibis.*, 41) orandi causa, clam a suis adire solebat et frequentabat.—*Ibid*, 44

[56] Et sollenne diei Dominice conservetur, ab hora nona Sabbati usque ad lucidum diei Lune (*Leges Regis Eadgari*, in Thorpe, *Ancient Laws*, ii 508) " And let Sunday's festival be held from the noon of Saturday until the dawn of Monday, and every mass-day's festival," &c —*Ibid*, 363.

and before dawn, uht-song (matins), and in the morning come with their offerings to the celebration of the Mass."[57]   A list of

The Service-Books for the Liturgy among the Anglo-Saxons

might easily be drawn up from the chance notices of such codices to be found amid the records of their times. Ælfric says :—" He (the mass-priest) shall also have for the (17) spiritual work, before he be ordained, these weapons ; that is, these holy books ; the psalter, and epistle-book, gospel-book, and mass-book, song-book (our breviary), and hand-book, numeral, and pastoral, penitential, and reading-book. These books the mass-priest should necessarily have, &c."[58]   And among the books bequeathed to the cathedral of Exeter by its Anglo-Saxon bishop Leofric, were several of such volumes.[59]   The whole series of that liturgical

---

[57] *Ecclesiastical Institutes, ibid.,* 421

[58] *Canons of Ælfric,* in Thorpe, *ibid,* ii 351   Long before Ælfric's time, Archbishop Ecgbeiht had given the same advice Nunc ergo o fratres qui voluerit sacerdotalem auctoritatem accipere ; In primitus propter deum cogitet et preparat arma ejus, ante quam manus episcopi tangat caput , Id est psalterium, lectionarium, antifonarium, missale, baptisterium, martyrologium, in anno circuli ad predicationem cum bonis operibus, et compotum cum cyclo.—*Egbert Pontifical,* pref xiii xiv

[59] They were ii fulle mæsse bec, and i collectaneum, and .ii pistel-bec, and .ii fulle sang-bec, and i niht-sang, and i ad te leuaui, and i. tropere, and ii salteras, and se þriddan saltere swa man singð on Rome and ii ymneras, and i deorwyrðe bletsing-boc, and iii. oðre, and ii. sumer raeding-bec, and i winter raeding-

service which Austin brought with him from
Pope Gregory, for the newly-planted corner of
the Church among the Anglo-Saxons, was contained in two great works : the Antiphoner, and
the Book of the Sacraments.   In the Antiphoner
were set down not only all the canonical hours,
both in their nightly and daily courses, but every
thing that the clergy had to sing in the choir
while the priest was offering up, at the altar, the
holy sacrifice of the mass : along therefore with
the words, might be found the (18) music to which
they were to be chanted.   The Book of the Sacraments contained not only the ordinary form of the
mass, and whatever belonged to its celebration
throughout the year ; but, besides this, it had in
it the forms of the other six sacraments, and the
rubrics for their administration.   As may be sup-
posed, the Antiphoner and the Sacramentary were
works of too unwieldy a bulk to keep, for any
length of time, their first size : both of them got
broken up, and each of their constituent parts was
made to form, by itself, a small and handy liturgical codex.   Out of the Antiphoner, even when it
had already been apportioned into four volumes,[60]

---

boc, and Regula canonicorum and Martyrologium, and 1. canon on
Leden, and 1 scrift-boc on Englisc, and 1. full spel-boc wintres
and sumeres, &c —Kemble, *Cod. Dipl. Anglo-Sax*, iv. 275.   *Cf.*
Leofric Missal, Introd , xxii , xxiii (ed Warren)
   [60] Inventa copia antiphonariorum, id est, tria volumina de noc-
turnali officio, et quartum quod solummodo continebat diurnale —
Amalarius, *De Ordin. Antiphonarn,* prolog., Hittorp, 503

came forth the full song-book or whole service for
the canonical hours, and which was called in old
Catholic England the "portous," but now the
"breviary"—the summer reading-book or-lessons
at matins, &c. throughout summer and autumn,
and the winter reading-book, the same for winter-
tide and spring—the responsorial or book of
responses—the antiphoner, strictly so called,
having in it the anthems sung during the canonical
hours—the collectaneum, or book of the collects
—the graduale, having in it the introits, the
graduals, the tracts, &c. sung by the choir at mass
(a book the Romans called "cantatorium,"[61] the
Anglo-Saxons "Ad te (19) levavi," because those are
the words of the introit for the first Sunday in
Advent with which this codex begins, the English,
Grail). The Sacramentary became subdivided into
the full mass-book, or missal properly so named—
the pontifical, or book for those rites which a bishop
only may perform[62]—a blessing-book, or the different forms of episcopal blessing bestowed upon
the people solemnly at mass each Sunday and
festival in the year[63]—the hand-book, or form for

---

[61] Notandum est, volumen quod nos vocamus Antiphonarium,
tria habere nomina apud Romanos   Quod dicimus Gradale, illi
vocant Cantatorium · qui adhuc juxta morem antiquum apud illos
in aliquibus ecclesiis in uno volumine continetur   Sequentem
partem dividunt in duobus nominibus   pars quæ continet respon-
sorios, vocatur Responsoriale; et pars quæ continet antiphonas,
vocatur Antiphonarius.—*Ibid*, 504

[62] Called by the Council of Chalkhythe, *Liber Ministerialis*, as we
before noticed, vol. 1. 143

the administrations of the priesthood in those
sacraments and blessings which they are allowed
to give.

Besides these, there were other liturgical codices
in use among Anglo-Saxon churchmen. From
the subdeacon upwards, every clerk must have
either known by heart,[64] or possessed a codex of,
the psalter with its rubrics to show what psalms
were to be said at matins, lauds, and even-song,
each day throughout the week. The "numeral"
was a calendar or directory which told the variations in the canonical hours and the mass, caused
by saints' days and festivals. The penitential,
a book which only shrift-fathers or priests who
heard shrifts (that is, confessions) might read,[65]
contained the penances decreed by the Church
for the different kinds of sin. The pastorale,
St. Gregory's work, and the "regula canonicorum," were each a looking-glass, as it were,
in which the clerk was to behold what manner
of man, to be worthy of his calling, he ought to
make himself. No sooner was the use (20) of metrical compositions allowed in the several canonical
hours and at the holy sacrifice, than the codices
wherein they were written, became requisites:
the song-book corresponded with the Salisbury

---

[63] One of such codices, the *Benedictional of Æthelwold* (mentioned
before, vols i. pp 24, 152, ii p 78), is among the most beautiful
manuscripts in this or any other country.

[64] See vol. iii p 4.

[65] *Excerpt. Egberti,* in Thorpe, *Ancient Laws,* ii 97.

portous and the Roman breviary; the hymnar contained those various hymns chanted at matins, lauds, prime, tierce, sext, none, even-song, and complin, all the year round; and the troper was a book having in it, besides other things, those verses to be sung along with the introit, the *Kyrie*, the *Gloria in excelsis*, the *Sanctus*, and the *Agnus Dei*, on the high festivals and chief saints' days in the calendar. Since of all these books, the only one now quite fallen into disuse, is

THE TROPER,

it may not be amiss to let the reader know what that liturgical codex contained, and the origin of its contents.

As those metrical compositions which, in contradistinction to the canticles of Holy Writ, we call hymns, were not sung, during the first ages, at any of the canonical hours, so neither was any kind of metre allowed in the solemnisation of mass. Towards the second half of the eighth century our own Alcuin had awakened among churchmen a strong and abiding taste for liturgical studies: our far-famed countryman was the first who drew up a list of masses to be said on each day of the week;[66] and ever since till now, the Church has gone on sanctioning this ritual practice, upholding it particularly as regards the

---

[60] See vols 1 p. 63, 111 p 154.

mass of the B. V. Mary for Saturdays. By his old schoolfellow Eanbold, made archbishop of York, Alcuin was sent in A.D 781 to Rome to fetch him back the pall (21) from Adrian I. The Roman pontiff and the Anglo-Saxon monk became warm friends, and both having kindred likings and a taste for the same sort of studies, Alcuin, who was so able, helped Adrian in a revision of the Antiphoner, an undertaking which, most likely, he had been himself the first to whisper into that pontiff's ear.

Long before Alcuin's time, had there crept into the ritual for high mass some customs which, though few and unimportant, are not without a certain interest. Of these, one was, at most of the festivals,—by way of showing the Church's gladness upon that particular occasion,—to keep on singing the last syllable in the *Alleluia* at the end of the gradual, for many minutes; and this drawing out of the notation for the *Alleluia*, they called the sequence. Another of these customs was to sing, besides this long chant of wordless notes, a rhythmical composition termed a " prose," in further honour of the occurring more solemn feast. A third practice which had also grown up, especially in the north and western quarters of Christendom, was that of weaving certain pious sentences, called by the Romans "festive praises," by the Franks " tropes," between the words of the psalm in the introit at mass, as well as all through the *Gloria in excelsis*, the *Sanctus*, and the *Agnus Dei*.

On all lower feast days the sequence, that is, the gradual *Alleluia*, with what would now be called its many bars of notes, was sung: on all higher festivals, besides this sequence, the rhythm called the prose, which generally consisted of between twenty and thirty verses, was likewise chanted. This long long roll of notation for the sequence, afterwards, in St. Osmund's times, got to be thought wearisome; it therefore became shortened, little by little, till at last this music for the *Alleluia* at the gradual, in losing its lengthsomeness, also lost its name. As, (22) however, the proses had always been loved by our people, they were not laid aside. But filling up, as they seemed to do, the room of the olden notation for the *Alleluia*, these proses dropped their own name, and took that of "sequence," under which those rhythms are known even now.

Through the sloth or forgetfulness however of the singers, the above-mentioned ritual practices were let to slip almost out of use, when Adrian I, at the warm beseechings of Alcuin, as well as to yield to the wishes of Charlemagne, brought them back again, especially with regard to the proses, or, as we now call them, the sequences, for which both our Anglo-Saxon monk and his friend and pupil, the Frankish emperor, had shown so strong a fondness [67] This was not all: at the beginning

(23) of the Antiphoner—as sent out after revision by Adrian I.—were some hexameters to the memory, and in praise, of St. Gregory the Great.[68] These verses, according to a practice followed on a few other occasions, used to be sung before, and not mixed up with, the introit, on the first Sunday in Advent:[69] as on that day commences the eccle-

---

[67] Hic (Adrianus Papa II, A.D. 867-872) constituit per monasteria ad missam majorem in solemnitatibus præcipuis, non solum in hymno angelico, *Gloria in excelsis Deo*, canere hymnos interstinctos quos "Laudes" appellant, verum etiam in psalmis Davidicis quos "Introitus" dicunt, interserta cantica decantare quæ Romani "Festivas Laudes," Franci "Tropos" appellant . quod interpretatur "Figurata ornamenta in laudibus Domini." Melodias quoque ante Evangelium concinendas tradidit quas dicunt "Sequentias"; quia sequitur eas Evangelium. Et quia a Domino Papa Gregorio primo et postmodum ab Adriano una cum Alcuino abbate delicioso magni imperatoris Caroli, hæ cantilenæ festivales constitutæ accommodatæ fuerant, multum in his delectato supradicto Cæsare Carolo, sed negligentia cantorum jam intermitti videbantur, ab ipso almifico præsule (Adriano II) de quo loquimur ita corroborat.e sunt ad laudem et gloriam Domini nostri J C. (*Vita Hadriani II*, in the *Liber Pontificalis*, quoted by Lebœuf, *Traité historique sur le Chant ecclésiastique*, p 103, &c., from a manuscript in the Bibliothéque du Roi, at Paris). Neither the Vatican, nor the other manuscripts upon which the two Vignoli, uncle and nephew, founded their valuable edition of the *Liber Pontificalis*, are whole in the life of Adrian II , not so the Paris codex, which gives that pontiff's acts entire, and for the knowledge of which we are indebted to the above-named learned French ecclesiastic

[68] Hic (Adrianus II) antiphonarium Romanum, sicut anterior Adrianus, diversa per loca corroboravit, et secundum prologum versibus hexametris ad missam majorem in die primo Adventus Domini J C decantandum instituit, qui similiter incipit sicut anterioris Adriani prœmium quod ille ad omnes missas in eadem dominica prima Adventus decantandum strictissimum confecerat, sed pluribus iste constat versibus —*Ibid*, p 103

[69] These hexameters, the first of which are

Gregorius præsul, meritis et nomine dignus
Unde genus ducit, summum conscendit honorem, &c,

siastical year, it was deemed fitting that the very
first service in a book like the Antiphoner, which,
for its arrangement and musical notation, owed so
much to the care of that illustrious pope, St.
Gregory, should begin with a thankful remembrance of him and his holy labours.   Hence
happened it, that to sing high mass on any festival, with all the solemnities due to such a day,
besides the (24) Antiphoner, it became necessary
to employ the troper,[70] or codex, which had in it,
—along with what of old were known as the sequences and proses,—also the introits, the *Kyrie*,
the *Gloria in excelsis*, the *Sanctus*, and *Agnus Dei*,
each mixed with words peculiar to the occasion,
and meant by the Church to tell her feelings, at
that time, of love, or gladsomeness, or thanksgiving, as it might be

Alcuin, it is allowed, was the best scholar in
Europe of his own times, and stood, in the world's
estimation, as high for his poetical as he did for
every other kind of composition.   Are we not
then warranted in thinking that, not only the

---

may be found at the beginning of most of the early codices of the
Roman Antiphoner · those which Tomasi gives (*Opp*, ed Vezzosi,
v. 1) no doubt furnish us with Pope Adrian I's "præmium,"
lengthened, as we learn, from the manuscript quoted in our last
note, by his namesake and aftercomer, Adrian II

[70] Hæ cantilenæ festivales . ab ipso almifico præsule (Adriano II) de quo loquimur ita corroboratæ sunt ad laudem et
gloriam Domini nostri J C, ut diligentia studiosorum cum antiphonario simul deinceps et tropiarius in solemnibus diebus ad
missam majorem cantilenis frequenteter honestis.—*Liber Pontif.*,
quoted by Lebœuf, *Traite hist*, &c, p. 104

verses at the head of Adrian's revised Antiphoner, but also those tropes and proses (now called sequences), scattered over it, and which, when picked out and written in a book by themselves, formed what was called the "Troper," came from the pen of our learned and liturgical Anglo-Saxon countryman? Be it so or not, this one thing is undoubted, that to Alcuin the troper of the middle ages owed a great deal; and in Alcuin do we behold the earliest discovered writer of those rhythms known to us as sequences.[71]

(25) Since among liturgical rarities, a troper is one of the rarest, our readers may therefore like to see a few extracts, which will show, at one glance, what those old tropes were, and how they used to be twined and threaded into the words of the daily service. Of Anglo-Saxon tropers, a copy was (perhaps yet is) in the library of St. Bavon's, Ghent; another is to be found amid that splendid collection at the Bodleian. Extracts from the codex in Belgium have been given by Pamelius,[72] and the following are drawn from the very valuable

[71] The passage we gave just now (note 67), from the Paris manuscript, with the life of Adrian II in its entire form, while it overthrows the learned Cardinal Bona's opinion (*Rer Liturg.*, ii. 3, 6), that the monk of St Gall, Notker (c A D. 904), was the inventor of sequences, helps us to win that liturgical honour for Anglo-Saxondom and Alcuin.

[72] At the end of his *Liturgicon*, ii. 611. From what Pamelius says in his preface to the first volume (fol iv), it would seem that the sequences were accompanied by an Anglo-Saxon translation

Oxford manuscript.[73] As a specimen of an introit, may be taken this:

DOMINICA DIE PALMARUM.

Israhel eggregius psaltes, clarusque propheta.
Sic quondam Christo dauid cantauerat almus,
Domine ne longe. *Sed celeri succurre mihi*
pietate paterna, Ad defensionem. (26) *Qui cupit*
insontem morsu lacerare ferino: Et a cornibus.
Ps. Deus deus meus respice.[74]

The *Kyrie eleison,* &c., was thus mixed with the tropes: *Xp̄e redemptor miserere nobis, Kyrrie-leison eia omnes dicite,* Kirrieleison, Kirrieleison, Kirrieleison.

O bone rex qui super astra sedes et domine qui cuncta gubernas eleison. Xp̄e eleison Xp̄e eleison. *Tua deuota plebs implorat iugiter ut*

---

[73] Under the press-mark, *Bod* 775 From one of the supplications in the litany Ut Æthelredum regem et exercitum Anglorum conservare digneris (fol. 18ᵛ), this codex must have been written out some time during Ætheldred II's reign, which lasted between A D 976-1016 Each of the "prosæ," which are at the latter end of the manuscript, had, at first, its own music written over every word Now, however, there are several of these proses, in which the old notation has been scratched out, and three red lines ruled Upon these lines other notes have been pricked But this second way of writing music is later than Guido d'Arezzo's times These alterations have been so nicely done, that some liturgical students might easily be led into the supposition that the beginning of this codex had been written a long while before the latter portions [See the edition of the Henry Bradshaw Society, vol viii, *The Winchester Troper,* and Frere, *Bibliotheca Musico-Liturgica,* i 69]

[74] *Winchester Troper,* 16

illi digneris eleison, Kirrieleison, Kirrieleison, Kirrieleison.[75]

The verses scattered through the angelic hymn were made to speak the feelings of the Church at the occurring festival; for example, at Christmas it was sung thus:

Gloria in excelsis Deo et in terra pax hominibus bone uoluntatis. *Pax sempiterna Christus illuxit gloria tibi pater excelse*. Laudamus te. *Hymnum canentes hodie quem terris angeli fuderunt Christo nascente.* Benedicimus te, &c.[76]

At the beginning of the different then called sequences, that is, chants for the *alleluia* at the gradual, we have this rubric: "Here for thee, the chanter, are all the sequences at hand which in their fair order are sung in the course of the year."[77] On some of the greater festivals, along with this *alleluia* (27) were joined a few words bespeaking the dignity of the day, or the honour of the saint, [or the name of the melody], thus, *Beatus vir Stephanus, alleluia,* with a very long

---

[75] *Ibid*, 47   Besides the above, there are twelve other forms of the *Kyrie*, with the appropriate variations; and the rubric at the head of the first is   *Incipiunt laude preces, quæ uoce latina hoc resonant, Miserē tuis O Christe misellis*

[76] *Ibid.,* 54   Then follow twelve other "laudes," for the *Gloria in excelsis,* and the rubric says   *Incipiunt Sancti modulamina dulciter ymni   Quem cecinere chori Christo nascente superni*   At p 60 we have   *Hymnus Angelicus Græca lingua compositum*   It is also given in the MS at fol 28, with its music in Anglo-Saxon notation, as well as at fol 72

[77] Hic tibi cantori sunt cuncta sequentia præsto
Que circulo annorum modulantur ordine pulchro. *Ibid*, 70

notation to it : *Justus Johannes ut palma florebit in cælo,*[78] in the same manner.

After these sequences came the *prosæ,* or proses, a kind of composition which, though the name may seem to us now to mean that they were unfettered by any law of scansion, were, nevertheless, written after some rule, if not indeed of the stubborn classic, yet of that easy, bending prosody set up in the middle ages, which sought for rhyming cadences rather than rhythm. The rubrics scattered through these proses show that, to each great festival of the year there was allotted its own, and that they used to be sung just after the sequence: *Incipiunt prosæ. De Nativitate Domini, Alleluia.*

> Celica resonent clare camenas agmina
> Nunc regis celebrando gratulanter nuptias
> Lux nova jam terras illustrat veteres pellens tenebras.[79]

Prosa ad sequentiam, Cithara, De Ascensione Dñi.

> Rex omnipotens die hodierna
> Mundo triumphali redempto potentia, &c.[80]

Prosa ad seq., In omnem terram, alleluia.

> Laude jucunda melos, turma, persona, &c.[81]

Prosa de omnibus sanctis ad Preciosa, alleluia.

> Alme cælorum turmæ concrepent alleluia
> In die hac sacrosancta sanctis omnibus splendida
> Que nobis extat annua sed his est continua

---

[78] *Ibid.,* 70.
[80] *Ibid.,* vii. 72.
[79] *Analecta Hymnica,* vii. 21
[81] *Ibid.,* vii. 183.

Celsa angelorum agmina laude iocunda Xp̄o resultent organa,
Mundanaque modulamina jam nunc intonant preconia cum
  letitia, &c

Followed by more than twenty other verses.[82]

(28) For the *Sanctus* we have :

Sanctus. *Admirabilis splendor inaccessibilisque
lux Pater Deus.* Sanctus. *Verbum quod erat in
principio apud Deum.* Sanctus Dominus. *Para-
clitus utriusque Spiritus.* Deus Sabaoth, &c.[83]

At the *Agnus Dei* there is a like mixture of
verses.[84]

After its canonical hours, and church-books,

The Missal Rites

of the Anglo-Saxon liturgy ask our next attention.

As their strong love for their mother in belief,
the apostolic see, had led the bishops of Anglo-
Saxondom, as early as the council of Clovesho
(A.D. 747)[85] to decree the adoption of the Roman
ceremonial, those rubrics themselves laid down
by Rome in those times, and the commentaries
on them, will show us what must have been the
ritual observances during the same period in this
country.

Of the altar, shrouded in its purple pall, overspread by white linen cloths, we have before

---

[82] *Analecta Liturgica,* 441

[83] *Winchester Troper,* 65, 66, and rubricated : *Incipiunt laudes
ad dulcia cantica* Sanctus

[84] *Ibid ,* 67, headed by · *Incipiunt laudes resonant quae dulciter
Agnus, Qui ueniens peccata pius tulit impia mundi.*

[85] See note 1, p. 1, of this volume.

spoken.[86] If, upon the hallowed board itself, there stood no candlesticks, hard by it, at least, lighted tapers were to be seen burning throughout the holy sacrifice ; for it had been enacted that always there should be burning lights in the church while mass was sung.[87] Very likely these candles were set upon those beautiful ornamented metal hoops called crowns, and hung from the church's roof. With a crowd of clerks, among whom seven acolytes carried each his burning (29) taper, and other three, as many kindled thuribles,— with seven,[88] five, or three deacons,[89] and the same number of subdeacons,—the bishop, arrayed in his chasuble, and having the book of the gospels borne before him, just at the moment that the choir began to sing the introit, walked forth into church, and on reaching the foot of the altar bowed himself lowly down, along with all his ministers, in worship of the divine Eucharist, which had been brought thither, and placed upon the holy table. Having blessed himself with the sign of

---

[86] Vol 1 pp. 211, 212.

[87] Thorpe, *Ancient Laws of England*, ii. 253.

[88] Beda must have had before his eye these seven deacons, when he said : Hinc jam decreverunt apostoli, vel successores apostolorum, per omnes Ecclesias septem diaconos, qui sublimiori gradu essent cæteris, et proximi circa aram quasi columnæ altaris assisterent, et non sine aliquo septenarii numeri mysterio —*In Acta Apost*, vi. [*P L*, xcii 956] That more than one deacon officiated on Good Friday, is clear from a rubric in the Leofric missal, which we have given in another part of this work (vol. i. p 109, note 9).

[89] Amalarius, *De Ecc Offic*, iii 5, Hittorp, 401

the cross, he bestowed the kiss of peace upon all the deacons, and, going·up the steps to the altar, kissed it, as well as the book of the gospels, which had been laid there wide open; then, walking up to his chair, he stood by it, having his seven deacons about him, while the subdeacons stayed below in the presbytery; and,

Corona above the Altar.

behind them, the seven acolytes, who, as soon as the *Kyrie* began, lowered their candlesticks, and put them in a row, from north to south, upon the floor. Two of the chanters,—known afterwards in St. Osmund's rite as the rulers of the choir,—at the proper time, uplifting their voices, sang together a call unto the bishop, bidding him to intone the angelic hymn: *Cantores gemini resonant hæc verba canentes.* Sacerdos dei excelsi, ueni ante sanctum et sacrum altare & in laude regis regum uocem tuam (30) emitte ; supplices te deprecamur, eia dic domine.[90] Turning himself about to the people as he stood at the altar, the bishop then gave out the *Gloria in excelsis*, which was taken up and ended by the choir. This hymn being sung, the bishop, with his face still beholding his flock, wished them peace in these words, *Pax vobis;* and then turning about, so as to look towards the east, he sang the collect, holding his outstretched hands uplifted all the while of this and other such prayers.[91] After the collect, the bishop sat down, the acolytes shifted their seven candlesticks, so that they might stand east and west, and one of the subdeacons went up into the ambo, or pulpit, on the south side of the choir, where he read, in a sort of chant, the epistle, during which all sat down.[92] Then the

---

[90] *Winchester Troper*, 54   See note 73, p 28, for a description of this important manuscript.

[91] Unde corpus illius (Elphegi, archiep. Cantuar et martyris) tanta attenuatum est macie, ut tempore sancti sacrificii, cum manus ecclesiastico more tensas in altum porrigeret, per medias palmarum juncturas claritas aeris perspici posset —Osbern, *Vita S. Elphegi, AA SS Aprilis,* ii 634   When Byron sang of Francesca's ghost on the shore at Corinth ·

> " Once she raised her hand on high,
>   It was so wan and transparent of hue,
>   You might have seen the moon shine through ; "

little did he dream that this beautiful thought of the transparent hand had been, eight hundred years ago, forestalled by a Canterbury monk.

[92] Amalarius, *De Eccl Offic*, iii 10, Hittorp, 407

precentor, standing on the lower step of this same ambo, intoned the gradual; and afterwards, if the solemnity of the day allowed it, the sequence, or prose, was also sung. The gospel followed, every thing belonging to the singing of which was done with much of the ritual's splendours   (31) The *textus*, or *evangeliarium*, was always beautiful, often quite magnificent. Though no other parts of Holy Writ were in this codex but the four gospels, whence the Anglo-Saxons called it "Christ's Book," still, of itself, it made a tall and bulky tome. Sometimes not a few of its leaves were dyed purple, whereon the writing was traced in golden or silver characters, and many a page glowed with elaborate and dazzling illuminations. Sheets of gold, studded with large pearls and precious stones, were not thought too good to be its binding.[93] Kneeling at the bishop's feet,—which he kissed, and then craved a blessing,—the deacon

---

[93] By far the most gorgeous and beautiful *evangeliarium* I have ever yet beheld is now in England, in that truly magnificent collection of manuscripts belonging to, and brought together by, one of our peers. This large glorious codex is bound between two plates of the purest gold, both of which are exquisitely worked, one side, as is usual, is much more elaborately wrought than the other, and for this reason, that it alone could be seen while the deacon was carrying the volume in procession to the pulpit or ambo This upper side is figured with a crucifixion in low relief, and our Redeemer's head is crowned with a royal diadem — not with thorns The whole surface glistens with pearls and gems curiously and admirably set. This binding is a sample of goldsmith work in the eleventh century, but the manuscript within it is of an earlier date.

who was about to sing the gospel, arose and
went to the altar, and kissed the *evangeliarium*
which lay there, and taking up that *textus* (always
large in size, and often quite heavy with its
beautiful adornments), leaned it against his right
shoulder athwart his breast, and so carried it
to the ambo on the north side of the choir.
Thither went before him two acolytes with their
tapers, and two subdeacons with thuribles sending forth clouds of incense: the former stopped
below, and put their candlesticks on the ground;
the (32) latter walked through the ambo, mount-
ing by one flight of stairs, and going down by the
other. When he got into the ambo the deacon,
with his face towards the men's side, or south,
hailed all present in these words, *Dominus vobiscum;* then, making the sign of the cross upon
his forehead and breast, as did every one in
church, he gave out from what evangelist the
gospel he was about to sing was taken [94] While
this procession was on its way from the altar, all
had risen to their feet and stood bareheaded; and
such among the old and weakly as might have been
leaning until then upon their staves, laid them
down. The gospel having been chanted by the

---

[94] At the beginning of every book of the gospels, in the celebrated Durham codex (*Nero* D.IV.), there is a list of those festivals
the gospels for which are taken out of that particular evangelist
In the published Anglo-Saxon versions, rubrics, to say at what
part of the chapter the gospel of each particular day begins, are
written all through the text

deacon, one of the subdeacons took the codex,
and going first to the bishop, held it open up
for him to kiss, and afterwards carried it about
to all the clergy as well as to the people, for
them to bestow a like mark of love and reverence
upon Christ's book. At this part of the liturgy,
the acolytes' seven tapers were all blown out;
and the sermon was preached [95] (33) Then came
the *Credo*,[96] which was no sooner intoned by the
bishop than the thuribles were carried waving
about the altar; and, as the fragrant cloud floated
by him, each one drew some of its smoke, with
his hand, towards his nostrils   When the *Dominus vobiscum* and the *Oremus* had been said,
the offertory was chanted by the choir.   The
subdeacon now came forth, bearing in his right
arm the paten, in his left the chalice, upon which
lay the linen cloth called the "corporal," or
"winding-sheet," which the deacon took off,
and having unfolded it, threw one of its ends
to the second deacon, so that both of them

---

[95] Ut omnibus festis et diebus Dominicis unusquisque sacerdos Evangelium Christi prædicet populo —*Excerpt Ecgberti*, in
Thorpe, *Ancient Laws*, ii 98

His ille (B Dunstanus) alloquiis cæterisque prædicamentis
salubribus ter sub una diei ipsius celebratione commissorum
corda affatim permonuit· primo enim ut ecclesiasticus ordo
post lectionis Evangelium jure insinuat, secundo post gratuitam
collatæ sibi potestatis benedictionem, tertio vero post piæ pacis
conferentiam quando communi carmine cecinimus, "Agnus Dei
Qui tollis peccata mundi, miserere nobis."—*Vita S Dunstani*,
ab auctore coævo, *AA SS Maji*, iv. 358 [*R S*, lxiii 51].

[96] The Nicene creed is, in more instances than one, called by
the Anglo-Saxons the "mass-creed"—Thorpe, *Ancient Laws*, &c,
ii 334, 344

could spread it out smoothly over the altar.
Waited on by the elder clergy, the bishop now
walked down to the edge of the presbytery, and
took from the people's selves their offerings of
bread and wine, which they brought to him,[97]
having their hands muffled up in a very clean
fine linen cloth or offering-sheet. The men first,
and then the women, came with their cake and
their cruse of wine. The bread-offerings the
bishop handed to a subdeacon, who dropped
them into a sheet, or a dish, carried by two
acolytes;[98] the wine to the archdeacon, who
poured it into (34) a large chalice held near
him by another subdeacon. Going to his chair,
the bishop, after washing his hands,[99] sat down,

[97] The *Ecclesiastical Institutes* say that it is fitting for all
Christian men on Sunday morning to come to church with their
offerings, to the celebration of mass —*Ancient Laws*, ii 421.

[98] Such sheets and dishes were thought worth being given
and received as bequests thus Queen Ælfgyfu (A D 1012) leaves
by will, annæ offring disc into Nunna mynstaer,—Kemble, *Cod
Dip Anglo-Sax*, iii 360, and in Wynflaed's will (A.D 995) we
read that Hio becwið into Cyrcan hyre beteran ofringsceat —
Ib., vi 130

[99] At his ordination the subdeacon received a basin, ewer, and
towel, to tell him one part of his ministry at the altar would be
to help at the washing of the celebrant's hands Besides being
made of the precious metals, these basins and ewers must, at
times, have been beautiful as works of art St Dunstan, among
other things, bestowed upon Malmesbury minster a fine one,
which bore upon it these verses —In hydriola quam, ut ministris altaris lympham funderet, fabricari fecerat (S Dunstanus),
hæc vidimus metrico scripta

Idriolam hanc fundi Dunstan mandaverat archi-
Præsul, ut in templo sancto serviret Aldhelmo

—*Vita S Aldhelmi*, in *AA. SS Maji*, vi 90 William of Malmesbury
gives the same verses, *Gesta Pontif*, v. 255 [R S, iii 407].

while the archdeacon put out upon the corporal
as much bread, and wine mingled with a little
water,[1] as would that day be wanted for the
communion. When the altar had been thus got
ready for him, the bishop went thither, and
received from the priests and deacons their offering of bread without any wine; this done, he
censed the sacred table, and turning about to
the people, said, *Orate, fratres*—Pray, brethren,
or words of the like meaning, to which all
answered by repeating the second, third, and
fourth verses of the xixth [xxth] psalm, or
sentences to the same effect. In the mean while
the deacons ranged themselves behind, the subdeacons before, the bishop. As the altar, in those
days, as we have noticed,[2] used to
stand by itself under a canopy, some
little way from the church's eastern
end, whether their numbers might
have been three, five, or seven, the
subdeacons could easily place themselves, at its further side, in front of
the bishop, while the deacons stood
behind his back, thus:

(35) After saying to himself a prayer, which
was hence called the "Secret," the bishop raised
his voice, and began the Preface. At those

---

[1] Amalarius, *De Eccl. Offic*, iii 19, 417, Hitt. See also in this
work, vol. i p 120

[2] Vol i pp 151, 152, of this work.

words, *Sursum corda*,[3] in it, an acolyte, with his hands muffled in the folds of a veil or scarf, which hung about his shoulders, took from off the altar the paten, and so held this broad, shallow kind of dish until the *Te igitur*, or the first words of the canon, when he carried and gave it to one of the subdeacons, who held it, with his naked hands uplifted, at his place in front of the bishop, till the *Pater noster*.[4] No sooner did the choir begin the *Sanctus, Sanctus, Sanctus*, after the Preface, than both the deacons and subdeacons bent their heads, and so stood keeping them bent—the deacons until the end of the *Pater noster*,[5] or those words, *Libera nos a malo*[6]—the subdeacons till *Nobis quoque peccatoribus*.[7]

(36) The whole of the canon of the mass was uttered, not aloud, but to himself,[8] by the bishop.

---

[3] How St. Cuthbert used to be often stirred to tears at mass, the while, uplifting his voice, he began the preface, is beautifully told by the venerable Beda Tantum autem compunctioni erat deditus, tantum cœlestibus ardebat desideriis, ut missarum solemnia celebrans, nequaquam sine profusione lacrymarum implere posset officium. Sed congruo satis ordine dum passionis dominicæ mysteria celebraret, imitaretur ipse quod ageret, seipsum, videlicet, Deo in cordis contritione mactando, sed et adstantes populos sursum corda habere, et gratias agere Domino Deo nostro, magis ipse cor quam vocem exaltando, potius gemendo quam canendo admoneret —St Beda, *Vita S Cuthberti*, xvi. [*P.L.*, xciv. 756]

[4] *Ordo Romanus*, in Mabillon, *Mus. Ital.*, ii. 49

[5] Amalarius, *De Ecc Offic*, iii 23, 420, Hittorp

[6] *Ib*, 27, 429, Hitt.   [7] *Ordo Rom*, in Mabillon, ii. 49.

[8] Amalarius, *Ecloga*, xxvii, in Georgi, *De Liturgia Rom. Pont.* iii. 363, and *De Ecc. Offic.*, iii 23, 421, Hittorp.

In the early part of it he prayed for the pope, and for all then in church ;[9] he brought to mind and honoured the memory of the B. V. Mary, the apostles, martyrs, and other saints, by whose merits and prayers he begged to be helped and defended ; in the latter part, he called upon God to be mindful of and take pity on, the souls of his dead brethren and friends, and all the faithful departed.

Whilst they stood yet bent, all the deacons washed their hands in water, which the acolytes brought them. As he said *Supplices Te rogamus*, the celebrant bowed himself down before the altar: at the words, *Nobis quoque peccatoribus*, all the subdeacons uplifted their heads, and looked full in the bishop's face. After the *Per quem omnia*, the first deacon, raising himself upright, took with both his hands the two-handled chalice muffled in an offertory-towel, and held it up towards the bishop, who touched the inside of this chalice with the host, making at the same time two signs of the cross with the body over the blood in the chalice.[10] At the end of the *Libera nos*, &c., this same head deacon, taking the paten, stretched it forth to the bishop's lips for being kissed, after which the same

---

[9] Una cum beatissimo famulo tuo ℟ et antistite nostro ℟ et omnibus, &c Such is the form in the Canon, in the *Leofric Missal* [60], for praying, first, for the Pope, then, for the bishop of the diocese

[10] *Ordo Romanus*, in Mabillon, *Mus Ital.*, ii 42.

minister gave it into the hands of the second deacon, that he might hold it.[11]

(37) It was just when this last prayer had been said, that among the Anglo-Saxons, as well as in several other parts of Christendom,—though not at Rome, nor where the Roman "ordo" was followed to the letter,—the bishop gave his benediction after a solemn manner, now laid aside.[12] Looking towards the people, the head deacon cried out, and said to them, "Bow yourselves down for the blessing," and then gave the benedictional to the bishop, who held that codex in his left hand; and having read the form allotted for the day, bestowed his blessing on the bended crowd, after the usual fashion, with his uplifted right hand, the thumb and first two fingers of which were outstretched, but joined, as an emblem of one God in three persons.[13]   The

---

[11] Amal, *De Ecc Offic*, iii. 27, Hittorp 428.

[12] Nonnulli sacerdotes post dictam orationem dominicam statim communicant et postea benedictionem in populo dant, quod deinceps interdicimus   sed post orationem dominicam, et conjunctionem panis et calicis, benedictio in populum sequatur, et tunc demum corporis et sanguinis Domini sacramentum sumatur, &c —*Concil Tolet* iv, can xviii in Coleti, *Concil Gen.* vi, 1457, Venet. 1728   From this canon of the iv council of Toledo (a d. 633) it would seem that in Spain all priests gave a blessing at this part of the mass

[13] Ille (archidiaconus) autem ut episcopus dicit, "Da propitius pacem," patenam illi accommodans, humerum ejus osculetur, statimque episcopo dicente, "Per omnia secula seculorum," accipiat benedictionalem librum, et conversus ad populum dicat, "Humiliate vos ad benedictionem," et clero respondente, "Deo gratias," porrigat episcopo librum   Expleta autem benedictione, veniens presbyter, accipiat pacem ab episcopo, eandem cæteris

wording of this episcopal benediction (38) varied
with the Sunday and the festival, and was, often
—though not always—gathered out of the day's
gospel: sometimes it spoke the church's thankfulness for the mystery, sometimes it unfolded
the ghostly meaning of the feast then celebrated.
But that the reader may see the form of an old
rite employed in the Sarum as well as the Anglo-
Saxon use, we set before him the following—one
for Christmas Day, the second for Maundy Thursday, the third for the festival of SS. Peter and
Paul.

Benedictio in die Natalis Domini.

Benedicat vos Omnipotens Deus vestramque
ad superna excitet intentionem, qui hanc sacra-
tissimam diem nativitate Filii sui fecit esse
sollempnem.   Amen.

Et qui eum qui panis est angelorum in presepi
æcclesiæ cibum fecit esse fidelium animalium,
ipse vos, et in presenti sæculo degustare faciat
æternorum dulcedinem gaudiorum, et in futuro

---

oblaturus, &c (*Ordo Romanus,* in Hittorp, *De Div in   Cathol.
Eccl. Officiis,* p 8)   This "Ordo" was, no doubt, arranged for
the use of some German cathedral, maybe that of Cologne, but
in it we behold a likeness to the Anglo-Saxon rubric   An illumination on p 116 at the end of Æthelwold's Benedictional,
shows us the bishop in the act of giving his benediction as above
described.   [An illustration of this has been given already in this
work; see vol 1 p 152.]   The instance of St. Dunstan's bestowing
his blessing at high mass, just before the "pax" or kiss of peace,
is mentioned in the extract from his life quoted just now, note
95, p. 37.

perducat ad satietatem æternorum premiorum. Amen.

Quique ejus infantiam vilibus voluit indui pannis, ipse vos cœlestium vestimentorum induat ornamentis.

Quod ipse prestare dignetur cujus regnum et imperium sine fine permanet in secula seculorum. Amen.

Benedictio Dei patris et filii et spiritus sancti, et pax Domini sit semper vobiscum.[14]

(39) Benedictio in Cena Domini.

Benedic quæsumus Domine universum hunc populum ad cene convivium evocatum. Amen.

Protege eum tuæ scuto defensionis, pro quo dignatus es opprobria sustinere passionis. Amen.

Defende eum a diri serpentis incursibus atque a cunctis absolve sordibus qui in hac die pedes discipulorum humiliata maiestate propriis lavasti manibus. Amen.

Benedicat vos omnipotens Deus qui in hac die cum discipulis suis cenans, panem in corpus suum, calicemque benedicens consecravit in sanguinem. Amen.

Ipseque vos faciat pura conscientia mundaque ab omni sorde peccati imminentem paschæ sollemnitatem cum exultatione placita sibi celebrare qui

---

[14] *Egbert Pontifical*, 83

cum discipulis discumbens desiderio in quid desideravi hoc pascha manducare vobiscum. Amen.

Ipse mentem vestram sanctificet et vitam amplificet castimoniam decoret atque sensus vestros in bonis operibus semper ædificet. Amen.

Quod ipse præstare dignetur, &c [15]

BENEDICTIO IN NATIVITATE APOSTOLORUM PETRI ET PAULI.

Benedicat vos Deus, qui nos beati Petri saluberrima confessione in æcclesiasticæ fidei fundavit soliditate. Amen.

Et quos beati Pauli sanctissima instruxit prædicatione, sua tueatur gratissima defensione. Amen.

Quatenus Petrus clave, Paulus sermone, utrique intercessione, ad illam vos certent patriam introducere, ad quam illi, alter cruce, alter gladio, hodierna die pervenere. Amen.

Quod ipse. Amen. Benedictio, &c.[16]

(40) That such episcopal blessings formed a part of the old liturgy followed by the Gauls long before Pope St. Gregory's and St. Austin's days, we learn from the fact that St. Cæsarius of Arles,[17] who

---

[15] Ætheluold Benedictional, 76

[16] Egbert Pontif, 87

[17] Ideo qui vult Missas ad integrum cum lucro animæ suæ celebrare, usquequo oratio Dominica dicatur, et benedictio populo detur, humiliato corpore et compuncto corde se debet in ecclesia continere —St Cæsarius, Hom XII, in Binius, Bib Pat. v, part III, 757. Unius aut duarum horarum spatium patientiam habeamus, donec in illa spirituali mensa animarum cibus apponitur,

lived almost a whole century before those apostles
of our Anglo-Saxon fathers, speaks of this rite as
a thing practised everywhere about him.   Know-
ing then, as we do, from the formal and public
visit made to the church in this island by SS.
Germanus and Lupus, how the British and the
Gallic churches were knit together, not only by
the feelings of religious friendship, but by the
oneness of true belief, we are warranted in thinking that a ceremonial then in common use throughout a neighbouring country with which this land
kept up such an intimate connection in matters of
faith, must have been common here too; so that
our bishops among the Britons, like their brethren
beyond the sea in Gaul, used to bestow their episcopal blessing at this part of the holy sacrifice.

(41) After he had thus given his benediction,
the bishop, at the words, *Pax Domini sit semper
vobiscum*—The Peace of the Lord be with you
evermore,—sent forth the kiss of peace.   This he
did by kissing, first, the altar, or the paten, then
the head deacon; who carried this apostolic
token of brotherly love and goodwill down to the

---

et sacramenta spiritalia consecrantur. Et quia præmissa oratione
dominica benedictio vobis non ab homine sed per hominem datur,
grato et pio animo, humiliato corpore et corde compuncto, rorem
divinæ benedictionis accipite. — Id., *Hom* VIII, in Gallandius,
Vet. Pat Bib., XI 12   A few years afterwards, it was enacted
(A D. 538) in the third council of Orleans De Missis nullus
laicorum antea discedat, quam dominica dicatur oratio, et si
episcopus præsens fuerit, ejus benedictio expectetur. — *Concil.
Aurelian.* III., can. XXIX in Coleti, *Concil. Gen*, v 1281.

next in rank; and thus did it pass from one to
the other among all those about the altar and in
the choir.[18] Thence went it unto the people; from
man to man on the men's side, from woman to
woman on the women's side, as each sex stood
apart by itself in the holy building.

The fragment that had been left from the mass
last offered, was, before giving the *Pax*,[19] put into
the chalice by the bishop, who, from the host he
had just then hallowed, broke off two small pieces,
one of which he dropped into the chalice, the
other he laid aside upon the altar, to be kept
until the morrow or another day, when the holy
sacrifice should be next celebrated Thus a portion of the eucharist, under one kind alone, was
always reserved in the church, from each mass to
the other.   Leaving the altar, the bishop went
to his chair, and standing thereat received the
euchaiist, which was brought to him,—the body
upon a wide paten, and the blood in a large chalice,
out of which he drank through a golden or silver
pipe or reed.   [See illustration, vol. i. p. 331.]
Along with him partook of this holy sacrifice all
his attendant clergy and the singers, as well as
very many among the people.   No sooner had the
celebrant walked to his chair, before he received
the communion, than the choir began to sing
Agnus Dei, &c, which was thrice repeated, and

---

[18] Amal, *Ecloga*, xxx., in Georgi, iii 369
[19] Amal, *De Ecc. Offic*, iii 31, Hittorp 432

ended the third, as well as the other two times,
with *Miserere nobis.*[20]   After himself and the
clergy had (42) received, he went down to distribute
the holy communion to the lay-folks.   As from off
the paten, carried by two deacons, he took and
gave to each person our Lord's body, our Lord's
blood was presented to the same individual by the
head deacon's allowing this communicant to sip
up a small draught, through the reed, from out
the large two-handled chalice, which that minister
bore in both his hands as he followed close behind
the bishop.   All the while the eucharist was being
thus distributed to the people, the choir sang the
whole or part of a psalm, called, from that circum-
stance, the "Communion."

When all had thus partaken of the eucharist,
the bishop returned to the altar, and, having read
the prayer of thanksgiving,—then called "Ad
complendum," now the "Post-communion,"—bestowed another blessing upon the crowd, whom
one of the deacons afterwards told that, as the
holy sacrifice was done, they might go away, as in
a loud tone of voice he sang, *Ite, missa est.*   With
the seven candles borne before him by as many
acolytes, and the thurible by a subdeacon, the
bishop and his ministering clergy then left the

---

[20] Such is the form given in the *Leofric Missal,* 62 [but without any
indication that it was to be sung three times; the *Canterbury
Missal* at Corpus Christi College, Cambridge, marks the repetition
and the change to *Dona nobis pacem*   Ed Rule, 44]

church, and went to do off their liturgical garments in the vestry.

With such a ceremonial used solemn high mass, as we have good reasons for thinking, to be celebrated among our Anglo-Saxon fathers, whenever a bishop pontificated. For the common week-day service, when the priest offered up the holy sacrifice in his parish church, after that way which we now call "low mass," the outline of the rubrics and the order of the prayers were exactly the same, and the only difference between these two forms of the liturgy was, that in the first there was much more of ritual splendour besides the crowd of ministering clergy.

The time for the parochial mass used to be, except on days of fasting, immediately after undern-song or tierce, (43) that is, about nine o'clock in the morning;[21] and to eat any thing before this service had been ended at church, either on holydays or Sundays, was strictly forbidden. Hence, say the *Ecclesiastical Institutes*, "we command those mass-priests who, both on Sundays and other mass-days, wish to sing before

---

[21] Beda incidentally tells us this as he speaks of the miraculous way in which the captive Imma's chains were loosed every morning his brother the priest said mass for his soul, thinking him to be dead ·—A tertia autem hora, quando missæ fieri solebant, sæpissime vincula solvebantur —*Hist Eccl*, ii 22 Hence arose the custom of breakfasting at undern-time among the Anglo-Saxons, as Beda likewise lets us know Ut horam diei tertiam etiam cibo reficiendus exspectaret, rogavit, ne si jejunus iret, &c . . expletis horæ tertiæ precibus vescendi tempus aderat, &c —*Vita S Cuthberti*, vii [*P.L.*, xciv. 743]

the high mass, that they do so privately, so that they draw off no portion of the people from the high mass . . . but we command that no man taste any meat before the service of the high mass be completed, but that all, both females and males, assemble at the high mass, and at the holy and spiritual church, and there hear the high mass and the preaching of God's word." [22]

Whether young or old, every woman came to church with a veil on her head. This we learn from Beda, who gives us the symbolic meaning for a custom yet followed in the southern countries of Europe; in obedience to the injunction of the Apostle (1 Cor. xi. 10), women cover their heads in church " because of the angels," who not only stood by the dead Body of our Saviour in His tomb, but are also present when that same holy Body is specially with us in the Holy Eucharist, after the prayer of consecration. [23]

(44) To give solemnity, and to bring as much grandeur as possible to the services of the church, music in both its kinds, vocal and instrumental, was not wanting. Winchester minster had an organ that would have rivalled in size the largest

---

[22] Thorpe, *Ancient Laws of England*, ii. 449; and vol 1 p 138 of this work.

[23] Quomodo autem posito in sepulchro corpori Salvatoris angeli astitisse leguntur, ita etiam celebrandis ejusdem sacratissimi corporis mysteriis tempore consecrationis assistere sunt credendi, monente Apostolo mulieres in Ecclesia velamen habere propter angelos—*Expos Lucæ Evang.* xxiv., *in Opp* ed Giles, xi. 375 [*P.L.,* xcii 623]

ones built in the present age : its double row of ſ ſ ſ'
keys, its four hundred pipes, its twenty-six feeders, ſ ſ.
and the seventy strong men required to blow them ;   ſ.
the soft sweetness of its tones, and its thunder-like
peals of sound, which it could roll forth to be
heard everywhere about the city, are all enumerated by Wolstan, the poet-monk, who had seen
and often listened to it.[24]   But this was not all :

---

[24]   Talia et auxistis hic organa qualia nusquam
            Cernuntur, gemino constabilita solo
      Bisseni supra sociantur in ordine folles
            Inferiusque jacent quatuor atque decem.
      Flatibus alternis spiracula maxima reddunt,
            Quos agitant validi septuaginta viri
      Sola quadringentas quæ sustinet ordine musas
            Quas manus organici temperat ingenii .
      Considuntque duo concordi pectore fratres
            Et regit alphabetum rector uterque suum. .
      Inque modum tonitrus vox ferrea verberat aures,
            Prætor ut hunc solum nil capiat sonitum. . .
      Musarumque melos auditur ubique per urbem.

—Wolstan of Winchester, *Lib de Vita S Swithuni*, ed Mabillon,
AA SS O B. vii 617 [*P.L*, cxxxvii 110]   Malmesbury minster
had a fine organ, which St Dunstan caused to be built there, in
honour of St Aldhelm, as the Latin verses on it testified In
organis scilicet, quæ ad tanti patris honorem archipræsul dederat,
hæc sunt æneis litteris assignata carmina.

      Organa do sancto præsul Dunstanus Aldhelmo
      Perdat hic æternum qui vult hinc tollere regnum

—*Vita S Aldhelmi* ab anonym Malmes in *AA SS Maji* vi 90
See also Will Malmesbury, *Gesta Pontif*, v 255 [*R S*, lii 407]
Between two and three hundred years before St Dunstan's time,
the world of sound which the organ could pour out had been more
than once mentioned by St. Aldhelm ·—

      Quamvis millenis collaudent ora loquelis,
      Sicut folligenis respirant organa flabris,
      Musica concisis, et clamat barbita bombis

—*De Octo Princip Vitiis* [*P.L.*, lxxxix. 287] ; and again,'*De barbito
sive Organo.*

(45) besides a variety of wind instruments, a sort of hoop, sheathed in plates of gilt silver, and having bells hung all about it, and made so as to twirl easily, the Anglo-Saxons brought into use for the sake of awakening the people's greater devotion on the higher holy days.[25] Throughout the whole church, but more especially about the altars and (46) where the shrine stood, the ground was strewed with rushes or sweet-smelling herbs.[26]

Here, perhaps, the reader would like to know

Quamvis ære cavo salpinctis classica clangant
Et citharæ crepitent, strepituque tubæ modulentur
Centenos tamen eructant mea viscera cantus·
Meque strepente stupent mox musica corda fibrarum.
—Ibid , Epist. ad Acircium [P L , 185]

[25] Præterea fecit vir Athelwoldus quandam rotam tintinnabulis plenam, quam auream nuncupavit, propter laminas ipsius deauratas, quam in festivis diebus ad majoris excitationem devotionis reducendo volvi constituit —Registrum de Abbendon, Cotton MS , Claud B vi, in Mon Angl , i 516 [R S ii 1 345] Some at least of these hoops with bells were small enough to be carried about, as may be guessed not only from the costliness of the precious metal out of which they were made, but also from the following lines, which seem to indicate this kind of musical instrument as borne about in the procession at the hallowing of Winchester cathedral, enlarged by Æthelwold —

Et simul hymnisona fratrum coeunte corona
Quisque tuum votum, qua valet arte canit
Cimbalicæ voces calamis miscentur acutis
Disparibusque tropis dulce camœna sonat

—Wolstan of Winchester, Lib de Vita S Swithuni, ed Mabillon, AA. SS O B vii 619 [P L , cxxxvii 112]

[26] Abp Theodore tells us of the "stramen" (Lib Pænit xxxix , § 10, in Thorpe ii 47), and that fennel often lay scattered on the floor about St Etheldreda's shrine in Ely, we learn from the record of a miracle wrought by one of the sprigs of that herb picked up there Accipientes surculos marathi unde fuerat cooperta totius superficies pavimenti, &c.—Acta S Etheldredæ, in AA SS. Junii iv., 521.

how these several functions at the altar were distributed, and unto whom they officially belonged. In answer to such a wish, a word or two must be said on

The Lower and Higher Orders in the Anglo-Saxon Hierarchy.

Of these various persons among the clergy ministering about the altar, from the bishop downwards to the lowliest little singing boy, we find the respective form by which each, in due turn, came to be hallowed unto the service of God's one Church on earth. That precious and venerable manuscript known as the Egbert Pontifical lets us see all those ordination-services through which the clerk had to go from the lowest to the highest step in the hierarchy. The youth who wished to become

A Singer

could be admitted into the choir by a priest, with the form, "See that what thou singest with thy mouth thou believest with thy heart; and what thou believest with thy heart thou commendest by thy life." [27]

---

[27] *Egbert Pontifical*, 10. *Psalmista, id est cantor, posteaquam ab archidiacono instructus fuerit, potest absque conscientia episcopi, sola jussione presbiteri, officium suscipere cantandi, dicente sibi presbitero* Vide ut quod ore cantas, corde credas, et quod corde credis, operibus probes

(47) The seven steps or degrees in orders—
from the lowest of which each one must begin
and go regularly through the rest, before he
may reach the bishophood,—and how Christ
himself, after a manner, went through them all,
Egbert's Pontifical thus sets forth

De vii *gradibus Ecclesie quos adimplevit Christus.*

Ostiarius fuit, quando conclusit et aperuit
archam Noe, et portas inferni aperuit; unde
modo hostiarii qui dicuntur, ecclesie ostia et
sacrarii, et tangere signum ut occurrant omnes,
custodiri jubentur. Lector fuit, quando aperuit
in sinagoga Judeorum librum Isaiæ prophetæ et
legit, Spiritus domini super me *et cetera*. Sunt
igitur lectores qui verbum Dei predicant, quibus
dicitur, Clama ne cesses, quasi tuba exalta vocem
tuam. Exorcista fuit, quando ejecit septem de-
monia de Maria Magdalene. Exorcistæ ex greco
in latino adjurantes vocantur. Invocant enim
super catecuminos, vel superbos qui habent
spiritum inmundum, nomen Jesu, adjurantes
per eum, ut egrediatur ab eis. Subdiaconus fuit,
quando benedixit aquam in Chana Galileæ, et
convertit in vinum. Subdiaconus vero oportet
apostolum legere, vestire et honestare altaria, et
ministrare diacono. Diaconus fuit, quando con-
fregit quinque panes in quinque milia hominum,
et vij^m panes in iiij^{or} milia, sive quando lavit

pedes discipulorum suorum. Diaconus namque oportet ministrare ad altare, et evangelium legere in æcclesia, baptizare et communicare in vice presbiteri, peregrinorum pedes lavare, et mortuorum corpora sepelire. Presbiter fuit, quando accepit panem in suis sacris manibus, similiter et calicem, respiciens in cœlum ad Deum Patrem suum, gratias agens, et benedixit. Presbiteros autem merito et sapientia dici non ætate intelligendum est. Presbiterum autem oportet benedicere, offerre, et bene praeesse, predicare, et baptizare, atque communicare, quia his supradictis gradibus senior est, et vicem (48) episcopi in æcclesia facit. Non enim propter decrepitam senectutem, sed propter sapientiam presbiteri nominantur. Quod si ita, mirum cui insipientes constituuntur. Episcopus fuit, quando elevatis manibus benedixit discipulos suos apostolos in Bethania, et educens eos foras elevatus est in cœlum. Episcopum oportet judicare, et interpretari, consecrare, et consummare, quin et ordinare, offerre, et baptizare. Episcopus autem grece latine superinspector, quia omnia prospicere debet et ordinare.[28]

The times during the year for giving orders, were the Saturdays of the four Ember weeks.[29] To begin with

---

[28] *Egbert Pontifical,* 10, 11.
[29] Tempore statuto sabbatorum diebus per tempora mensium. *Ibid ,* 11.

The Door-keeper.

As his office was to lock up and unlock the church, and to ring the bells, at his ordination the bishop put into his hands the church keys, and the archdeacon led him down to the threshold, where he made over to him, as it were, the keeping of the doors: then followed the prayers, in which the bishop prayed over the door-keeper.[30] This youth's next step was when he became

Reader.

As such, he had to sing—or merely read, as it might be—those lessons which come in the different services of the church. Within his hands when he was ordained the bishop put a book of the lessons, telling him to be a trustworthy bearer of the word, and to fulfil his office of reader (49) with steadfastness; and then he said a prayer of blessing over him.[31]   As

---

[30] *Ostiarius cum ordinatur, postquam ab archidiacono instructus fuerit, qualiter in domo Dei debeat conversari, ad suggestionem archidiaconi tradat ei episcopus claves de altari, dicens* ✠ Sic age quasi redditurus Deo rationem pro his rebus, quæ istis clavibus recluduntur   *Et tradat ei archidiaconus ostium æclesiæ   Ibid , 11, 12.*

[31] *Lector cum ordinatur, faciat de illo verbum episcopus ad plebem, indicans ejus fidem ac vitam atque ingenium   Post hæc, expectante plebe, tradat ei codicem de quo lecturus est, dicens* Accipe et esto verbi Dei delator habiturus, &c   *Benedictio Lectoris   Ibid., 12*

The Exorcist

got a power from the Church of praying over
those who were worried by evil spirits, to drive
away the foul fiend, therefore did the bishop
bestow upon him, as he gave him ordination, a
book of the exorcisms, telling him to learn them
by heart, and to receive authority for the laying
on of his hands over possessed people.[32] The
highest of these four lower orders was that of

Acolyte,

who, at his ordination, after being first told of
his liturgical duties by the bishop, received from
the archdeacon's hands a candlestick with its
taper, and an empty cruet. The candlestick was
meant to say how unto him was more especially
entrusted the care of looking after the church
lights; the cruet let him understand that another
part of his office would be to carry unto the altar
the wine and water needed for working the
mystery of Christ's blood at the offering up of
the eucharist.[33] In one of the prayers over the

---

[32] *Exorcista cum ordinatur accipiat de manu episcopi libellum, in
quo scripti sunt exorcismi, dicente sibi episcopo* ✠ *Accipe et com-
menda memoriæ, et haboto potestatem imponendi manum super
inerguminum, sive baptizatum, sive catæcuminum* After this
follow the blessings.—*Ibid*, 13

[33] *Accolitus cum ordinatur, primum ab episcopo doceatur qualiter
in officio suo agere (50) debeat Sed ab archidiacono accipiat cero-
ferarrium cum cera, ut sciat se ad accendenda ecclesiæ luminaria
mancipari Accipiat et urceolum vacuum ad fundendum vinum in
Eucharistia corporis Christi. Ibid*, 13, 14.

acolyte, the bishop asked that he might prove faithful in this duty.[34] The next step took the acolyte to

The Subdeaconship.

He who was called to this ministry, had, at his ordination, put into his hands, by the bishop, an empty paten and an empty chalice,—by the archdeacon, a basin and ewer, with a towel. While warning him of the duties belonging to his new office, the bishop gave the subdeacon to know, among other things, that he must always set for consecration as much bread, out of the offerings, upon the altar, as would be enough, considering the number of people present at the holy sacrifice; and another of his obligations would be to wash the altar-cloths, for which purpose he should have two distinct vessels,— one exclusively for the upper sheet, called the "corporal," because on it lay, and within it was wrapped, the body of Christ at mass,—a second basin, for the under cloths, two or three of which were spread out upon the altar beneath the corporal. The water in which this linen was rinsed had to be thrown into earth through the

---

[34] Ita benedicere digneris hunc famulum tuum ✠ in officio accoliti, ut . . . ad suggerendum vinum et aquam ad conficiendum sanguinis tui ministerium in offerendo Eucharistiam sanctis altaribus tuis fideliter subministret Accende, Domine, ejus mentem, &c Ibid, 14

baptistery drain.[35] In due time the subdeacon was raised to

The Deaconship.

Before the ordination either of a deacon or a priest, the bishop first blessed the attire with which those ministers were to be arrayed whensoever they had to go about their holy office at the altar;[36] and from one of the prayers said over those garments, we know, by the specification of them, what they were : the chasuble, the *poderis*—a long gown, answering to our cassock[37] —the alb, the stole, the girdle, and the amice.[38] Having hallowed these vestments, the bishop cast the stole upon the intended deacon's neck, saying to him the while those words of our Lord, " my

---

[35] *Subdiaconus cum ordinatur, quia manus impositionem non accipit, patenam de manu episcopi accipiat vacuam, et calicem vacuum. De manu vero archidiaconi accipiat urceolum cum aquamanili ac manutergium. Exhibeatur in conspectu episcopi patena et* (51) *calix vacuus, et dicat episcopus subdiacono* . Oblationes quæ veniunt in altare panes propositiones appellantur, de ipsis oblationibus tantum debet in altare poni, quantum populo possit sufficere, ne aliquid putridum in sacrario remaneat Pallæ vero quæ sunt in substratorio in alio vase debent lavari, in alio corporales pallæ Ubi pallæ corporales lavatæ fuerint, nullum linteamen ibidem aliud debet lavari, ipsa aqua in baptisterio debet vergi . . *Et tradat et calicem et patenam, et manipulam Ibid*, 14, 15

[36] *Ibid*, 16, 17.

[37] We have spoken of this under the name "subucula" before, vol. 1., pp 374, 375.

[38] Domine Deus Pater omnipotens . . . exaudi propitius orationem nostram, et hanc planetam famuli tui, ✠ seu pudorem (poderem), albam, ac stolam, cingulum, orariumque dextera tua sancta benedicere, sanctificare, consecrareque, et purificare digneris, &c.—*Egbert Pontifical*, 17.

yoke is sweet, and my burden light." [39]   To this
followed, first, a prayer, then a short discourse, or
"Sermo Innocentii Papæ de vii. gradibus æccle-
siae ordinandis." [40]   This done, the bishop hung
the (52) stole upon the shoulder of the postulant
for the deaconship, and put into his hands a copy
of the evangelists, saying, "Take this book of
the gospels, read, understand, and give it to
others; and do thou in thy work fulfil it." The
bishop alone laid his hands upon the new deacon's
head, reciting a short prayer over him. [41]   Then
came what was called the " consecration," which
ended with the bishop's anointing of the deacon's
hands with holy oil and chrism. [42]

When the deacon had reached the prescribed
age, and been called to take upon himself

The Priesthood,

the first ceremony at his consecration unto this
new dignity was to alter the way of wearing the
stole.   From waving, as it had been left to do

---

[39] *Ibid*, 17   [40] *Ibid.*, 18.

[41] *Diaconus cum ordinatur, circumdetur ejus humerus sinister cum
stola ab episcopo, et tradat ei sanctum Evangelium, et dicat sibi,* ✠
Accipe istud volumen Evangelii, et lege, et intellege, et aliis trade,
et tu opere adimple   *Deinde solus episcopus, qui eum benedicit,
manus super caput illius ponat, quia non ad sacerdotium, sed ad
ministerium consecratur* —*Ibid.*, 18, 19

[42] *Consecratio manuum Diaconi de oleo sancto et chrisma*   Consecrentur manus istæ, quæsumus Domine, et sanctificentur per
istam unctionem, nostramque benedictionem, ut quæcumque benedixerint benedicta sint, et quæcumque sanctificaverint sanctificata
sint —*Ibid*, 21   The deacon's hands are not anointed now at his
ordination

heretofore, loose behind and before, on the left
shoulder, the bishop now shifted this liturgical
ornament, and put it about the neck, so as to
make its two ends fall down in equal lengths,
on both sides, low in front of the wearer.[43] In
behalf of his clerical brother kneeling before him,
the bishop now breathed many and warm en-
treaties unto heaven, that it would send down
its ghostly strength into the soul of one who,
as its priest, would have to offer up to it a
sacrifice, in which, by Christ's own words, bread
and wine are transformed—transubstantiated into
Christ's own flesh and blood.[44] As he clothed
him with the chasuble, the bishop besought a
blessing from above on this priest, that his might
be a hallowed priesthood, and that he might offer
up to Almighty God atoning sacrifices for the
people's sins.[45] His hands were next anointed

[43] *Presbiter cum ordinatur, circumdentur humeri ejus cum stola ab
episcopo. Et ibidem tuteletur (53) specialiter ad qualem ecclesiam debeat ministrare Et benedicente eum episcopo, manus super caput ejus
teneat Similiter et presbiteri, qui presentes sunt, manus suas juxta
manum episcopi super caput illius teneant —Ibid*, 21

[44] Tu, Domine, super hunc famulum tuum ℞., quem ad presbiteri honorem dedicamus, manum tuae benedictionis infunde
. ut purum atque immaculatum ministeri tui donum custodiat
et per obsequium plebis tuae, corpus et sanguinem Filii tui immaculati transformet, &c —*Ibid*, 23

[45] *Hic vestes eum casula* Induct te Dominus vestimento salutis,
et coronam lætitiae ponat super caput tuum Benedictio Dei
Patris, et Filii, et Spiritus Sancti descendat super te, et sis benedictus in ordine sacerdotali, et offeras placabiles hostias pro
peccatis atque offensionibus populi Omnipotenti Deo, &c. —
Ibid., 23.

with chrism; and the prayer then said warned
the priest again of his sacerdotal duty of offering up sacrifice to appease God for the guilt and
short-comings of the people, and of hallowing,
by a benediction with those hands, such things as
the people needed.[46]   Besides the hands, the
head also of the newly-made priest was anointed;
but in this unction the holy oil, and not the
chrism, used to be employed.[47]

Upon the last and loftiest step of holy order
stood

The Bishop,

for the hallowing of whom the ceremonial was
longer and more diversified.   As he knelt before
the metropolitan (or, in his stead, the consecrating
bishop), two other bishops upheld a book of the
gospels, as it lay open, and resting on the head
of the priest about to be made bishop, while
some prayers were said by all the other bishops
who happened to be there, and the other clergy
outstretched their hands over him.[48]   After being

---

[46] *Consecratio manus.* Benedic, Domine, et sanctifica has manus
sacerdotis tui ⊞ ad consecrandas hostias, quae pro delictis atque
negligentiis populi offeruntur, et ad cetera (54) benedicenda quae ad
usus populi necessaria sunt &c *Faciens crucem sanctam de chrismate in manibus ejus, et dicis* Consecrentur manus istae, quaesumus
Domine, et sanctificentur per istam sanctam unctionem et nostram invocationem, adque divinam benedictionem, ut quodquod
benedixerint, sit benedictum, et quodquod sanctificaverint, sit
sanctificatum Per —*Ibid* , 24.

[47] *Consecratio capitis oleo* Unguatur et consecretur caput tuum
coelesti benedictione in ordine sacerdotali, in nomine Patris, &c.—
Ibid., 24

told, among other things, that he had been called
to the work of the full priesthood—ad summi
sacerdotii ministerium [49] — and to rule God's
Church from the episcopal chair — tribuas ei
(Domine) cathedram episcopalem ad regendam
Æcclesiam tuam [50]—his hands were anointed with
chrism (55) and holy oil [51] Upon his head also was
poured the holy oil; the kiss of peace was given
him. The pastoral staff was next put into his
hands with an admonition to be at the same time
strict, just and merciful; and afterwards the
episcopal ring was given to him and placed
upon his finger. [52] The ceremony ended by leading the new bishop to an episcopal chair, whereon
he sat the while was prayed a prayer, which
told him, in beautiful words, how, by God's
kindness, he had been brought to be, as it were,
one of the links in the apostolic succession within
that one church which Christ our Lord had
raised for himself, and had left to be taught
and governed by his apostles and their after-

---

[48] *Episcopus cum ordinatur, duo Episcopi ponant et teneant Evan-
geliorum librum super cervicem ejus, et unus fundat super cum benedictionem, et postea istas tres orationes omnes Episcopi, qui adsunt,
recitare debent, reliqui vero manus suas super caput ejus teneant —
Ibid, 1*   [49] *Ibid., 2.*

[50] *Ibid, 2*   [51] *Ibid, 3*

[52] Accipe baculum pastoralis officii, et sis in corrigendis vitiis
sæviens, in ira judicium sine ira tenens, cum iratus fueris miseri-
cordiae reminiscens *Cum anulus datur haec oratio dicitur* Accipe
anulum pontificalis honoris, ut sis fidei integritate munitus —
Ibid, 3

comers in the apostleship.[53]   The service then
ended with a special blessing.[54]

(56) But many of

THE FESTIVALS OF THE YEAR,

as they came about, brought with them each its
own little variations that spoke of itself or that
tide, and wrought a slight change, for the day,
in those rubrics at mass, as well as at the other
services of the church.   Though the liturgy followed by the Anglo-Saxons was that of Rome,
still, along with their growth as a Christian
people, there sprang up among those forefathers of ours some few ritual peculiarities,
which, however, were unimportant as far as belief went; or, if anything, only more energetic
exponents of Catholic teaching even than the
Italian ceremonial.   These observances they loved

---

[53] *Modo mittendus est in cathedram episcopalem, et haec oratio dicenda
est* Omnipotens Pater, Sancte Deus æterne .. in novo (testamento)
por Filium tuum Jesum Christum apostolos sanctos ex sanctis
omnibus elegisti, primum Petrum apostolum in cathedra honoris, et
Mathiam ejusdem consortem in apostolatum atque cathedram
honoris enumerasti,   da similem gratiam fratri nostro ✠ ad
instar sanctorum apostolorum tuorum sedentium in cathedra
honoris et dignitatis, ut in conspectu majestatis tuae dignus
honore appareat   Per
Domine Jesu Christe, tu præelegisti apostolos tuos, ut doctrina
sua nobis præessent, ita etiam vice apostolorum hunc episcopum
doctrinam docere, et benedicere, et erudire digneris, ut immacu-
latam vitam et inlesam conservet   Per omnia —*Ibid* , 4

[54] *Benedictio ejusdem sacerdotis.*   . Sit Deus pater tuus, sint
angeli amici tui, sint apostoli fratres tui, et apostolatus tui
gradum custodiant, &c.—*Ibid* , 5

because they were their own. Such national feelings, the most learned and holiest men of this land, instead of trying to weaken, did their best to make stronger. The great St. Dunstan forbade the churchmen of his day to lay aside any of this country's liturgical usages that were befitting, which had come down to them from their elders.[55] To hear the

Church bells

going was what every Anglo-Saxon loved ; hence from childermass-tide, all through the holydays, a full peal was rung for matins, mass, and even-song.[56] All the Christmas (57) festivals were hallowed after a becoming manner ; but

[55] Honestos huius patriæ mores ad Dominum pertinentes, quos veterum usu didicimus nullo modo abjicere sed undique uti diximus corroborare decrevimus —*Reg Conc*, 85

[56] His autem diebus inter Innocentium festivitatem, et octavas Domini, quia *Gloria in excelsis Deo* ob tantæ festivitatis honorificentiam ad missam celebratur, ad nocturnam, et ad vesperam, uti ad missam sicut in usum huius patriæ indigenæ tenent, omnia signa pulsantur (*Ibid*) Among other works of art wrought by the hands of our great St Dunstan, was a bell which, for many ages after that saint's death, hung in Canterbury cathedral, and was deemed one of the sweetest in England Tunc pulsato signo beatissimi patris nostri (Dunstani), quod ipse manibus suis olim fecisse dicebatur, quo nullum dulcius neque ad commovendos hominum animos flebilius, concurrit universa civitas (Cantuariensis) Osbern, *Vita et Mirac S Dunstani*, in *AA SS Maji* iv 379 [*R.S*, lxiii 138]. Abingdon could also boast of two bells made by the same saint, as well as of other two the work of its founder St Æthelwold Fecit (Athelwoldus) etiam duas campanas propriis manibus, ut dicitur, quas in hac domo (de Abbendon) posuit cum aliis duabus majoribus quas etiam beatus Dunstanus propriis manibus fecisse perhibetur --*Registrum de Abbendon*, MS Cotton, Claudius B. vi, in *Mon Anglic*, i. 516 [*R S*, ii 1 345]

St. Stephen's day

was distinguished by the deacons singing some short versicles just before the introit of high mass This short musical service was performed by these ministers alone, who for the purpose divided themselves into two choirs, one answering the other's song, thus : *Versus ante officium in festivitate Sancti Stephani Protomartiris Primo dicant leuitae canentes,* Cui adstat candida contio omnis, &c. *Tunc respondeant illis alii dicentes,* Optamus regi regum dicere odas, &c. *Item prætitulati cantores dicant,* Laudabile est Christo, &c. *Item leuitae,* Alleluia nunc leuitae, &c.[57] Because the protomartyr had himself been one of the seven deacons ordained by the apostles, the Church in this land, not only in Anglo-Saxon but in later times, bade her deacons look upon and honour him as their patron (58) saint. While teaching the people their duty in his sermon for

The Purification,

Ælfric lets us see, as it were, that procession in which the Anglo-Saxons—men and women— walked, each one bearing in his hand a lighted taper, hallowed at the beginning of that day's service in his parish church, for the ceremony. " Be it known also to everyone," says the homilist,

---

[57] *Winchester Troper,* 6.

" that it is appointed in the ecclesiastical observances, that we on this day bear our lights to
church, and let them there be blessed . and that
we should go afterwards with the light among
God's houses, and sing the hymn that is thereto
appointed. Though some men cannot sing, they
can, nevertheless, bear the light in their hands ;
for on this day was Christ the true light borne to
the temple, who redeemed us from darkness, and
bringeth us to the Eternal Light, who liveth and
ruleth for ever "[58] Of this rite itself, and how it
used to be kept throughout this country in his
own days, Beda tells us, as he happens to glance
at the heathenish lustration of old Rome ordained
by Numa. This heathenish lustration was adopted
by the Christian Religion with suitable alterations
for use on the Festival of Our Lady's Purification.
All the faithful carried lighted tapers and went in
procession round the church and through the
streets, after the manner of the five wise virgins
in the parable.[59] The form for hallowing these

---

[58] *Homs.* ed Thorpe, 1 151

[59] Sed hanc lustrandi consuetudinem bene mutavit Christiana
religio, cum in mense eodem die sanctæ Mariæ plebs universa,
cum sacerdotibus ac ministris, hymnis modulatæ vocis per ecclesias,
perque congrua urbis loca, procedit, datosque a pontifice cuncti
cereos in manibus gestant ardentes, et augescente bona consuetudine, id ipsum in cæteris quoque ejusdem beatæ matris et perpetuæ
virginis festivitatibus agere didicit, non utique in lustrationem
terrestris imperii quinquennem, sed in perennem regni cœlestis
memoriam, quando, juxta parabolam virginum prudentium, omnes
electi, lucentibus bonorum actuum lampadibus, obviam sponso ac
regi suo venientes, mox (59) cum eo ad nuptias supernæ civitatis
intrabunt *De Tempor. Ratione,* xii [*P L*, xc. 351, 352]

tapers, and the ceremonial of carrying them processionally, may be found in the Anglo-Saxon liturgy; Egbert's Pontifical gives the prayer of blessing, thus .—*Benedictio Luminis in Purificatione Domine Sanctæ Mariæ.* Sancte Pater, Omnipotens, æterne Deus, benedicere et sanctificare digneris istum ignem quem nos indigni suscipimus, per invocationem Unigeniti Filii Domini nostri Jesu Christi, quem, hodie in templo presentatum, justum Symeonem diu exspectantem in ulnas suscipisse novimus, et salutare tuum ante faciem omnium populorum esse, lumen scilicet gentibus et gloriam plebis tuæ Israel, prophetico spiritu docuisti. Te quæsumus Domine benedicere digneris lumen istud, et omnibus hoc manibus gestantibus illud verum lumen tuæ majestatis concede, ut te agnoscentes per viam virtutum ad te valeant pervenire, &c.[60] Besides this same prayer in the Leofric missal,[61] we have as follows :—*Oratio super cereos. In Purificatione Sanctæ Mariæ,* . . Te humiliter (Domine Deus) deprecamur ut has candelas ad usus hominum et animarum, siue in terra, siue in aquis, per inuocationem sanctissimi nominis tui, et per intercessionem Sanctæ Mariæ genetricis tuæ, cuius hodie festa percolimus, per precesque omnium Sanctorum tuorum benedicere et sanctificare digneris; ut hæc plebs tua illas (honorifice) in manibus portans, cantando teque

---

[60] *Egbert Pontifical,* 132   [61] Ed Warren, 204.

laudando tueatur; uocesque illorum de cęlo sancto tuo exaudias, &c [62] *His peractis cantetur antiphona ad stationem Sanctæ Mariæ*, Aue gratia plena, Dei genetrix, uirgo (with the Anglo-Saxon notation for the singing)—*His finitis, accensis luminaribus materialibus, in cordibus nostris amore Christi ardentes, in obuiam Christo uero sponso æcclesię venturi* (60) *sperantes, uerum lumen, a quo inluminamur confitentes, ternis trino antip(h)onis collectisque laudato, et in sinibus æcclesię fidelium accepto congratulantes, missæ sollempnia donec finiantur expectemus.*[63]

From the foregoing rubrics we gather that there used to be two distinct blessings; one over the unlighted wax tapers, the other over the fire (very likely a burning candle) from which they were afterwards all lit. This procession took place before mass, and on getting back again to their church, the people stopped for the offering up of the Holy Sacrifice

When Septuagesima Sunday—the third before Lent—came, *Alleluia* was left out by the Church from all parts of her service. Then did she begin to read, for the lessons at matins, the book of Genesis, which tells of man's fall: in sorrow for Adam's weakness, and bearing in mind that the season for her yearly fast was not far off, she now hushed this her usual song of ghostly joy. That

---

[62] *Ibid*, 203, 204   [63] *Ibid*, 204

among our Anglo-Saxons the *Alleluia* used to be
laid aside with some ritual formality, we may
gather from the fact that they had, in their liturgy,
a hymn which they sang on the occasion, and
which began thus :—

> Alleluia dulce carmen
> Vox perennis gaudii, &c

One of its strophes was :—

> Alleluia non meremur,
> Nunc perenne psallere ,
> Alleluia nos reatus
> Cogit intermittere ;
> Tempus instat quo peracta
> Lugeamus crimina.[64]

(61) *Shrove-tide, or the week before Lent,*

brought along with it more than one religious and
ritual observance.   The very name which our
Anglo-Saxon sires had given to this time, said
how they had ever looked upon it as the particular
season of shriving themselves, that is, going to
their shrift-father or parish-priest, and in sacra-
mental confession telling him their most hidden
sins.   "In the week immediately before Lent,
every one shall go to his confessor," said the
Ecclesiastical Institutes, "and confess his deeds ;
and his confessor shall so shrive him as he then
may hear by his deeds what he is to do : and he

---

[64] Hymnus in LXX^ma, id est, in Clausula Alleluia —*Latin
Hymns of the Anglo-Saxon Church,* ed. Surtees Society, p 56

shall command all his parishioners, with God's
command, that if any of them have any enmity
against any man, that he make peace with him;
but if any one will not agree to that, then he may
not shrive him, but then he shall acquaint the
bishop, that he may turn him to right . . . then
with minds thus purified, let them enter on the
tide of the holy fast, and by penance purify themselves against the holy Easter, &c." [65] In his
homily for Shrove Sunday or Dominica in Quin-
quagesima, Ælfric says· "Now is a clean and
holy tide drawing nigh, in which we should make
amends for our heedlessness; let, therefore, every
Christian man come unto his confessor, and confess
his secret guilt." [66] If those who had sinned
hiddenly, now bethought themselves how they
might best do hidden penance for their secret
guilt during the coming Lenten fast, that man
who had, with open shamelessness, broken God's
behests, was now called upon by the Church to
take away, by his open sorrow, the scandal which
he had thrown in the path of his brethren. For
such an end, as well as to strike a wholesome
dread into the hearts of all, (62) every public sinner
was, at that season of the year, made to undergo
the infliction of

[65] Thorpe, *Ancient Laws*, ii. 433.
[66] *Homilies*, ed Thorpe, i 165

Public Penance.

Barefoot and bareheaded, with nothing on them
but a short rough garment of sackcloth, those
men came to the church door at early morn on
Ash Wednesday.   To each one among them was
allotted a course of penitential works and prayer
proportionate to his guilt, by the proper official
for whose guidance in such matters Theodore
archbishop of Canterbury, and Egbert archbishop
of York, had severally drawn up a hand-book
known as the "penitentiary."   By the bishop
these public penitents were afterwards brought
into church, where casting himself with them outstretched on the ground, he and his clergy said
the VII penitential psalms.   Arising, the prelate
next spread forth his hands over them, sprinkled
them with holy water, put ashes first, then sackcloth, on each one's head, and, with sighs, told
them that like as Adam at his fall had been driven
out of paradise, so they too for their sins must be
sent out of the Church.   At the bishop's bidding,
some of the clergy, who went chanting the
words, "In the sweat of thy face shalt thou eat
bread," &c, led these public penitents back again
beyond the church door, which was to be shut
unto them till Maundy Thursday.   This we learn
from the writings of archbishop Theodore.[67]   But

---

[67] De pœnitentibus, ut in capite ieiunii omnes publice pœni-
tente sin civitate veniant ante fores ecclesiæ, nudis pedibus, et

Ash Wednesday

had its ceremonial of strewing ashes upon, not
merely the public penitent, but all; and thereby
spoke its awful teachings and its warning unto
all—unto the young and old, the guiltless and
the guilty.   As soon as none-song was over, that
is, about mid afternoon, the ashes were hallowed,
and then put upon each one's forehead.[68]   From

cilicio induti episcopo suo se repraesentent   In capite Quadrage-
simae omnes poenitentes, qui publicam suscipiunt vel susceperunt
poenitentiam, ante fores ecclesiae se repraesentent episcopo sacco
induti, vultibus in terram prostratis, reos se esse ipso habitu et vultu
proclamantes.   Ibi adesse debent archipresbyteri parochiarum, id
est, presbyteri (63) poenitentium, qui eorum conversationem
diligenter inspicere debent, et, secundum modum culpae, poenitentiam per praefixos gradus injungant   Post haec in ecclesiam
eos introducat et cum omni clero septem poenitentiales psalmos,
in terram prostratus, cum lachrymis, pro eorum absolutione de-
cantet   tunc resurgens ab oratione, juxta quod canones iubent,
manus eis imponat, aquam benedictam super eos spargat, cinerem
prius mittat, deinde cilicio capita eorum cooperiat, et cum gemitu,
et crebris suspiriis eis denunciet quod sicut Adam proiectus est de
Paradiso, ita et ipsi pro peccatis ab ecclesia abiciuntur   Post haec
iubeat ministris, ut eos extra ianuam ecclesiae expellant; clerus
vero prosequitur eos cum responsorio, "In sudore vultus tui," &c
ut videntes sanctam ecclesiam pro facinoribus suis tremefactam
atque commotam, non parvipendant poenitentiam   In sacra autem
Domini coena, rursus ab eorum presbyteris ecclesiae liminibus repre-
sententur   *Cap et Fray* in Thorpe, *Ancient Laws*, ii 70   The "Ordo
agentibus publicam poenitentiam" may be seen in the *Leofric
Missal*, 73   This rite is more than once noticed in our national
records, of St Elphege I, bishop of Winchester. William Malmesbury tells us that —Dies erat Cinerum, et pontifex pro more
poenitentes ecclesiae liminibus excludebat, ceteros adhortatus est
ut ieiunio et castitati vacantes, etiam uxorias delicias abiicerent
illis diebus —*Gesta Pontif*, ii. 75 [*R S*, iii 164].

[68] The form for blessing these ashes may be seen in the *Leofric
Missal*, 204   *Benedictio super cineres .   . cineres, quos causa pro-
ferendae humilitatis, atque promerendae ueniae capitibus nostris de-
cernibus(m) benedicere pro tua pietate digneris, &c.

(64) their own parish church, the people then went in procession to some other church, and on coming back heard mass. Then, and only then, did such as were bound, and able to fast, take any kind of food.[69]

All through Lent, as well as on the ember days, the deacon and the subdeacon wore, at high mass, a chasuble like the priest's. This vestment the subdeacon laid aside for the time, before he sang the epistle, but put it on again immediately afterwards; the deacon, however, ere going to chant the gospel, took off his chasuble, and, folding it into a long narrow band, fitted it, thus rolled, upon his left shoulder, so that it fell thence, beltwise, on both sides, about his breast and back, meeting beneath his right arm, where he fastened its ends together by the girdle of his alb; and went through his ministrations so arrayed, till after the communion, when he undid and shook out his rolled-up chasuble, and wore it after the ordinary manner. [See the picture in vol. 1. p 314] The rubric itself, with the hint of its antiquity, comes in St. Dunstan's *Rule* [70]

---

[69] Quarta feria capitis ieiunii (writes St Dunstan) nona decantata, abbas stola ornatus benedicat cineres quibus benedictis eat ipse abbas, et imponat capitibus singulorum, quia ejus est pœnitentiam illis imponere, &c , tunc vadant quo ire habent canentes antiphonas quae in Antiphonario continentur· venientes ad ecclesiam, quo eunt, iterum agant orationem, &c., et ibi incipientes litaniam revertantur ad matrem ecclesiam, ac dehinc more solito agatur missa, &c —*Reg Conc*, 85

[70] Tunc induti casulis sacerdos, diaconus ac subdiaconus peragant ministeria sua Hic autem (65) mos casularii, tantummodo quadra-

The way of keeping Lent,

both with regard to its fastings and players, is
well shown in a very precious memorial of those
olden times, the Anglo-Saxon *Ecclesiastical Institutes* · "The Lenten fast ought to be kept with
very particular care, so that there be no day, except only the Sundays, on which any one may
take any meat, before the tenth or the twelfth
hour; except any one who is so weak that he
cannot fast, and young men who have not the
age, who may dispense with the fast; because
these days are the tithing-days of the year, and
we should therefore solemnize them with all piety
and holiness. It is a custom that people often,
for love of friends, redeem other fasts with alms,
but this may, on no account, be broken. . . It
is daily needful for every man that he give his
alms to poor men; but yet, when we fast, then
ought we to give greater alms than on other days;
because the meat and the drink which we should
then use if we did not fast, we ought to distribute
to the poor; because if we fast, and reserve the
morning repast for the evening refection, then is

gesimali et quatuor temporibus usu præcedentium patrum observetur Subdiaconus quoties casula induitur exuat eam dum
legit epistolam, qua lecta, rursus ea induatur Diaconus vero
antequam ad evangelium legendum accedat, exuat casulam, et
duplicans eam circumponat sibi in sinistra scapula annectens
alteram summitatem ejus cingulo albæ Peracto communionis
sacramento induat eam antequam collecta finiatur —*Ibid*, 85

that no fast, but the hour of meat will be deferred, and the evening refection doubled.   It is the custom of many men, when they fast, that, as soon as they hear the none-bell, they take to (66) meat, but it is not allowable that that be a fitting fast, but it is right that, after none-song, mass be heard, and after the mass, even-song at the time; and after the even-song, let every one give his alms, so as his means will permit him, and after that take to meat.   But if any one be constrained by any occupation, so that he cannot come to the mass nor to the even-song, then at least let him continue fasting until he know that the mass and the even-song have been sung; and then, having thus completed his own prayers and his alms, let him enjoy his good things and take refection.   At this tide there should be abstinence from all delicacies, and soberly and chastely we should live. If any one, at this holy tide, can forego cheese, and eggs, and fish, and wine, it is a very strict fast; but for those who, from infirmity, or any other reasons, cannot forego them, it is needful that they enjoy them moderately, and at the times when they are allowed, that is, after the even-song; and let him take neither wine nor other drink, for any drunkenness, but for his heart's refection, &c.   Every Sunday, at this holy tide, people should go to housel, except those men who are excommunicated, &c "[71]   From these extracts

---

[71] Thorpe, *Ancient Laws*, 11 435, &c

we learn that, under the Anglo-Saxon ritual, mass was never said, on the week-days during Lent, till late in the afternoon, and no food was eaten until almost sunset.

The advice which St. Paul gives to married folks (1 Cor. vii. 5), our Anglo-Saxons not merely heard, but heeded.[72]   (67) They were taught to follow it whenever they partook of the adorable eucharist; for " to the people it is to be said, that at those tides, when they receive the holy mystery of Christ's body and blood, that is, the holy housel, that they do so with great awe and piety, and that they previously, both with fasts and with alms, both purify themselves and refrain from conjugal act," &c.   But this apostolic teaching were they taught to obey more especially all through the time of Lent: " For those married it is also very needful that they hold themselves chastely at this holy tide, without defilement of any cohabitation, that they, through pious life, with purified heart, and their bodies' chastity, with acceptable deeds, may come on the holy Easter-day; because the fast avails nought that is defiled with conjugal act," &c.[73]

---

[72] Qui in matrimonio sunt, abstineant se in III xL^mas, et in Dominica nocte, et in Sabbato, et feria IIII et VI quæ legitimæ sunt, et III noctes abstineant se antequam communicent, et I postquam communicent, et in Pascha usque ad octabas, inde ait Apostolus. 'Nolite fraudare invicem, nisi ex consensu, ut vacetis orationi ad tempus "—Theodore, *Liber Pœnitent*, in Thorpe, *Ancient Laws*, ii 12

[73] *Ibid*, 441

Thus did they go through this solemn fast. As its end drew nigh they were thus warned : "This tide from (the fifth Sunday in Lent) until the holy Easter tide, is called CHRIST'S PASSION-TIDE, and all God's ministers in the holy Church, with their church services honour, and in remembrance hold, His passion, through which we were all redeemed. Our books also say that we should hold these fourteen days with great earnestness, on account of the approaching of the holy passion and honourable resurrection of our Saviour. On these days we omit, in our responses, *Gloria Patri*, on account of our lament for the holy passion, unless some high festival-day occur during them."[74] In his sermon for

Palm Sunday,

Ælfric says : "The custom exists in God's Church, by its (68) doctors established, that everywhere in God's congregation the priest should bless palm-twigs on this day, and distribute them, so blessed, to the people ; and God's servants should then sing the hymn which the Jewish people sang before Christ when he was approaching to his passion. We imitate the faithful of that people with this deed, for they bare palm-twigs, with hymn, before Jesus. Now we should hold our palm until the singer begins the offering-song,

---

[74] *Homilies*, ed Thorpe, ii 225

and then offer to God the palm for its betokening.
Palm betokens victory. Victorious was Christ
when he overcame the great devil, and rescued
us; and we should also be victorious, through
God's might, so that we overcome our evil practices, and all sins, and the devil, and adorn our-
selves with good works; and, at the end of our
life, deliver the palm to God, that is our victory,
and thank Him fervently that we, through His
succour, have overcome the devil, so that he could
not deceive us." [75] The blessing of those boughs
—called, from the Sunday's service, palms—the
procession wherein they were afterwards borne
by clergy and people, singing as they went, along
the highways and the fields, from one church to
another, and the carrying them up afterwards,
and handing them, as their offering-gift, to the
sacrificing priest, at the offertory of the mass,
are all duly noticed in the Anglo-Saxon rituals.

In the Egbert Pontifical we have the following prayers:

Ad Palmas benedicendas vel Ramos

Domine Jesu Christe, qui ante mundi principium venisti, &c.

Deus, qui temporibus Noe famuli tui, per colum-
bam ramum olive virentibus foliis in ore defer-
entem, post diluvii effusionem, cum pace hominibus

---

[75] *Ibid*, II 219

reddita nuntiare voluisti, et qui Unigenito tuo
Domino nostro Jesu Christo ad Jerosolimam (69)
properanti pueros Ebreorum cum ramis palmarum
obviam venientes, laudesque decantantes, et voce
elevata dicentes, Osanna in excelsis, Benedictus
qui venit in nomine Domini, Rex Israel, voluisti
benedicere; sanctificare atque consecrare digneris
hos palmarum ramos diversarumque frondium vel
florum, ut omnes, qui ex eis in manibus accipere
voluerint tibi placere possint, et in die judicii cum
palma victoriae et fructu justiciae ad judicium pervenire mereantur, et exinde gloriam accipientes
indefectivam tecum sine fine vita aeterna per-
manere.   Per.[76]

Leofric's missal lets us behold how the ceremony used to be done in the south-west parts
of Anglo-Saxondom:[77] but it is St Dunstan who
sets out, in his famed *Rule*, the ceremonial of this

---

[76] P. 128 Another, and still longer form, is given on pp. 135,
136 Martene was mistaken when he said (*De Antiq Ecc Rit*,
iv. 20) that in archbishop Egbert's Pontifical no trace of blessing palms could be found   This however is true, that our Anglo-
Saxon archbishop of York's codex is the earliest book yet known
which gives such a blessing

[77] *Deinde accedat episcopus et benedicat ramos ita dicendo, &c
Deinde spargentur rami palmarum cum aqua benedicta, et turifi-
centur cum incenso et thimiamate, et diuidantur, primo clero, deinde
populo .   Finita antiphona pergant ad processionem cum candelabris
et turibulis   Antiphone ad processionem,* Cum appropinquaret. . .
*Tunc episcopus siue presbiter faciat sermonem de sancta cruce, et in-
cipiat antiphonam* Aue, rex noster, *Et omnes prosternant se ad terram.
Finita antiphona, cantor incipiat   R   In die qua . .   procedant pueri
duo aut tres, et canant hos,* Gloria, laus et honor.   *Tunc portetur
crux in antea, et cum introrerint ecclesiam, sequente clero ac populo,
dicat cantor R ,* Ingrediente Domino, &c.   Ed Warren, 255, 256

day at greatest length. (70) All were to go, clad in albs and repeating psalms silently, to the church where the palms were to be blessed, and there to pray, invoking the Patron Saint. After the deacon had read a gospel, the palms were blessed, sprinkled, censed and distributed, and meanwhile antiphons were sung. Then followed the procession · at the return to the church the hymn *Gloria, laus* was sung by the boys with its refrain, and, on entering, a respond. The palms were retained in the hands of the people and offered at the offertory.[78]

One of those anthems sung the while the palms are being given out, the then venerable antiquity

---

[78] Dominica die Palmarum, quia maior restat processio agenda, illa quae solet in claustro agi, interim dum matutinalis missa canitur, agatur a sacerdote tantum conspersionem et benedictionem agente Finita illa missa, agatur illa maior processio, in qua sicut in priori diximus agendum, ita agatur, id est, ut ad illam ecclesiam ubi palmae sunt, sub silentio ordinatim eant dediti psalmodiae omnes, si fieri potest et aura permiserit, albis induti, quo cum pervenerint, agant orationem, ipsius sancti implorantes auxilii intercessionem, cui ecclesia dedicata est Finita oratione, a diacono legatur evangelium, *Turba multa usque mundus totus post ipsum abiit,* quando sequatur benedictio palmarum Post benedictionem, aspergantur benedicta aqua et thus cremetur Dehinc pueris inchoantibus antiphonas, *Pueri Hebreorum,* distribuantur ipsae palmae, et sic maioribus antiphonis initiatis egrediantur, venientes ante ecclesiam subsistant, donec pueri qui praecesserunt, decantent *Gloria laus* cum versibus omnibus, sicut mos est, *Laus et Gloria* respondentibus, quibus finitis, incipiente cantore responsorium, *Ingrediente Domino,* aperiantur portae ingressi, finito responsorio, agant sicut supradictum est; et tenant palmas in manibus usque dum offertorium canetur, et eas post oblationem offerant sacerdoti

Ea die ad passionem, dicitur *Dominus vobiscum,* sed *Gloria tibi, Domine,* non respondetur · similiter et in reliquis passionibus, excepta Parasceuae passione ubi neutrum dicatur nec *Dominus vobiscum,* nec *Gloria tibi, Domine* —*Reg. Conc ,* 86

of this ghostly song, the joyous strains in which
the two bands of singers used to chant it, are all set
forth by one of the earliest (71) lights of the Anglo-
Saxon priesthood, the holy bishop Aldhelm.[79]

The remaining part, especially the last three
days of

Holy Week,

then, as now, drew forth the Church's sorrows,
which she so feelingly showed to the world by
so many of her heart-reaching ceremonies.   For
Maundy Thursday, as well as for Good Friday and
Holy Saturday, the matins and lauds, which, in
these our times, and all through several bygone
ages, have been called

Tenebræ,

were sung by the Anglo-Saxons with the same
accompaniment as ours, of lighted tapers, to be
put out, one by one, as the psalms went on.   A
scholar of our Alcuin, Amalarius, has a short
chapter, "De extinctione luminum" in which he
gives a mystical explanation of this unwonted
ceremony.[80]

---

[79] De quo lætantes evangelici consona vocis harmonia psallentes
concorditer cecinerunt · *Benedictus qui venit in nomine Domini*
Cujus rei regulam nostra quoque mediocritas, authentica veterum
auctoritate subnixa, in sacrosancta Palmarum solemnitate binis
classibus canora voce concrepans, et geminis concentibus *Osanna*
persultans, cum iucundae iubilationis melodia concelebrat.—*De
Laudibus Virginitatis* [*P L* , lxxxix. 128]

[80] Quod lumen ecclesiæ extinguitur in his noctibus, videtur
nobis aptari ipsi soli iustitiæ, qui extinctus est, et sepultus

Besides telling us that the tapers were put out then, as now, at the office of Tenebræ, a rubric of St. Dunstan's speaks of a short ceremony, at present nowhere kept up, which used to be observed, perhaps not in all, though in very many of our Anglo-Saxon minsters. It consisted in the chanting of the *Kyrie eleison* by two boys on the right side of the choir, who were answered by other two on the left, with *Christe eleison ;* then a third couple of youths, from the west end, sang *Domine miserere nobis*, and the whole choir

tribus diebus et tribus noctibus . Tot enim (lxxii) discipulos misit Christus binos et binos prædicare ante faciem suam Igitur per singulas noctes memoratarum feriarum viginti quatuor lumina accenduntur Et quia ipse sol significat solem nostrum qui occubuit vespere passionis, per lumen quod nos possumus accendere et extinguere, instar ortus solis et occasus, (72) demonstramus ortum et occubitum veri solis aliquo modo Illuminatur nostra ecclesia vigintiquatuor luminibus, et per singula cantica, in quibus nos oportet exultare, decidimus mœstitia, quia verus sol noster occubuit, et sic per singulas horas defectus solis augetur, usque ad plenam extinctionem Hoc enim fit ter, quia triduo recolitur sepultura Domini —Amalarius, *De Eccl Offic*, iv. 22 [Hittorp, 471] Elsewhere he lets us know that when he wrote (c A D 830), this rite of putting out the candles was not followed at Rome Mos ecclesiæ nostræ obtinet per tres noctes, id est, per feriam quintam, quae vocatur Cœna Domini, et per sextam, quae vocatur Parasceve, et per septimam quae vocatur Sabbatum sanctum, ut extinguantur luminaria ecclesiæ in nocte. De more sanctæ matris nostræ Romanæ ecclesiæ interrogavi archidiaconum Theodorum memoratæ ecclesiæ scilicet Romanæ . Nihil enim ibi in eadem nocte (de Cœna Domini) observatur de extinctione luminum, &c *De Ordine Antiph*, 44. Bearing in mind the weight which our Anglo-Saxon countrymen, by whose missionary toils so large a part of Germany was brought within the fold of Christ, must have had upon the church service of Mentz, where Amalarius was deacon, we are fully warranted in thinking that such a ceremony began in this island and hence spread itself to the other parts of Christendom

joined in singing *Christus Dominus factus est obediens*, &c. After this had been thrice repeated, prayers followed.[81]

(74) Early on the morning of

---

[81] (73) Quinta feria quæ et Cœna Domini dicitur, nocturnale officium agatur secundum quod in Antiphonario habetur. Comperimus etiam in quorumdam religiosorum ecclesiis quiddam fieri, quod ad animarum compunctionem spiritualis rei indicium exorsum est, videlicet ut peracto quicquid ad cantilenam illius noctis pertinet, evangeliique antiphona finita, nihilque iam cereorum luminis remanente, sint duo ad hoc idem destinati pueri in dextra parte chori, qui sonora psallant voce, *Kyrie eleison*, duoque in sinistra parte similiter qui respondeant *Christe eleison*, necnon et in occidentali parte, duo qui dicant *Domine miserere nobis* quibus peractis respondeat simul omnis chorus, *Christus Dominus factus est obediens usque ad mortem* Demum pueri dexterioris chori repetant quae supra eodem modo quo supra, usquequo chorus finiat quae supra. idemque tertio repetant quae supra, eodem ordine. Quibus tertio finitis, agant tacitas genu flexo more solito preces, qui ordo trium noctium uniformiter teneatur ab illis Qui, ut reor, ecclesiasticæ compunctionis usus a Catholicis ideo repertus est ut tenebrarum terror qui tripartitum mundum Dominica passione timore perculit insolito ac apostolicæ praedicationis consolatio quae universo mundo Christum Patri usque ad mortem pro generis humani salute obedientem revelaverat, manifestissime designetur Haec ergo inserenda censuimus, ut si quibus devotionis gratia complacuerint, habeant in his unde huius rei ignaros instruant, qui autem noluerint ad hoc agendum minime compellantur —*Reg Conc*, 86 Writing on the liturgy as followed in his own country, which had been won from heathenism to a belief in Christ by Anglo-Saxon missioners, Rupert, abbot of Duyts, lets us see how, till his days (c A.D. 1111) this very rite of the Anglo-Saxon Church was still kept up on the banks of the Rhine —Plerisque moris est, ut extinctis luminaribus, in ipsis tenebris lugubres tropi, præcinentibus cantatoribus et choro respondente, flebili modulatione decantentur, incipientibus a *Kyrie eleison* Significant autem lamenta sanctarum mulierum, quae, ut in Evangelio legimus, lamentabantur Dominum, sedentes contra sepulchrum —*De Divin Offic*, v. 27 [Hittorp, 1 953].

Maundy Thursday

all the younger clerks went to church, and, bare-foot, washed its pavement the while the priests, with their deacons and subdeacons, and other attendants, were going about washing each one of the altars there, with water hallowed for that especial purpose.

What Christ did to his apostles after the last supper,[82] the clergy, in commemorating it, now did very solemnly to the poor, and then to one another —wash their feet. For this purpose, in some fitting place out of the church itself, were gathered, before the hour for mass, a number of aged men, some-times the poor of the neighbourhood, sometimes wandering beggars, or pilgrims. Kneeling before these poor men, the younger among the clergy washed their feet, which, having wiped them dry, they kissed. These same poor people were after-wards fed, and while they ate, waited on by those clerks, who, ere letting their lowly guests take leave, gave unto each of them a small piece of money.[83]

---

[82] St John xiii. 5.

[83] Facto namque capitulo (feria v in coena Domini), discalcient se fratres, et intrantes ecclesiam, more obedientiæ, lavent pavimenta ecclesiæ, sacerdotibus interim cum ministris altaris, benedicta aqua, sacra altaria lavantibus

Ea enim die non fit celebratio missæ in aliquo altari donec lavetur.

(75) Quibus peractis, lotis pedibus, recalcient se. Sexta peracta, celebretur missa.

Pauperibus ante ad hoc collectis secundum numerum quem abbas præviderit, dehinc collectis in locum congruum, eant fratres

Those public sinners who had, on Ash Wednesday, been openly put out of the church, when known to have fulfilled the austerities allotted them during the Lenten fast, and to have become truly sorrowful, were on this day again openly brought back within its walls, and thus restored among their brethren to that place which, by their guilt, they had forfeited. Over these penitents, as they lay stretched upon the ground outside the church-door, the bishop or the priest, as it happened to be, read several prayers; after which, as an anthem was being sung, he raised them up, and then gave them absolution,[84] as is witnessed not only by Egbert but by Leofric also.[85] That the absolution, if not always, was sometimes at least, spoken in the Anglo-Saxon tongue, seems certain,

---

agendum mandatum, ubi canentes antiphonas eidem operi congruentes, lavent et extergant pedes pauperum, atque osculentur, et data aqua manibus eorum, dentur etiam eis cibaria, fiatque secundum abbatis arbitrium in eis distributio nummorum. —*Reg Conc.*, 87

[84] *Oratio ad Reconciliandum Pœnitentem, Feria v, in Cœna Domini.* Adesto, Domine, supplicationibus, &c *Alia.* Presta, quæsumus Domine, huic famulo tuo dignum pœnitentiæ fructum, &c Deus, humani generis, &c. *Oratio super pœnitentem* Da nobis, Domine ut sicut publicani, &c *Hic levas eos de pavimento his verbis dicendo, cunaturque antifona* Ant. Vivo ego, dicit Dominus, nolo mortem peccatoris, &c. *Psalmus,* Miserere mei Deus. Absolvimus vos vice beati Petri Apostolorum principis cui Dominus potestatem ligandi atque solvendi dedit, &c —*Egbert Pontifical*, 123, 124

[85] The same service, as it used to be administered in the south and western parts of this land, may be (76) seen in the Leofric missal [ed Warren, 92], where it is noticed thus —*Feria v., quæ est Cœna Domini* Præsentatur pœnitens in gremio ecclesiæ, et prostrato omni corpore in terra, dat orationem sacerdos ad reconciliandum ita. *An.* Cor mundum, &c.

from the fact that in the Egbert Pontifical, on the leaf at this place, is stitched a small strip of vellum written with the following tianslation of the Latin text :—h. Broðor ða leofestan, we onlysað eow of synna bendū on gewrixle ðaes eadegan Petres ðaia Apostola ealdres, ðam ðe ure dryhten ðone anweald sealde synna to gebindienne 7 eft to onlysenne. Ac swa miclum swa eow to belimpð eowra synna gewregednes 7 us to gebyreð sio forgifenes, sie God aelmihtig lif 7 haelo eallum eowrum synnum forgifen ðurh ðone ðe mid hun leofað 7 ricsað geond world aworld. Am̄ [56]

Some time after mid-day, and when none-song had been sung, a procession, formed of the clergy arrayed in their vestments, and bearing along with it a staff, the end of which was in the shape of a serpent, went down to the church-door. There, from out a flint, was struck fire, which was first hallowed,[57] and then used for lighting a candle that came out of the serpent's mouth. This staff, (77) with its burning tapei, was next given over to the head-sacristan, who carried it back in the

---

[56] *Egbert Pont* 158 [xvii]

[57] The Egbert Pontifical [129] gives the prayer for this blessing, thus —*Benedictio Ignis* Domine Deus noster, Pater Omnipotens, exaudi nos, lumen indeficiens tu es sancte conditor omnium luminum, benedic, Domine, hoc lumen quod a te sanctificatum atque benedictum est Tu inluminasti omnem mundum ut ab eo lumine accendamur, et inluminemur igni claritatis tuæ, sicut ignem inluminasti Moyse, ita inluminabis cordibus et sensibus nostris, ut ad vitam æternam pervenire mereamur Per The *Benedictio [Consecratio] ignis et ceræ* comes in the *Leofric Missal,* 223

procession to the choir; and from that candle
alone were lighted all the others needed that day
in the church, or about the altar. The same
ceremonial was repeated on Good Friday and
Holy Saturday.

Immediately after this procession, then began
high mass, in which the kiss of peace was not
given at the *Agnus Dei*, unless the celebrant
was a bishop. On this day, all partook of the
blessed sacrament; and at this day's sacrifice,
there was made a particular

Reservation of the Eucharist,

so that, under one kind, there might be not only
the viaticum as usual if needed for the dying,
but enough for the communion of all the people
and clergy, and an especial particle for the celebrant on the morrow, Good Friday, the one day
throughout the year whereon the church then
forbade, as she yet forbids, the holy mysteries
to be consecrated. The eucharist so reserved was
reverently carried to a place set aside for it in
the sacristy.[88]

---

[88] Dehinc hora congrua agatur nona, qua cantata, ob arcanum
cuiusdam mysterii indicium, si ita placuerit, induant se fratres,
et pergant ad ostium ecclesiæ ferentes hastam cum imagine
serpentis, ibique ignis de silice excutiatur, illo benedicto ab
abbate, candela quæ in ore serpentis infixa est, ab illo accendatur,
sicque edituo hastam deportante cuncti fratres chorum ingrediantur, unusque dehinc cereus ex illo illuminetur igne. Sexta
feria, eodem ordine agatur, ac a decano portetur Sabbato similiter, a præpositoque deferatur Et post hæc celebratio missæ, ad

But the most striking feature in this day's ceremonial, was the

Hallowing of the Holy Oils.

An ampul of gold held the chrism; other two of silver were got ready; one for the oil of exorcism, the other for the oil of the sick. The purest olive oil was sought for the purpose, but along with that for the chrism or creme, they mingled sweet smelling balsam. Then, as now, this chrism used to be employed in the consecration of bishops and priests, at the coronation of kings, and for the latter of the two unctions given at baptism, for the sacrament of confirmation, for anointing altars and the walls of a newly built church, and the blessing of bells. But besides these occasions, the Anglo-Saxons applied chrism to their deacons' hands in ordaining them, as well as for the blessing of crucifixes, when made of gold or silver.[89] The oil of exorcism

quam *Dominus vobiscum* minime dicatur nisi ab episcopo tantummodo ubi chrisma conficitur, a quo, etiam, in eucharistiæ acceptione, pacis osculum praesbyteris, ter (78) *Agnus Dei* decantato, solummodo detur, ab aliis vero minime praesumatur: in qua missa, sicut et insequentium dierum communicatio præbetur tam fratribus quam cunctis fidelibus, reservata nihilominus ea die eucharistia quae sufficit ad communicandum cunctis altera die. —*Reg. Conc*, 87.

[89] Of this chrism, and its several ritual uses, thus speaks Beda In urbe Judææ, quæ vocatur Engaddi, nobiliores cæteris vineæ nascuntur, utpote de quibus liquor non vini, sed opobalsami defluit . Namque in vineis Engaddi, ut præfati sumus, balsamum gignitur, quod in chrismatis confectione, liquori olivæ admisceri, ac pontificali benedictione solet consecrari, quatenus fideles omnes

was then, as now, (79) employed for the first of the unctions at baptism: the Anglo-Saxons, besides this, had other ritual and pious uses for it. The oil of the sick was used for aneling those whose sickness threatened them with speedy death.

In his epistle entitled *Quando dividis Chrisma*, Ælfric states to what parochial purposes these holy oils were applied :—" O ye mass-priests, my brothers, we will now say to you what we have not before said, because to-day we are to divide our oil, hallowed in three ways, as the book points out to us ; *i.e.*, oleum sanctum, et oleum chrismatis, et oleum infirmorum ; that is, in English, holy oil, the second is chrism, and sick men's oil: and ye ought to have three flasks ready for the three oils, for we dare not put them together in one oil vessel, because each of them is hallowed apart for a particular service. With the holy oil ye shall mark heathen children on the breast, and betwixt the shoulders, in the middle, with the sign of the cross, before ye baptize it in the font-water ; and when it comes from the water, ye shall make the sign of the cross on the head with the holy chrism. In the holy font, before ye baptize them, ye shall pour chrism in the figure of Christ's cross, and no one

cum impositione manus sacerdotalis, qua Spiritus sanctus accipitur, hac unctione signentur, qua etiam altare dominicum, cum dedicatur, et cætera quae sacrosancta esse debent, perunguntur.—*In Cantica Canticorum*, ii [*P L*, xci. 1097, 1098]

may be sprinkled with the font-water after the chrism is poured in." [90]

The oleum infirmorum, or oil for the sick, was blessed by the bishop, ere he began that short prayer in the canon, *Per quem : Through whom, O Lord, thou dost always create, sanctify, quicken, bless, and give us all these good things, &c.*, which goes immediately before the *Pater noster.* Unshrouded by any sort of veil, the ampul which held this oil was brought by a deacon to the bishop, who, stepping somewhat aside from the altar, then said (80) the prayers of blessing over it. When hallowed, this oil was either put to stand upon a column which had been set there for the purpose, or carried away and laid by at once in its own place; and the bishop went forwards with the holy sacrifice. Having ended mass, the bishop walked to his episcopal chair, and waited there for the procession, which, with much ritual solemnity, was about to fetch unto him from the sacristy, for consecration, the oil and balsam, or the chrism, and the oil of exorcism to be used at baptism.

In this procession walked acolytes, having lighted tapers in their candlesticks, clerks bearing crosses, thurifers with their smoking censers, and a deacon having in his hands a golden-bound book of the Gospels. The chrism, and the oil

---

[90] Thorpe, *Ancient Laws,* II 391

of exorcism or catechumens, were each carried
muffled within the folds of a silken scarf, which
fell about the shoulders of its bearer, though
the oil for the sick had been taken before, un-
covered, up to the bishop. Next came, arrayed
in chasuble, and walking two and two, those
priests, usually twelve, who were to bear witness,
and help in the hallowing of these oils. This
long line ended with a crowd of singing-boys,
who as they went chanted that beautiful hymn,
Audi, judex mortuorum When the chrism had
been breathed upon, and signed with the cross,
and God's blessing called down, and it had been
duly hallowed by the bishop, the golden ampul
which held it was carried round, in a subdeacon's
hands, to be kissed by all those about the altar.
A like token of respect was also shown to the
oil of exorcism, as it was borne in the hands of
an acolyte to its proper place. The ceremonial
for this function is set forth in more than one
Anglo-Saxon codex. The Egbert Pontifical has
full rubrics.[91]

---

[91] *Feria v in Cena Domini hora vi^ta celebratur missa ad Lateranis
sic incipiens Pontifex dicit,* (81) Oremus *Tunc ponuntur in altare
Sancta ; et altare est cavum. Omnibus rite in altare compositis, oblata
et libamenta, paucaque per ecclesiam luminaria accensa, diaconi dalmaticis vestiti, cerostata iiiij. ante altare posita. Stante ante altare
pontifice, et elevata dicente voce,* Sursum corda *Respondet populus,*
Habemus ad Dominum, &c . . . *Finito* Vere dignum *Dicit omnis
clericus et populus,* Sanctus, Sanctus, Sanctus *Sic intrat in missam
usque* Sed venie, quæsumus Domine, largitor admittas Per
Christum. *Tunc diaconus cardinalis sumet oleum pro infirmis, portet
usque ad pontificem, at ille paululum divertens se ab altare, stans in*

In the Leofric Missal there are two services for
the hallowing of the oils : the first is headed thus :
Feria v Cœna Domini in ultimo ad missam, &c.
Conficitur chrisma ;[92] but the second, which was
in all likelihood written some few years later,
gives the rubrics at much greater length [93]

---

*suo gradu, signans oleum in manu diaconi, et orationem institutam
supra tacite dicens.*

Emitte, Domine Spiritum, Sanctum tuum Paraclytum de cœlis in
hanc pinguedinem olivæ, &c   *Oratione finita, ponebatur oleum supra
columnam quandam, et sacerdos missam ordine sua celebrans dicit,* Per
quem hæc omnia, Domine, &c . . . Libera nos, &c., *Et pontifex tacite
signat calicem cum oblata sanctificata, nemine respondente. Diaconi
cooperiant sacramenta   Facta missa, iterum in altare ascendente pontifice ad sedem suam, tunc archidiaconus ascendens cum chrismate,
ampulam auream cum pallio albo habens in manu sua, et illud pallium
mittens ex parte supra dexteram scapulam, stansque ante pontificem, et
omnes episcopi et presbyteri et diaconi in circuitu ejus   Et ille pontifex
tribus vicibus sufflans in ampulam tangens sua manu, dicit magna
voce,* Sursum corda.   .

Benedictio chrismatis principalis.   Vere dignum.   Qui in principio, &c .   *Et pontifex signat in modum crucis tribus vicibus cum
pollice, et insufflat iterum tribus vicibus, cum halitu signat in crucis
modum.   Et subdiaconus suscipiens de manu archidiaconi portat
cunctis in presbiterio stantibus ad osculandum.   Alter vero cardinalis
diaconus sequitur cum ampulla habens oleum exorcizatum, argenteo
vestitus pallio fusco expansum supra humerum sinistrum (82) suum,
ascendit ad pontificem   Et ille oleum signans, oratione consecrationis,
nullo respondente, submissa quasi tacita magis voce benedicens   Exor-
cismus olei incipit,*

Deus qui virtute Sancti Spiritus tui imbecillarum mentium
rudimenta confirmas   .

*Finita oratione consecrationis, ab accolitis ad salutandum propheratur,
et in secretario ponatur.   Communicante clero omnique populo, dicit
pontifex omnibus communicantibus,* Accepit Jesus panem   Oremus.
Dicta oratione, respondit omnis populus Amen —*Egbert Pontifical,*
120–122

[92] *Leofric Missal,* 222

[93] *Feria v. hoc est in Cœna Domini. . .   Ante missam uero faciant
mandatum cum peregrinis et hospitibus. . . .   Et ita per ordinem usque
Per quem hęc omnia   Tunc offerantur pontifici oleum de ampullis*

(84) But besides such a solemn hallowing of the holy oils, our Anglo-Saxon brethren observed, during this day's mass, another rite, which consisted in

quas offerunt populi, unguendos tam infirmos quam energuminos Et in ultimo, antequam dicatur Per quem hęc omnia, exorcizet et benedicat illud, tam ipse quam omnes presbiteri qui assunt, ita ut tantum possit a circumstantibus audiri. Item benedictio eiusdem olei, ad omnem languorem, quocumque tempore. . Et oleum reportetur et in loco suo conseruetur. Missa uero ordine suo agatur usque dum benedictiones episcopales (83) soluantur Et Pax Domini sit semper uobiscum Tunc communicet solus pontifex ante altare, et diaconus offerat ei calicem, et non frangat oblatas, nisi eam solam unde ille communicat illo tantum die Postquam communicauerit episcopus, ponat diaconus calicem super altare. Deinde acceptam a subdiacono patenam ponat iuxta calicem de latere sinistro, et statim a duobus subdiaconis utrimque cooperiatur de sindone munda, quam prius preparauerant in ora altaris e regione pontificis, post corporalem expansam Tunc domnus episcopus uadat ad sedem suam cum diaconibus, et expectet

Ordo de Consecratione principalis crismatis *Expectante uero in sede sua pontifice, ueniant ad sacrarium .xii presbiteri, et ceteri clerici, quantum opus sit ad deferendum cum omni decore oleum crismale, ac oleum catecuminorum et neophitorum, usque in ecclesiam ante episcopum Sint enim idem presbiteri parati, et cum eis ceteri clerici casulis et sollempnibus uestimentis Tunc duo acoliti accipientes illas duas ampullas, quę ad crisma et ad oleum catecuminorum consecrari debent, inuolutas cum sindonibus de albo serico, ita ut uideri possint a medio. Teneant in brachio sinistro, proiectis sindonibus super scapulam sinistram, ita ut pertingant ad scapulam dextram, quatinus possint dependentia retineri. Et procedant, et ordinent se illi presbiteri et predicti clerici rite et ordinabiliter, ita ut primum ambulent duo acoliti cum candelabris et ardentibus cereis Deinde portentur duę cruces, et inter illas medium crismale oleum Post eas portentur duo turibula cum incenso, et inter illa medium oleum catecuminorum. Deinde portetur euangelium, ut impleatur omne bonum. Postea sequantur, bini et bini, illi xii presbiteri, testes et cooperatores eiusdem sacrosancti crismalis mysterii Tunc uero subsequantur pueri, in laudem eiusdem mysterii concinentes hos uersus ad hoc congruentes Audi, iudex mortuorum, una spes mortalium Ibid, 256-258.*

The blessing of Milk and Honey.

A short time before the celebrant came to the words *Per quem*, &c. in the canon at which, as we said just now, the oil for the sick was hallowed, a cup having in it milk mingled with honey was set on the altar, and over it he spoke this blessing-prayer, so that it might end that sentence, "through whom, O Lord, thou dost always create, sanctify, quicken, bless, and give us all these good things," &c.[94]

The Washing of Feet,

or the "mandatum," or maundy, as it came to be called from those words of Christ, *Mandatum novum do vobis*—A new commandment I give you (St. John xiii. 34)—when He washed His apostles' feet,—and sung then, as now, by the Church on this occasion, was another religious rite, which, though practised at many (85) other times in the year, the clergy of a cathedral, and the monks in their minsters, observed, with more than usual

---

[94] The form in the Egbert Pontifical is somewhat shorter than in other codices · *In Cœna Domini antequam dicatur* Per quem haec omnia. *Benedictio lactis et mellis.* Benedic, Domine, has creaturas fontis lactis et mellis, et pota famulos tuos de hoc fonte perenni, qui est Spiritus veritatis, et enutri eos de hoc melle et lacte, tu enim, Domine, promisisti patribus nostris Abrahae Isaac et Jacob dicens Introducam vos in terram repromissionis, terram fluentem lacte et melle ... Conjunge, Domine, famulos tuos Spiritu Sancto, sicut conjunctum est hoc lac et mel in Christo Jesu Domino nostro, qui tecum *Egbert Pontifical*, 129 The Leofric Missal gives a like form (p. 224), and a longer one may be seen in the *Rituale Ecclesiæ Dunelmensis* [ed Surt Soc., p 129]

solemnity, on the day itself, commemorative of the Last Supper. A portion of the morning's earlier functions had already consisted in the ceremonial of washing the feet of the neighbouring poor and stranger-pilgrims; [95] but it was when evening came, and they went through this observance a second time, that the rite could be witnessed in all its fulness. As soon as even-song was over, a procession led the celebrant from the choir to the chapter-house, or some building beyond the church walls. Amid the crowd of clerks might be seen a deacon vested in a festive dalmatic, and carrying a large richly jewel-studded Gospelbook, to honour which, acolytes with lighted tapers in their hands, and a thurifer with a burning thurible, walked before him. On reaching the spot, whereat all due preparations had been made, the bishop washed, and dried, and kissed the feet of his upper clergy, or the abbot those of the elder monks in his house, as it might happen · the like was then done to this same personage, by the official next in dignity to himself. At this part of the ceremony used, in all likelihood, to be sung the hymn, *In Cœna Domini*, Tellus ac æthra jubilant; the strophes of which speak of those works of love wrought by Christ for man this day, and remembered in its rites, thus:

[95] In the *Leofric Missal* [p. 256, ed. Warren] we find this rubric *Feria v hoc est in Cœna Domini. . . . Ante missam uero faciant mandatum cum peregrinis et hospitibus.*

Hac nocte factor omnium
Potenti sat mysterio,
Carnem suam cum sanguine
In escam transfert animæ

(86)   Pallet servus obsequio
Cum angelorum Dominum
Ferendo lympham linteo
Cernit cœno procumbere

And truly may we believe that, like the other peoples of Christendom in those ages, our Anglo-Saxon fathers were taught to let, more especially upon this solemn day, the bondsman go free for the love of their common Lord and Redeemer :—

Nexi solvuntur hodie
Carnis ac cordis carcere
Unguen sacratur chrismatis
Spes inde crescit miseris [96]

When the washing of feet was done, they went in procession to the eating-hall; there the love-cup was sent about, and every one without exception sipped of its wine, along with which had, no doubt, been mixed a little of that milk and honey blessed before at that day's mass. All this while, the deacon, from a high reading-desk, con-

---

[96] In a codex of the missal written out at the desire, and for the use, of Ratold, abbot of Corbie (who died A D. 986), Dom. Menard found this hymn, and has published it, together with its old notation, among his notes on the *Liber Sacramentorum* of St. Gregory [*P.L*, lxxviii 326]. As the reading of this MS is evidently truer than that in the *Latin Hymns of the Anglo-Saxon Church* (ed Surtees Society, p 80), we have given it the preference.

tinued to recite that chapter in St. John's Gospel
(xiii. 1), descriptive of the Last Supper and the
washing of feet.[97]

The Still Days

was a name which the Anglo-Saxons gave to
Maundy Thursday, Good Friday, and Holy Saturday. The bells in all likelihood were not rung
during these last three days of Holy Week, but
the people were called to church (88) by the loud
strokes from an iron knocker, or a wooden mallet

---

[97] The following rubrics from St Dunstan's pen, sketch out to
us a picture of a ceremony which, we may be sure, took place on
this day in every large church throughout Anglo-Saxondom

Peracta missæ celebratione, omnes ad mixtum pergant   (87) post
mixtum, quos voluerit abbas ex fratribus, secum adsumens suum
peragat mandatum , quo peracto, vesperas celebrent, dehinc refectionem fratrum agant   post quam tempore congruo, eorundem
agatur mandatum , qui tamen fratres prius pedes suos diligenter
emundent, venientesque ad mandatum hebdomadarii ministri,
secundum morem suum abbatem antecedentes, mandatum agant,
quos sequitur in chonca sua singulorum pedes lavans ministran-
tibus sibi quos voluerit ad hoc obsequium, quos extergat, et osculetur   Quo peracto, resideat abbas in sede sua, veniantque priores,
et ei eadem exhibeant   Inde vero dum manus lavant, diaconus
hebdomadarius, et reliqui ministri eant et induant se, signoque
collationis moto, ingrediantur, diacono dalmatica induto cum textu
Evangelii, præcedentibus cereis, et turibulo , legaturque Evangelium secundum Johannem *Ante diem festum* donec tintinnabulum
pulsetur   tunc præcedente processione subsequatur omnis congregatio, cunctisque in refectorio residentibus, idem diaconus stans
prosequatur Evangelii sequentia imposito super ambone Evangelio
Interim abbas propinando circueat fratres cum singulis potibus
singulorum osculans manus , qua peracta ministratione, residente
abbate dicatur *Tu autem Domine*   Tunc a priore propinetur abbati,
et reliquis ministris qui assistebant, Evangelioque finito potibusque
haustis, procedat processio, et exuant se fratres, sintque cum reliquis ad complendum —*Reg   Conc* , 87

on a board that was light enough to be carried
in the hands of a youth about the town, as
Amalarius tells us.[98] Of this same time, too,
Ælfric says: "Church customs forbid any
sermon to be said on the three still days."[99]
As on the last, so on this night "Tenebræ"
were sung and accompanied with the same ceremonial.

Good Friday

brought along with it its own rites still peculiar
to that mournful day. In the afternoon, about
none-song tide, the people went to church, and
there had read to them the Passion from St.
John's gospel. At those words out of the Psalms,
"They have parted my garments among them,"
two deacons, hastily as it were, stripped the altar
of its linen cloth · then began the ceremony for

Kissing the Cross.

After the collects had been said, and while the
choir was wailing forth those sorrowful yet love-
sweetened upbraidings from Christ unto the Jews,
" My people, what have I done to thee," with the

---

[98] Omnis salutatio deest in istis tribus diebus, sive noctibus
ad vitandam salutationem pestiferam, qualem diabolus Judas
exercuit Necnon etiam altitudo signorum quæ fiebat per vasa
ærea deponitur, et lignorum sonus usquequaque humilior æris
sono, necessario pulsatur, ut conveniat populus ad ecclesiam —
De Eccl Offic, iv 21 [Hittorp, 471]

[99] Homilies, ed. Thorpe, i 219

response of the Trisagion first in Greek and then in Latin, a muffled crucifix was held up by two deacons, who stood half-way between the choir and the altar. From this spot they carried this veiled rood towards the altar, before which they laid it down on a pillow. After due time this crucifix was unshrouded by the two (89) deacons, who, in doing so, uttered in a low chant, "Behold the wood of the Cross." Then barefoot, as he and all the other clergy were from the very beginning of this day's service, whoever happened to be the celebrant, whether bishop, abbot, or priest, came forward, and halting thrice on the way to throw himself on the ground, in most lowly wise kissed the crucifix After him followed the clergy, then the people, to offer the same token of homage to their crucified Lord. All the while this kissing of the cross was going on, the choir sang those anthems — Ecce lignum crucis, Crucem tuam adoramus, Dum fabricator mundi, and the hymn Pange Lingua. At the conclusion of it all returned to their places [1]

---

[1] Inde Parascevæ agatur nocturna laus sicut supradictum est post hæc venientes ad Primam, discalciati omnes incedant quousque crux adoretur Eadem enim die, hora nona, abbas cum fratribus accedat ad ecclesiam, &c Legitur *Passio Domini nostri Jesu Christi secundum Johannem* Ad illam passionem, diaconus non dicat *Dominus vobiscum,* sed *Passio Domini* et reliqua, nullo respondente *Gloria tibi Domine,* et quando legitur in evangelio *Partiti sunt vestimenta mea* et reliqua, statim duo diaconi nudent altare sindone quæ prius fuerat sub evangelio posita, in modum furantium post hoc celebrentur orationes, et veniens abbas ante altare incipiat

The following is the rubric for the Good Friday service as contained in the Leofric Missal : *The bishop approaches alone and first adores, then kisses the cross. Then the priests, the deacons, and the rest come in their turn; and afterwards the people.*[2]

Besides the seven penitential psalms, special prayers of humble supplication, and adoration of the Crucified were sometimes said by the cele-

---

orationes solemnes quæ sequuntur Quibus expletis per ordinem, statim præparetur crux ante altare, interposito spatio inter ipsam et altare, sustentata hinc et inde a duobus diaconibus Tunc cantent *Popule meus*, respondentes autem duo subdiaconi stantes ante crucem canant Græce, *Agios o theos, Agios yschiros, Agios athanatos eleyson emas* Itemque schola idipsum Latine *Sanctus Deus* Deferatur tunc ab ipsis diaconibus ante altare, et eos acolitus cum pulvillo sequatur, super quem sancta crux ponatur, antiphonaque finita quam schola respondet Latine, canant ibidem sicut (90) prius *Quia eduxi vos per desertum*. Idem vero respondeant subdiaconi Græce sicut prius *Agios* ut supra, itemque schola Latine ut prius *Sanctus Deus*, itemque diaconi levantes crucem, canant sicut prius *Quid ultra*, item subdiaconi sicut prius *Agios* ut supra, itemque schola Latine *Sanctus Deus* ut supra Post hæc vertentes se ad clerum, nudata cruce, dicant antiphonam *Ecce lignum crucis*, antiphonam *Crucem tuam adoramus*, antiphonam *Dum fabricator mundi Pange lingua* Ilico, ea nudata, veniat abbas ante crucem sanctam, ac tribus vicibus se prosternat cum omnibus fratribus dexterioris chori, scilicet senioribus ac iunioribus, et cum magno cordis suspirio septem pœnitentiæ psalmos cum orationibus sanctæ cruci competentibus decantando peroret . . et eam humiliter deosculans surgat Dehinc sinistra deosculans surgat Dehinc sinisterioris chori omnes fratres eadem mente devota peragant, nam salutata ab abbate vel omnibus cruce, redeat ipse abbas ad sedem suam usque dum omnis clerus et populus hoc idem faciat.—*Reg Conc.*, 87, 88

[2] *Uenit pontifex solus et adoratam deosculatur crucem Deinde presbiteri, et diaconi, et ceteri per ordinem, deinde populus* —Ed. Warren, 262

brant, as with his ministers he knelt before the cross ere he kissed it.[3]

---

[3] These prayers are given in the Egbert Pontifical, 134, 135. *Orationes dicendæ cum adoratur Sancta Crux* Domine Jesu Christe, gloriosissime conditor mundi, qui cum splendor gloriæ æqualis Patri Sanctoque Spiritui carnem inmaculatam assumere dignatus es, et gloriosissimas tuas sanctas palmas crucis patibulo permisisti configi, ut claustra dissipares inferni, et humanum genus liberares a (91) morte miserere mihi misero oppressum facinore, ac nequitiarum labe sordidatum, non me digneris derelinquere, gloriosissime Domine, sed dignare mihi indulgere quod malum egi, exaudi me prostratum ad adorandam vivificam crucem tuam, ut in his sacris sollempnis tibi merear assistere mundus qui vivis.

Alia

Domine Jesu Christe, adoro te in cruce ascendentem, spineam coronam in capite portantem, deprecor te, ut ipsa crux liberet me ab angelo percutiente

Domine Jesu Christe, adoro te in cruce vulneratum, felle et aceto potatum deprecor te, ut tua mors sit vita mea

Domine Jesu Christe, adoro te descendentem ad inferos, liberantem captivos deprecor te, ut non me permittas introire in pœnis inferni

Domine Jesu Christe, adoro te ascendentem in cœlo, sedentem ad dexteram Patris deprecor te, miserere mei

Domine Jesu Christe, adoro te venturum in judicio deprecor te, ut in tuo adventu ne intres in judicio cum famulo tuo, me peccatore, sed deprecor te, ut dimittas peccata mea ante quam judices Amen —*Egbert Pontifical*, 134, 135

In one of the oldest liturgical manuscripts belonging to our Anglo-Saxon period,—so old indeed that Wanley thinks it to be one of those sent over hither by Pope St Gregory to St Austin *Cat* 222),—we find the following addresses to the cross [written in the leaves at the end of the volume in a hand of the eleventh century]

(Oratio ad Crucem)

O sanctum et venerabile nostri Redemptoris signum, &c [f 157ᵛ].

(Alia)

[O Jesu Christe, crucifixe domine f 158]
Salve crux sancta et veneranda, &c [f 158ᵛ]

(Salutatio, sive oratio ad crucem)

Ave sancta crux omnium arborum gloriosissima [f 159]

(92) Though not insisted on for general observance, there was a rubric that allowed a rite, at
this part of the office, to be followed, which may
be called

The Burial of the Rood

At the hind part of the altar, and where the
hollow within might be easily laid open, there
was made a kind of sepulchre, hung all about with
a curtain.   Inside this recess, and just beneath
the altar-stone itself, the cross, after the ceremony
of kissing it had been done, was carried by its
two deacons, who had, however, first wrapped it
up in a linen cloth or winding-sheet.   As they
bore their burden along, they sang certain anthems till they reached this spot, and there they
left the cross ; and it lay thus entombed till Easter
morn, watched all that while by two, three, or
more monks, who chanted psalms through day
and night   When the Burial was completed the

(Alta)

Te Sancta Dei crux humiliter adoro [f 160].
Cotton MS Vespasian, A 1 in the British Museum —[Cat of Anct.
MSS , Pt II 8]
    Why such a secondary respect or lower kind of worship—a dis-
tinction which the Anglo-Saxons from the beginning had been
taught to know and make, as we said before (vol. III 155)—
should be shown to the cross, is set forth in another codex —
HÆ SUNT QUATUOR CAUSÆ QUIBUS SANCTA CRUX ADORATUR.
[Prima causa est ; qui in una die septem cruces addit, aut septies
unam crucem adoret, septem porto inferni clauduntur illi et
septem portæ paradisi aperiuntur ei Secunda causa est , si primum

deacon and sub-deacon came from the sacristy with the reserved host.[4] Then followed

The Mass of the Pre-sanctified,

the rubrics for which may be seen in the Leofric

---

opus tuum tibi sit ad crucem, omnes dæmones si fuissent circa te, non potuissent nocere tibi. Tertia causa est ; qui non declinat ad crucem non recepit pro se passionem Christi : qui autem declinat, recepit eam et liberabitur. Quarta causa est ; quantam temæ† pergis ad crucem, quasi tantum de hereditate propria offeras domino.] *Cotton MS. Titus, D.* xxvii. (sæc. x.) fol. 70. There is [at fol. 65ᵛ] an illumination of the crucifixion, and at the top these verses :

Haec crux consignet Ælfwinum corpore mente
In qua suspendens traxit Deus omnia secum.

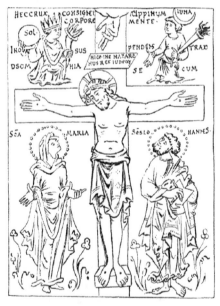

[4] Nam quia ea die (Paraschevæ) depositionem corporis Salvatoris nostri celebramus, usum quorundam religiosorum imitabilem ad fidem indocti vulgi ac neophitorum corroborandam æquiparando sequi, si ita cui visum fuerit vel sibi taliter placuerit, hoc modo decrevimus. Sit autem in una parte altaris qua vacuum fuerit,

Missal[5] and St. Dunstan's "Rule."[6] In this there
was no consecration, but after the reading of the
solemn prayers and lections of the day the reserved host was placed upon the altar with a
chalice of unconsecrated wine. The Lord's Prayer
was said as at the end of the Canon, with its
bidding before it and its embolism after it, and

---

quædam assimulatio sepulchri, velamenque quoddam in giro ten-
sum, in quod dum sancta crux adorata fuerit, deponatur hoc
ordine Veniant diaconi qui prius portaverunt eam, et involvant
eam sindone in loco ubi adorata est, tunc reportent eam canentes
antiphonam, *In pace in idipsum* (93) *habitabit*, item, *Caro mea re-
quiescet in spe*, donec veniant ad locum monumenti, depositaque
cruce, cum omni reverentia custodiatur usque dominicam noctem
resurrectionis Nocte vero ordinentur duo fratres aut tres aut
plures, si tanta fuerit congregatio, qui ibidem psalmos decantando
excubias fideles exerceant —*Reg Conc*, 88

[5] Quibus peractis, egrediantur diaconus et subdiaconus de sacrario cum corpore Domini quod pridie remansit, et calice cum vino
non consecrato, et ponant super altare Tunc sacerdos veniat
ante altare, et dicat voce sonora *Oremus*, *Praeceptis salutaribus
moniti*, et *Pater noster*, inde *Libera nos quæsumus*, *Domine*, usque
Per omnia secula seculorum, et sumat abbas de sancto sacrificio, et
ponat in calicem nihil dicens, et communicent omnes cum silentio.—
Ibid, 88

[6] *Incipit ordo Feria ii Passionis Domini*. *Hora nona procedant
omnes ad ecclesiam, et egreditur sacerdos e sacrario cum sacris ordinibus
nihil canentibus, et veniunt ante altare, postulet pro se orare, dicens,*
Oremus *Et adnuntiat diaconus*, Flectamus genua *Et post paululum,* Leuate *Et dat orationem hanc* Deus a quo et Judas reatus
sui pœnam, et confessionis suae latro premium sumpsit, conce-
(de) nobis tuae propitiationis effectum, ut sicut in passione sua
Jesus Christus, dominus noster diuersa utrisque intulit stipendia
meritorum, ita nobis ablato uetustatis errore, resurrectionis suæ
gratiam largiatur. Qui tecum uiuit. *Istas orationes expletas, in-
grediuntur diaconi in sacrario, et procedunt cum corpore Domini sine
uino consecrato, quod altera die remansit, et ponunt super altare et dicat
sacerdos* Oremus. Preceptis salutaribus moniti, et diuina insti-
tutione formati audemus dicere, Pater noster *Et adorata cruce,
communicent omnes.*—*Leofric Missal*, 94, 96

the commixture was made in silence. Then followed the communion of all who were present.

(94) The meaning of these customs is embodied in one of Ælfric's canons, which says "Housel may not be hallowed on Good Friday, because Christ suffered on that day for us; but there must, nevertheless, be done what appertains to that day; so that two lectures be read with two expositions, and with two collects, and Christ's Passion; and afterwards, the prayers. And let them pray to the holy rood, so that they all greet the rood of God with kiss. Let the priest then go to the altar of God, with the housel bread that he hallowed on Thursday, and with unhallowed wine mixed with water, and conceal it with the corporal, and then immediately say, ' Oremus præceptis salutaribus moniti,' and ' Pater noster,' to the end. And then let him say to himself, ' Libera nos quæso Domine ab omnibus malis'; and aloud, ' Per omnia secula seculorum.' Let him then put a part of the housel into the chalice, as it is, however, usual; then let him go silently to the housel; and for the rest, let look who will."[7]

On

Holy Saturday,

as on the two foregoing days, the service did not begin till the hour for singing none-song,

---

[7] *Canons of Ælfric,* in Thorpe, 11 359, § 36.

that is, in the afternoon ; and the first of its rites was the hallowing of

The Paschal or Easter Fire.

By this name must we call the blessing of the fire upon Holy Saturday among the Anglo-Saxons and such of the German nations as they brought, by the apostolic toils of St. Boniface, St. Wilbrord, and other missioners sent thither from this country, to believe in Christ. Not only here at home, but when they went to preach abroad, the (95) hallowing of fire on this day was done by the Anglo-Saxons with some liturgical splendour, and after a certain way almost peculiar to themselves. It would seem that the olden custom was to catch, by means of a burning-glass, the first spark of fire for this day's service from the sun, from heaven as it were, as often as the weather would allow ; but if the sky happened to be clouded, the fire was struck from out a flint.

All the peoples of northern Europe kept, until they threw off heathenism and became Christians, a great festival at spring-tide, in honour of the sun ; for they worshipped this luminary as the giver to the earth of light and heat. To make good come out of evil, and to bring men to yield their worship, not to the works themselves, but unto God who wrought them, the Church thought fit to snatch from this ceremony its heathenish, and bestow upon it instead a Christian, meaning ; and for this end she hallowed the new fire at Easter time.[8] In those ages, Easter Sunday was looked upon as the first day of the new year : fire, even to the last spark, was everywhere put out, in the public minster and parish church, as well as the private dwelling, from the king's house downwards to the hind's hovel. Late on the eve of the coming year, the Church hallowed while she renewed the fire for her own use in the ritual, and for her children's use within the walls of their private homes. To teach the world how everything must (96) come to us from God, it was from the sun's rays—from heaven as it were—that the Church fetched her new fire. After it had been solemnly blessed, light was taken from this flame to kindle the thurible, to light the lamps hung about the altar, and the tapers carried in the acolytes' hands at the holy sacrifice. That day men and women took home with them a light from the sanctuary ; and the hearth that had all day long been cold and brandless now became warm and bright once more, and the evening candle shone bright again, with a flame from the new hallowed fire. For church-use at least, this fire might truly be said to have lived the whole

---

[8] Thus did our St. Boniface in Germany, and a remembrance of it was, till a late period, kept up there — Inclytæ famæ, sumptuosarumque victimarum idolum cui Retto nomen, deturbavit (St Bonifacius) . Factum autem adhuc hominum memoria, ut in deturbatæ superstitionis memoriam luculentus ipso resurrectionis die, ignis qui Paschalis etiam alibi vocatur excitaretur — Serarius, *Moguntiacarum Rerum*, iii 474

year through, for as lamp was lighted from lamp,
it thus crept on burning from one Holy Saturday
to another. Our own Beda tells us, "that other
fire than what comes down from heaven may
not burn in the holy lamps nor be lighted on
God's altar."[9] This passage is quite darksome
to such as do not know the above-mentioned
fact; for him who does, our venerable countryman's words lend no small help to understand
the very custom from which they borrow their
own meaning. How this fire is to be got from
heaven, our St. Boniface indirectly hints, in the
question to Pope Zachary, whom he asks whether
at Rome they employed for that purpose a crystal,
no doubt as his own countrymen the Anglo-
Saxons did, like a burning-glass, to catch this
fire from above : the pontiff's answer shows that
it was not a Roman usage.[10]

From the olden ritual, and the early liturgical
writers in those parts of Germany which heard

---

[9] Nec ignis alius quam qui de cœlo descendit, vel in lucernis
sanctis ardere vel in altari Dei debet accendi —*De Tabernaculo*, III
I [*P L*, xci 463]

[10] De igne autem paschali quod inquisisti, a sanctis priscis
Patribus, ex quo per Dei et Domini nostri Iesu Christi gratiam,
et pretioso sanguine ejus Ecclesia dedicata est, quinta feria
Paschæ, dum sacrum chrisma consecratur (97) tres lampades
magnæ capacitatis, ex diversis candelis ecclesiæ oleo collecto, in
secretiori ecclesiæ loco ad figuram interioris tabernaculi insistente,
indeficienter cum multa diligentia inspectæ ardebunt, ita ut oleum
ipsum sufficere possit usque ad tertium diem. De quibus candelis
sabbato sancto pro sacri fontis baptismate sumptus ignis per
sacerdotem renovabitur De crystallis autem, ut asseruisti, nullam
habemus traditionem —Zacharias Bonifacio, in *Epist. S. Zachar*,
xiii [*P L*, lxxxix 951]

and took their Christian belief from Anglo-Saxon
preachers, we may fairly draw some few hints
of what must have once been the practice in
our own land. That this new fire, then, was
got, not only by striking sparks from a flint,
but also through a burning-glass, when the sky
was cloudless and the sun's rays strong enough,
we gather from Rupert abbot of Duyts (c. A.D.
1111).[11] In some ritual customs which St. Ulric
(who was made bishop of Augsburg A.D. 924)
first set forth, but in after times became adopted
for the guidance of their house by certain Cluniac
monks, we find that the burning-glass employed
for this liturgical purpose used to be carried, as
one of the Church's solemn appliances, in the
great procession on Holy Saturday, and afterwards
kept (98) with no small care. From its being
called a precious stone, or beril, we are led to
think that it generally was a fine large piece of
rock-crystal mounted in a frame of gold or silver:
the duty of keeping it, and of carrying it in the
procession belonged to the apocrisiarius, or
principal custodian of the church.[12] For this

---

[11] Amisso igne, qui ad matutinos . . extinguitur, ad lapidem
per eosdem tres dies confugimus, ut vel lapidem percutientes ex
abstrusis ejus venis ignem occultum eliciamus, vel liquidum crystalli lapidem sereno coelo soli objicientes, radium ejus trajectum
per ejusdem crystalli orbiculum spectabili miraculo in subjectam
suscipiamus escam —*De Divinis Officiis*, v 28 [Hittorp, 953]

[12] Post nonam statim sacerdote alba induto, et caeteris ad
majorem missam servituris, faciunt processionem ad novum ignem
consecrandum cantantes psalmum 50mum   Ante processionem

evening's service, and to burn at stated hours
through the period from Easter till Ascension
day—besides answering as a symbolical object—
there was got ready a tall, thick wax-light, called

The Paschal Candle,

that used to be set near the north ambo, upon
its own high candlestick.   Standing in this pulpit,
a deacon sang, after a particular and solemn
manner, the blessing of this candle, as well as
of the incense, large knobs of which, or as they
are now named, "grains," were stuck upon it
at one part of this ceremony.   Whether the
Anglo-Saxons wreathed this light with flowers,[13]

---

portatur crux, aqua benedicta et thuribulum, tamen sine igne,
ut novus ignis, postquam consecratus fuerit, aspergatur et in-
censetur ad benedicendum   .   Ipso die rite lumen in pertica
portatur a custode ecclesiae, in Parasceve a priore, in Sabbato
Sancto a domino abbate vel a sacerdote, lapis pretiosus berillus
in quo ignis est producendus, sub custodia apocrisain servatur,
quem tantum praecentori adhibet, ut ab eo ignis proferatur,
eumdemque ipso die, in processione idem major ecclesiae custos
bajulat —*Antiq Consuetudines*, 1 12 [*P I.*, cxlix 658]
[13] The Paschal candle having wreaths of flowers about it, with
the deacon in the ambo singing the "Exultet," is shown, from
a MS of the eleventh century, at vol 1 p 167 of this work, and
a like representation from another roll, with the "Exultet" of
the same period, may be seen in D'Agincourt's beautiful work,
plate 55, of painting   These *Exultet* rolls are some among the
rarest liturgical codices   Being much illuminated and narrow,
they stretched out to some length   one still kept at Monte
Casino is twelve feet long, and a little more than nine inches
broad   As the deacon went on unrolling it, that part which he
had sung fell before him outside the ambo, hence the illuminations, that they might be seen in their true position by the

as was done in those times abroad, (99) or
whether they followed the then Roman usage

The Deacon singing the *Exultet*.

people, had to be limned wrong-wise up with regard to the
writing. [These features are exemplified in the illumination
reproduced above from Brit. Mus. MS. 30,337, which is one
of these Italian *Exultet* rolls. The children are represented
gathered under the ambo in order to look at the picture; while
the illumination itself is set upside down on the roll as will be
seen; for on inverting the page, part of the Deacon's *Exultet* will
be recognised—*O vere beata nox*, &c., with its Lombardic neums
over it.] The usage itself, of twining the Paschal candle with
wreaths, is thus mentioned in an old Ambrosian missal :—Quid
enim magis accommodatum, magisque festivum, quam Jesseico

of writing upon it the date of the year, we do
not now know, though Beda distinctly speaks
of this latter custom.[14] In the Egbert Pontifical
there is a special rubric and prayer for the blessing of the incense.[15] The codex which is known as
the Leofric Missal, though it contains two Pontificals bound up into one volume, gives at full length
the blessing of the Paschal candle. When this
ceremony was done, and another smaller candle,
as well as the two acolytes' tapers, had been
lighted, a subdeacon went up into the south
side ambo, or pulpit, and read the lessons. These
over, there was sung the seven-form litany;[16]

flori floreis excubemus ut tedis ? præsertim cum et sapientia de
semetipsa cecinerit Ego sum flos agri et lilium convallium —
Ambros Missal. Ordo, in Pamelius, *Liturgicon*, 1 346

[14] Sancta siquidem Romana et Apostolica Ecclesia hanc se fidem
tenere et ipsis testatur indiculis, quae suis in cereis annuatim
scribere solet, ubi tempus Dominicae passionis in memoriam
populis revocans, numerum annorum   adnotat — *De Temp.*
Ratione, xlvii [*P L*, xc 494, 495]

[15] *Benedictio incensi in Sancto Sabbato antequam benedixeris cereum,*
et ipsum debes mitti in cereum in ipso loco ubi dicitur Suscipe incensi.
Deus Omnipotens, Deus Abraham, Deus Isaac, Deus Jacob, immitte
in hanc creaturam incensi vim odoris tui vel virtutem, ut sit
servulis tuis et ancillis munimentum tutelaque defensionis, ne
intret hostis in viscera eorum aditumque et sedem habere non
possit, per Te Jesum Christum Filium Dei, qui cum Patre et Spiritu
Sancto vivis et regnas per cuncta sæcula *Alia* Domine Deus
Omnipotens cui adstat exercitus angelorum cum (100) tremore,
quorum servitus in vento et igni convertitur dignare, Domine,
respicere et bene-dicere et sanctificare hanc creaturam tuam
incensi, ut omnes languores et insidiæ odorem ipsius sentientes
effugiant, et separentur a plasmatu quam pretioso sanguine redemisti, ut nunquam ledatur a morsu antiqui serpentis Per —
Egbert Pont, 130, 131

[16] It is thus described in an old "Ordo" Interim schola jussa
facit litaniam ad fontem ante altare, primo septenam, et spatio

the procession then went down, and carried to
the font the smaller wax candle alight, together
with the chrism and the oil of the catechumens,
for hallowing the baptismal font.   After the
blessing of these waters, and the administration,
to a few children, of baptism, solemn high mass
began.   By the time the celebrant had to give
out the *Gloria in excelsis Deo*, the whole church
glistened with the beams of a crowd of lamps
and (101) tapers newly lighted, and every bell
in the steeple swung out its gladsomeness.   While
the holy communion was being distributed to
those who wished to have their housel, *Alleluia*
burst forth from the singers' lips; a short psalm,
followed by an anthem and the *Magnificat*, was
chanted; and thus mass and even-song were
ended at the same moment.[17]   That the new-

---

facto, faciunt alteram quintam , ita enim inchoatur   Stat primi-
cerius unus in dextro choro, et dicit cum illo, "Kyrie eleeison,"
et respondet secundicerius cum sinistro choro, "Kyrie eleeison,"
usque ter.   Deinde, "Christe eleeison," usque ter hoc sunt septem
vices repetitae, unde et septenae dicuntur   Post haec, "Christe
audi nos," usque septies, et sic per ordinem   Hoc ordine, intervallo
facto sequuntur, ut praedictum est, litaniae quinque, id est, quin-
quies repetita —*Ordo Romanus*, Hittorp, 83 ,   See *Leofric Missal*, 96
[17] An outline of this day's ritual may be seen, as the pen of
St. Dunstan once sketched it   Sabbato Sancto, hora nona, veniente
abbate in ecclesiam cum fratribus, novus, ut supra dictum est,
afferatur ignis   Posito vero cereo ante altare, ex illo accendatur
igne   Quem diaconus more solito benedicens, hanc orationem
quasi voce legentis proferens dicat   *Exultet iam Angelica turba
coelorum.*   Tunc voce sublimiore dicat, *Sursum corda*, et reliqua
Finita benedictione, accendatur alter cereus, et tunc illuminantur
duo cerei tenentibus duobus acolitis unus in dextro cornu altaris
et alter in sinistro   Benedictione peracta, ascendat subdiaconus
ambonem, legat lectionem primam,   .   Finita oratione, inchoen-

born children, baptized to-day, were given, like those elder believers who had received the housel or eucharist on Maundy Thursday, to taste of milk and honey that had been blessed, seems probable, at least in the first ages of the Anglo-Saxon Church. To this end the cup of honey and milk was hallowed after the same way which we before noticed. For all, both young and old, —for the neophyte just baptized, as well as for him who had many years before been reborn through those same life-giving waters, Easter was a season of renewed strength. That her children might make holy their Paschal feast under the second and better dispensation, and taste of that ghostly happiness nowhere to be found but within her fold, the Church, in her services at Easter-tide, said unto them, in words like those spoken to the Israelites by Moses,—"The Lord hath brought you into a land that floweth with milk

---

tur litaniæ septenæ ad introitum ante altare Postea descendat abbas cum schola canentes litanias quinas ad fontes benedicendos Sequitur, *Omnipotens sempiterne Deus*, et praefatio His expletis, redeunt ad altare cum litania terna, et antequam cantatur *Gloria in excelsis Deo*, magister scholæ dicat alta voce, *Accendite*, et tunc illuminentur omnia luminaria ecclesiæ, et abbate incipiente, *Gloria in excelsis Deo*, pulsentur omnia signa Ante evangelium non portantur luminaria in ipsa nocte, sed incensum tantum Finito evangelio, dicat abbas, *Dominus vobiscum, Oremus* In ipso die non cantatur *Offertorium*, nec *Agnus Dei*, nec *Communio*, et pacem non debet dare nisi iis qui communicant, sed interim dum communicantur, *Alleluia*, et *Laudate Dominum omnes gentes* cantatur, dehinc antiphona, *Vespere autem sabbati*, et *Magnificat* Sic sacerdos missam ac (102) vespertinalem sinaxim una compleat oratione — *Reg Conc*, 89

and honey" (Exodus xiii. 5); and again, with
the prince of the apostles, begged of them
thus: "As new-born babes desire the rational
milk without guile, that thereby you may grow
unto salvation" (1 Peter ii. 2).

Easter Sunday

had one rite which exclusively belonged to itself,
and consisted in showing how the two Maries
and Salome made their sunrise

Visit to the Sepulchre

of our Lord. As the last lesson at matins was
being read, four members of the choir vested
themselves, three in copes, the fourth in an alb
only. This last personage went to the place at
the altar wherein, on Good Friday, had been
laid, as it were in the grave, a crucifix wrapped
up in an altar-cloth for a winding-sheet. Ere
he rang the (103) bell for matins, before break of
day, the sacristan had taken away this cross out
of the sepulchre, but left the linen shroud lying
at its mouth. The clerk, arrayed in an alb, and
holding a palm-branch in one hand, seated himself
by this tomb, and thus personified the watching
angel at Christ's burial-place in the garden. The
other three in copes, each carrying a thurible
that smoked with incense, and seemingly in
earnest search of something, crept on slowly

towards that spot. This they did, to represent
how "Mary Magdalen, and Mary the mother
of James, and Salome, brought sweet spices,
that coming they might anoint Jesus" (Mark
xvi. 1). As soon as these three got near him, the
one in the alb sang in a low soft mellow strain,
and asked whom they sought. Answering all together, these three chanted, "Jesus of Nazareth."
To this the other replied, "He is risen, He is
not here: behold the place where they laid Him.
Go and tell that He has arisen from the dead."
Turning about to the people, these three arrayed
in copes cried out, "Alleluia, the Lord is risen." [18]
Then the one personating the angel sang, "Come
and see the place"; after which he stood up
and showed them that the crucifix was gone from
out the tomb, and how there was nothing there
but a winding-sheet. On beholding this to be
so, they set their thuribles down and left them
within the hollow where the cross had lain,
singing, in the meanwhile, "The Lord is risen
from the sepulchre" When they had held up
this linen cloth to be seen all through the church,
they spread it on the altar. Then was sung by
the whole choir the hymn "Te Deum," and
immediately after followed lauds [19]

---

[18] See vol ii, p 345 of this work, for the Latin directions of the
Regularis Concordia

[19] The rubrics for the latter part of this liturgical representation
on Easter morn as given by St. Dunstan are (104) —Dicto hoc
rursus ille residens veluti revocans illos dicat antiphonam *Venite*

(105) At this morning's solemn mass, all kinds of food for man, but, in particular, what was meant to be for that Easter-day's dinner-meal, especially

Lamb or other flesh meat, was blessed

at the altar by the celebrant on coming to those words in the canon, "Through whom," &c.[20]

Every afternoon all through Easter week there was made, between even-song and complin,

---

et videte locum Hæc vero dicens, surgat et erigat velum, ostendatque eis locum cruce nudatum, sed tantum linteamina posita, quibus crux involuta erat, quo viso deponant thuribula quæ gestaverunt in eodem sepulchro, sumantque linteum, et extendant contra clerum ac veluti ostendentes quod surrexerit Dominus et jam non sit illo involutus, hanc canant antiphon, *Surrexit Dominus de sepulchro*, superponantque linteum altari Finita antiphona, prior congaudens pro triumpho regis nostri, quod devicta morte surrexit, incipiat hymnum *Te Deum laudamus*, quo incepto una pulsantur omnia signa, post cujus finem dicat sacerdos versum : *In resurrectione tua Christe*, verbo tenus, et initiat matutinas dicens *Deus in adiutorium meum intende*, &c —*Reg Conc*, 89

[20] The form for such a service may be learned from the following, out of the Egbert Pontifical —*Benedictio super carnem agni in Pascha antequam dicatur* Per quem hæc omnia Deus universe carnis, qui Noe et filiis suis de mundis et immundis animalibus precepta dedisti, qui agnum in Ægypto Moysi et populo tuo in vigilia Pasche comedere præcepisti in figura agni Domini nostri Jesu Christi, cujus sanguine omnia primogenita tibi de mundo redemisti, in nocte illa omne primogenitum in Ægypto peremisti, servans populum tuum agni sanguine pernotatum dignare, Domine Omnipotens, benedicere et sanctificare has ovium mundarum carnes, ut quicunque ex populis tuis fidelibus comederint, omni benedictione cœlesti, et gratia tua saturati repleantur in bonis Per. *Alia benedictio carnis quadrupedum ipso die Pasche.* Deus, qui ex divina providentia .   Te supplices exoramus et poscimus, ut hanc carnem quadrupedum seu volucrum benedicere et sanctificare digneris —*Egbert Pontifical*, 129, 130

A procession to the newly-blessed font ;

and the clergy, as they went down the nave, sang the CXII. [cxiii.] Psalm, "Praise the Lord, ye children," &c. ; and at the font itself was said a collect [21]

From Easter to Whitsuntide the custom was to pray, not kneeling as at other seasons of the year, but standing ; and while speaking of this ritual usage, our Beda affords us an explanation of it by connecting it with the fact that the Holy women, at the sight of the angels on the morning of the Resurrection, did not fall to the ground, but are said to have looked down to the ground.[22]

Every day throughout the same period, as well as upon all Sundays the year round (except from Septuagesima till Easter), *Alleluia* used to be sung, to betoken the Christian's hope of a happy

---

[21] Ad vesperam *Dixit Dominus, Confitebor, Beatus vir* cum antiphona sine capitulo, (106) grad *Haec dies,* sine versu, Alleluia cum versu, et sequentia Postea inchoetur antiphona in evangelio, et collecta dehinc eatur ad fontes, psalmum *Laudate pueri* cum antiphona canentes quem sequatur collecta Completorium more peragatur Canonicorum per omnia, &c Hic in reliquis sex diebus teneatur ordo —*Reg Conc ,* 90

[22] Et notandum quod sanctæ mulieres astantibus sibi angelis non in terram cecidisse, sed vultum dicuntur in terram declinasse. Nec quempiam sanctorum legimus tempore Dominicæ resurrectionis, vel ipso Domino, vel angelis sibi visis, terræ prostratum adorasse Unde mos obtinuit ecclesiasticus, ut vel in memoriam Dominicæ, vel in nostræ spem resurrectionis, et omnibus dominicis diebus et toto quinquagesimæ tempore, non flexis genibus, sed declinatis in terram vultibus oremus —*Expos in Lucæ Evang.,* xxiv. [*P L.,* xcii 624]

resurrection, and in praise of Christ's uprising from the grave upon the first day of the week, as the same light of the Anglo-Saxon Church, St. Beda, tells us.[23]

(107) The procession all about the fields and lanes of a country parish, and through the streets and alleys of the town, on the Monday, Tuesday, and Wednesday, before the feast of the Ascension, and now called Rogation week, but then

The Gang Days,

has been already noticed in this work (vol. iii., pp. 181, 182, 297). A theft committed on any one of these three days, was, by Alfred's laws, sconced in a two-fold "bot" or fine,[24] as if it had been a Sunday or one of the higher Church holydays. How all the gang-day service used to be performed — how a crucifix and the relics of the saints borne along in a shrine, were carried about the highways and byways of this land, the while the litanies were sung; and how, as the procession stopped every now and then on its road, the whole crowd of following people knelt down and begged forgiveness of God for their sins, may be found set forth by the council of Clovesho (A.D. 747)[25]

---

[23] Nam et Alleluia Dominicis diebus totoque Quinquagesimo tempore propter spem resurrectionis, quæ in Domini est laude futura, continue canit ecclesia —*Explan Apocal* xix [*P.L*, xciii. 188] The "Quinquagesimæ tempus" is the space between Easter and Whitsuntide   [24] Thorpe, *Ancient Laws*, 1. 64.

The Use of Lights

among the Anglo-Saxons in the liturgy, is brought
to our knowledge by many of their ritual observances, as well as through some of their laws
binding layfolks to bring, at (108) certain feasts,
a specified weight of wax for such a purpose.

At his ordination, the youth made acolyte had
a candlestick with a taper put into his hands, as
the bishop told him that his office would now
be to look after the church-lights. Beda's beautiful sketch of the abbot Ceolfrid's leaving the
minsters of Wearmouth and Jarrow to begin his
road Rome-ward, besides its glance at the liturgical employment of lights, sets before our eyes
that ritual form wherewith the Anglo-Saxons
speeded a well-beloved friend on his pilgrimage.
At day dawn, mass was sung in the church of
the ever-Virgin Mary, Mother of God: after
another mass in St. Peter's, and at which each
one present was houseled along with him,
Ceolfrid made himself ready to start. The
brotherhood met in the church · there, as with
a thurible in his hand, he stood upon one of

---

[25] Ut litaniæ, id est rogationes a clero omnique populo his
diebus cum magna reverentia agantur id est   . tres dies ante
ascensionem Domini in cælos, cum jejunio usque ad horam
nonam, et Missarum celebratione venerentur   cum timore et
tremore, signo passionis Christi, nostræque æternæ redemptionis,
et reliquis sanctorum ejus coram portatis, omnis populus genuflectendo divinam pro delictis humiliter exoret indulgentiam —
Cap xvi *De Diebus Litaniarum,* in Wilkins, *Concil* 1 97

the steps of the altar whereat he had, a moment
before, offered up incense and said a prayer,
Ceolfrid gave unto all the kiss of peace.   Hence
they led him forth, as they chanted the litanies
which their sobs and sighs often broke in upon.
At the head of this procession walked the deacons
of the church carrying a crucifix which was of
gold, and lighted tapers ; and these same deacons
not only went, like the rest, with their departing
abbot, to the water's edge, but got into the boat
which took him over the stream, on the other
side of which his horse awaited him   After he
had knelt and kissed this crucifix surrounded by
the lights borne about it, Ceolfrid mounted, and
rode off.[26]   How lighted tapers that had been
hallowed were (109) borne about in the people's
hands as all went a procession to honour the B V.
Mary, every year, upon that one of her festivals
which was therefore called " Candlemas," we have
already noticed.   [See p. 67 of this vol.]   The
Christian wife, too, who, xl. days after child-birth,
came, like our blessed Lady, to the house of God
for her churching, brought along with her, besides
some small offering gift, a wax-taper to be lit for
the ceremony,as we learn from Archbishop Theodore's Penitential.[27]

---

[26] Ascendunt et diacones accclesiæ cercas ardentes et crucem
ferentes auream, transit flumen, adorat crucem, ascendit equum
et abiit.—Beda, *Hist Abbat*, 17 [Plummer, 1 382]

[27] Mulier . .   post partum, XL diebus et noctibus, sive mas-
culum sive feminam genuerit , et tunc cum lumine et oblatione
intret ecclesiam —Theodore, *Lib. Pænit*, in Thorpe, 11 12.

In more than one passage of his writings, our Beda drops words which, though few and never meant for such an end, bring up before our eyes a glimpse of many an usage about which we can no where else find such a strong testimony. Wishful, by the easiest illustration that might be found anywhere, to make his readers understand how it happened that the moon, at the summer solstice, seems to be higher in the sky than the sun, our learned countryman, while choosing the two large chandeliers (called *pharus*), that hung far away from each other in a church, for his example, says to us, without a thought to do so, how the cathedrals and minsters of this country used, in those ages, to be lighted up at night, on the saints' festivals, with more or less brightness, according to that degree of veneration in which they happened to be held by the faithful who took such means for honouring God's now happy servants.[28]

In one of his homilies, Beda not only tells us that this "pharus" was a large bronze hoop studded with lamps, but he lets us know that to his mind,—and of course, he uttered the feelings of his own countrymen at that period,—the

---

[28] Intrabis noctu in aliquam domam praegrandem, certe ecclesiam, longitudine, latitudine, et altitudine praestantem, et innumera lucernarum ardentium copia, pro illius cujus natalis est martyris honore repletam, inter quas duae (110) maxime ac mirandi operis pharis suis quaeque suspensae ad laquearia catenis, &c.— *De Temp Ratione*, xxvi [*P L*, xc 410]

figure of the cross when wreathed in such a
crown of light had shown it a homage that
was but its due. What Beda praised was, no
doubt, practised at his time all over this country,
and a ring of light shone around the cross in
every large Anglo-Saxon church when the higher
festivals of the year were kept.[29] To find these
lights about the church and at the altar, it was
decreed that besides those willing gifts which
pious people might like to bestow for this purpose, each one according to the extent of land
he had, should pay into his parish church, thrice
a year (viz. at Candlemas, again at Easter, and
lastly at Allhallows'-tide), a certain quantity of
wax under the name of "light-shot." [30]

But if the tapers carried about on Candlemas
day, and the boughs of yew or flowery willow on
Palm Sunday, (111) were hallowed—if, indeed,
whatever happened to be put into use for God's
worship had first to be blessed, there was one
thing in every such benediction which the rubrics
always required to be employed, and that was

---

[29] Golgothana est ecclesia, quae inter alia ornamenta tali loco
congrua crucem argenteam habet pergrandem in loco quo Dominus
crucifigi pro nostra est salute dignatus, pendente magno pharo
desuper, id est aerea rota cum lampadibus, quae ipsam crucem
debita lucis veneratione coronent –Hom, ii 4 Infra octavas Pasch.
[P.L., xciv 153, 154]

[30] Let light-scot be paid at Candlemas, let him do it oftener
who will –Laus of K Ethelred, in Thorpe, i 343 And light-scot
thrice in the year, first, on Easter-eve, a halfpenny worth of wax
for every hide, and again, on Allhallows' mass, as much, and
again, on the Purification of St Mary, the like –Laus of K Cnut,
in Thorpe, i 367

Holy Water

Its use is one of the earliest rites to be found in the history of the Anglo-Saxon Church. "Tell our brother Austin," says Pope Gregory to Mellitus, "that having a long time thought over to myself the affairs of the English, I deem it best that the temples of the idols among that people should not be pulled down; but after the idols themselves have been broken, let holy water be blessed and sprinkled all over those temples, and then altars may be set up and relics put within them."[31]

That holy water was often taken home from church and cast about their houses by the believing Anglo-Saxons, we gather from the words of Archbishop Theodore, who says: "Let the inhabitants sprinkle their houses with hallowed water as often as they wish."[32] As the hand sprinkled this water, prayers beseeching God to shield that house and its inmates from harm of soul and body were said[33]

In the public trial by the hot iron ordeal the

---

[31] Dicite ei (sc fratri nostro Augustino episcopo) quid diu mecum de causa Anglorum cogitans tractavi, videlicet, quia fana idolorum destrui in eadem gente minime debeant, sed ipsa, quæ in eis sunt, idola destruantur, aqua benedicta fiat, in eisdem fanis aspergatur, altaria construantur, reliquiæ ponantui —Beda, *Hist Ecc*, i 30

[32] Aqua benedicta domos suas aspergant quotiens voluerint, qui habitant in eis —Thorpe, *Ancient Laws*, ii 58.

[33] *Durham Ritual*, 122

sprinkling of holy water upon all who bore a
part or stood witness in it, was not the least
conspicuous rite which had to be observed.
"Let," say the Laws of Æthelstan, "let the
(112) mass-priest sprinkle holy water over them
all, and let each of them taste of the holy water,
and give them all the book and the image of
Christ's rood to kiss." [34]   Then as now, a little
salt was mingled in the water after each had
been separately exorcised and hallowed, with the
self-same prayers which the Church still uses for
the purpose, as may be seen in the Egbert Pontifical,[35] and the so-called Durham Ritual.[36]

If holy water was often, oftener still was the

Sign of the Cross

employed at their public ritual and private devotions by the Anglo-Saxon people.   When he
raised his voice in witness of such an usage
throughout this his fatherland before and during
his own days, our Beda while thus following
the example of the great St. Austin, made his
words too his own, as he cried out with that
glory of the African Church:—"What is the
sign which every one knows, but Christ's cross?
Now unless this sign be employed—unless it
be made upon the forehead of him who be-
lieves, and traced over the water through which

---

[34] *Laws of K Æthelstan*, in Thorpe, 1. 227
[35] *Egbert Pontifical*, 34, 35   [36] p 120

he is reborn, or over the oil with which he
is anointed in confirmation, or over the sacrifice
by which he is fed, none of these rites are duly
performed." This, as well as St. Boniface's
anxiety to learn what was the proper number
of crosses to be signed over the blessed Eucharist,
has been already noticed.[37]

From Beda we learn that the sign of the cross
is one among other weapons to be wielded in the
fight against the devil, during the everyday life
of this world;[38] and that the man who wishes
(113) to drive away from himself foul evil thoughts,
must begin by tracing upon his breast this token
of redemption through Christ.[39] In the beautiful
letter which he wrote to Egbert of York, at that
bishop's own request, Beda calls upon his old
friend to be earnest in teaching his flock, among
other things, to strengthen themselves, by the
frequent sign of the cross, against the wiles of
unclean spirits.[40] And Alcuin tells us that the

---

[37] See vol 1, pp 66, 67, of this work, where the references to
these passages are given

[38] Moxque ubi futuras ejus (antiqui hostis) insidias perspicimus,
unicum nobis refugium foramina petræ nostræ, id est, Dominicæ
fidei præsidia intremus, ac signo nos passionis illius defensare
studeamus —*Exp in Cantic Canticor*, iv. [*P L*, xci 1164]

[39] Sed et noxios sæpe cogitatus, dum incauta mente voluimus,
ac subito respecti a Deo signum sanctæ crucis pectori imprimimus,
et quod nefarium tractamus, abjicimus, quasi vitta coccinea cap-
illos nobis ligamus, quia fluxa cogitationum trophæo sacri cruoris
comprimimus —*Ibid* iii [1132]

[40] Eorum quoque qui in populari adhuc uita continentur solli-
citam te necesse est curam gerere   . et hoc eos inter alia discere
facias   quam frequenti diligentia signaculo se Dominicæ crucis

first thing we should do when we awake in the
morning is to make upon our lips the sign of
the cross.[41]   That teaching like this was old
among the Anglo-Saxons, and had not been
thrown away upon them, we may gather from
all (114) their history ; and in the picture which
Beda draws of Caedmon's holy death, not the least
beautiful part is that wherein he shows us how,
after the poet had been houseled, he crossed himself, lay back and quietly died.[42]   In a record of
one particular event in the life of St. Guthlac,
Felix, the saint's contemporary, does not forget
that holy man's morning custom of crossing
himself.[43]

But our Anglo-Saxon fathers had another way
of making known what were their inward feelings of love towards Christ, through that outward homage for this emblem of the atonement
wrought by Him for mankind, and it was

---

suaque omnia aduersum continuas immundorum spirituum insidias
necesse habeant munire —*Epist ad Egbertum Episc* , 15 [Plummer,
1 418, 419]

[41] Ergo cum a somno evigilas, et crucis signum depingis in labiis,
tertio repete *Domine, labia mea aperies, et os meum annunciabit
laudem tuam* —Alcuin, *Lib de Psalm Usu*, 1 [*P L* , ci. 468]

[42] Signans se signo sanctæ crucis reclinavit caput ad cervical,
modicumque obdormiens, ita cum silentio vitam finivit —*Hist Eccl.*,
iv 24.

[43] Tunc indutos artus agresti de spatulo surgens arrexit, et
signato cordis gremio salutari sigillo, &c —*A A SS Aprilis*, ii 39

To stand in the Cross,

as they called it, the while they said their prayers. Such a devotional custom they went through after more forms than one. The first was when, standing upright, they kept their arms and hands spread out full length : thus they stood and prayed whenever they wanted to show much earnestness in their supplications, as we learn from the example of St. Ecgburga, who, to let St. Guthlac understand how strongly she besought him to take her gift of a leaden coffin and a winding-sheet for his burial, having uttered her wish aloud—with outstretched arms in the shape of the cross, like as she were praying—bade her messenger who was by and saw what she had done, to go, and, putting himself into the same attitude, say her errand to that holy ankret at Crowland.[44] The second way was to kneel down instead of standing, but with the arms still thrown wide open as before. Their third method consisted in casting themselves down upon the ground, and in thus remaining there in prayer, with arms and hands abroad in the form of the cross. Sometimes in one, sometimes in the other

---

[44] Ecgburgh . adjurans per nomen terribile superni Regis, seque ad patibulum Dominicæ crucis erigens, in indicium supplicis (115) deprecationis extensis palmis, ut in officium prædictum vir Dei illud munus susciperet, per nuntium alterius fidelis fratris præcipiens, ut hoc indicium coram illo faceret supplici rogatu mittebat *Ibid*, 47

of these last two positions, was it that public but
sorrowful sinners put themselves at church, as
they underwent their canonical course of pen-
nance. In his *Liber Pœnitentialis*, Archbishop
Theodore mentions this among penances [45] Again,
the canons enacted under Edgar, speaking of the
sinner who is a man of power and wealthy, say:
" By day and by night, the oftenest that he can,
let him remain in church, and, with alms-light,
earnestly watch there, and cry to God, and im-
plore forgiveness, with groaning spirit, and kneel
frequently in the sign of the cross (on rode
tacne); sometimes up, sometimes down, extend
himself, &c." [46]

In an age when even some kings could not
write, it became necessary to choose an easy common token, the signature of which to instruments
and documents should be held as giving them all
due legal strength. Among our Anglo-Saxons,
such a token was sought for from among the sym-
bols of their Christian belief; and all through
(116) their period, from Æthelbert's till the first
William's days,

The Mark of the Cross upon a Deed

was meant, by him who put it, to be a sign either
that he had tied himself down to the fulfilment of

---

[45] Qui psalmos non novit, et jejunare, sive vigilare, vel genu-
cleare, vel in cruce stare, aut sæpe prosternere, seu aliter pœnitere,
pro infirmitate non potest, eligat qui pro illo hoc impleat, &c —
Thorpe, *Ancient Laws*, ii 62   [46] *Ibid*, 289

its stipulations, or had agreed to accept its terms,
or had been present as a witness when it was
drawn up. The solemn making of this mark got,
from the first, to be looked upon, if not with all
the awe, at least with some of the feelings belonging to an oath : it was thought that he who so set
his hand to a written document of any kind, was
thereby deemed to say that, as he hoped and trusted
for the happiness of heaven through Christ crucified, he pledged himself to carry out, and wished
his aftercomers to stand by, his plighted word for
ever; or, if only a witness, that what he had so
attested he believed to be true. The custom of
thus ratifying and witnessing deeds of gifts and
every other sort of instrument by drawing the
sign of the cross with a pen, or laying the finger
on the gold or red cross already made by the scribe
upon the parchment, may be seen, and the weight
of the act felt, in these following extracts from our
Anglo-Saxon charters —

Hoc, cum consilio Laurencii episcopi et omnium
principum meorum, signo sanctæ crucis confirmavi
(Æthelbertus rex A.D. 604), eosque iussi ut mecum
idem facerent.[47] Pro confirmatione eius manu propria signum sanctæ crucis expressi (*ibid.*, 21);
ut ne aliquis in posterum sit adversitas, propria
manu signum sanctæ crucis expressi (*ibid.*, 31);
ad cuius confirmationem pro ignorantia litter-
arum ✠ signum sanctæ crucis expressi (*ibid,*

---

[47] Kemble, *Codex Dipl. Angl.-Sax*, 1. 1.

50); hanc donationem meam confirmando signo
sanctæ crucis munivi (*ibid.*, 65); ✠ hoc signum
ego Cyniheaιdus (117) indignus episcopus impressi
ad confirmandam roborandamque hanc cartulam,
quam huiusmodi conscriptam esse fateoι (*ibid.*,
126); in nomine Dei omnipotentis quιbusque
dignitatis ac conditionis hominibus præcipio, et
per crucem Domιnicæ passionis adιuro cuius
signum ad cumulum firmitatis in hac paginula
descripsi (*ibid.*, 133). At vero ut hanc donationem meam quilibet hominum aliquando non
possit irritam facere, manu propria signum sanctæ
crucis subtus in hac pagina facere curavi (Eg-
bertus   rex),   testesque   relιgiosos   ut   ιdipsum
facerent adhibeo (*ibid.*, 194).   Obsecro per
omnes vιrtutes cœlorum, ut nullus homo hanc
positionem crucis Chrιsti, quæ tantorum virorum
testimonio confirmata est, non præsumat mιnuere
(*ibιd.*, 228).   ✠ Ego Coenwulf rex Merciorum,
cum vιrtute sanctæ crucιs scribendo conroboravi
(*ibid.*, 256).   To bestow her formal sanction upon
such a pious usage, the Anglo-Saxon Church,
in the third council of Chalk-hythe (A.D. 816),
sent forth a decree that all documents bearιng
an authentic sign of the cιoss weιe bιnding and
ought to be obeyed and fulfilled :—De omni ιe,
quæcunque cum vexillo sanctæ crucis Christi
roborata est, sic stare servareque prœcιpimus, nιsi
forsan rex vel prιnceps antecessorum suorum
manuum impositιones pro nihilo ducant: et illud

non emendare neque cassare pertimescant, idipsum in se suisque hæredibus sustineant, sicut scriptum est · In quocunque judicio judicaveritis, judicabimini.[48]

Before, however, setting their mark to a deed, especially of high importance and amid circumstances of more than ordinary ceremonial, they took the hand of that personage to whom they were about pledging their word for the fulfilment of each condition in the document—or if he were away, his representative's hand—and upon its open palm (118) they drew a sign of the cross, with the thumb of their own right hand. Thus did Offa and Archbishop Lambert with his brother bishops, as they all promised the holy see, through Pope Adrian's messenger, to observe those decrees and canons which had been passed, under the presidency of that same pontifical legate, in the first council held at Chalk-hythe (A.D. 785), as we noticed in another part of this work.[49]

But new men brought in new customs, and under the first Norman king, the old Anglo-Saxon attestation—the sign of the cross—was laid aside, and waxen seals were strung to all instruments in its stead.[50] Some there were of the Church-

---

[48] Wilkins, *Concil*, 1 170. [49] Vol 111 400

[50] Alias etiam consuetudines immutabant Nam chirographorum confectionem Anglicanam quæ antea usque ad Edwardi regis tempora fidelium subscriptionibus cum crucibus aureis aliisque sacris signaculis firma fuerunt, Normanni condemnantes, chirographa chartas vocabant , et chartarum firmitatem cum cerea impressione per uniuscujusque speciale sigillum   . conficere

men in this country who strove to keep up such a seemly usage, and among them was Gundulf bishop of Rochester, who ratified a deed in these words: Et ut inperpetuum integra et inviolata permaneat, signo crucis Christi vice piissimi sanctorum Andree apostoli eam consigno et corroboro.[51] Strangely enough, however, the old Anglo-Saxon custom which grew out of their warm Catholic belief, still lives among Englishmen, and the person who cannot write—the marksman as he is called—even now is allowed to authenticate any deed or statement by making a cross before his name that another hand has traced.

---

constituebant.   Ingulph, in Gale, *Rer Anglic. Script*, 1. 70 [ed. Birch, p 122]
[51] *Registrum Roffense*, 33.

CHAPTER XII

Such then are the doctrinal, such the liturgical observances, which were every day set so strongly before the Anglo-Saxons by their Church in her religious services. However feebly this outline of them may have been drawn, it will be strong enough to show that there is no one article of belief, no one single element of ritual practice embodied in the treatise of the Norman Saint Osmund, or

The Use of Sarum,

which will not be found to have been, all along, in being among the Anglo-Saxons. How indeed could it be otherwise, when both people drank in their Christianity from streams which, though running through two different countries, took their rise from the same well-spring of truth—from Rome?

Not quite three centuries after the happy conversion of this island, when another horde of pagan Northmen, under Rollo, landed upon the opposite coast of France, and made themselves masters of a portion of that country, now known as Normandy; they, in their turn, soon stooped their necks to the sweet yoke of the gospel, and became Christians. Some time before, the whole of France, at the prayer of Charlemagne, had exchanged her national liturgy for that of the apostolic see. Thus it happened that the Northmen, on becoming Christians in Gaul, adopted the Roman ritual; so that when the descendants of these conquerors of the Franks came over to England with William, (120) they found among the Anglo-Saxons the very same liturgy to which they had always been accustomed in France ; and whatever difference was perceptible between the ecclesiastical practices of either people, they saw consisted not in anything material, but in a slight disparity in some rubrics or ceremonies with which the mass was offered up, and the sacraments and other rites of the Church were administered.

The labours of St. Osmund afford another of the many examples which show how that beautiful saying of the royal prophet has always been fulfilled, who, as he foretold the unity of doctrine which was ever to mark Christ's Catholic Church, sang thus of her : "Astitit regina a dextris tuis in vestitu deaurato, circumdata varietate"—the queen stood on thy right hand in golden clothing, surrounded with variety (Ps. xliv. [xlv.] 9). Notwithstanding the overthrow of kings, the changes wrought in the laws and the language of the country, the thraldom of the people under new lords ; notwithstanding the appointment to all

places of trust and of authority, of new men with
strangers' feelings and strangers' likings and dis-
likes,—still the same strong family resemblance is
ever to be witnessed between our old national religious rites and those of Rome ; and with becoming
thankfulness do we behold that the few peculiarities of our old English service-books only express
in another—nay, at times, a stronger—set of words
those self-same doctrines taught, not merely in the
Roman, but in every other liturgy used at any
period, or in any place within the Catholic Church.
Now should it be asked

*In what did the Sarum ritual vary from that of
Rome, and of the Anglo-Saxons?*

the question is readily answered by replying, that the
(121) difference was neither much nor important.
On comparing the Breviary, the Missal, and the
Manual of Salisbury, with such of the service-
books as have come down to us from Anglo-Saxon
times, and those books now in use at Rome, we
shall find that they agree with one another almost
word for word ; so much so, indeed, as to show
that St. Osmund did nothing more than take the
Roman liturgy as he found it at the time, ingraft
upon it some slight unimportant insertions, and
draw out its rubrics in such a way as to hinder the
ordinary chances of falling into any mistakes about
them from happening. He seems to have invented
nothing of himself in these matters, but to have

chosen out of the practices he saw in use around him, among the Anglo-Saxons here, and more especially among his own countrymen in Normandy; and it would appear he undertook nothing more than to arrange the church-offices in such sort that his clergy—composed as they must have been of Normans and Anglo-Saxons—might have one known uniform rule to lead them while going through their respective functions within the sanctuary, and their several duties amid their flocks. Our first notice shall be given to the codices for the

Choir Service

Like as in the Anglo-Saxon, so in the Sarum rite, all the hours of the office had the same component parts as are still to be found in the Roman and other breviaries. Matins consisted of an invitatory joined to Psalm xciv. [xcv.], *Venite*, a hymn; a certain number of psalms, with anthems; lessons, with responses and versicles; and the hymn, *Te Deum*. The invitatory, according to a venerable old English catholic writer, "ys as moche to saye, as a callynge, or a sturrynge Wherby eche of you sturreth, and exhorteth other to the praysyng of God. . . . And therby also, (122) ye calle them that here you · and desyre other that ar absente to come to prayse with you. And therto accordeth the psalme, *Venite*, that foloweth, and ys songe wyth the Inuitatory. But the

Inuitatory ys som tyme songe hole, and somtyme halfe." [*Myroure of Oure Ladye*, ed. J. H. Blunt (E. E. T. S.), p. 83.] These invitatories varied with the time of the year and the occurring festival; and many of them were the same as those still found in the Roman breviary. One was always said along with Psalm xciv., *Venite*, at the beginning of matins, except upon Maundy Thursday, Good Friday, and Holy Saturday, and at a dirge, and on All Souls' day; thus agreeing, with the exception of the service for the dead, with the Roman usage, according to which however an invitatory is always recited on All Souls' day, and at the dirge which is chaunted at a burial.

Of these Sarum matin hymns, the larger portion are the same as those now sung in the Roman breviary; while of the remainder, but a few are quite different, and the rest exhibit mere verbal variations.

For the great feasts, for the saints' days, for the Sundays, and for the week-days throughout the year, precisely the same arrangement in numbers, and the allotment, with a few exceptions, of the very same psalms for matins, as in the Roman, may be seen in the Sarum portous. In both, the Sunday's office, simply as such, consists of three divisions of psalms, called "Nocturns," the first of which contains twelve, the other two six psalms each. High feasts and the greater number of saints' days have three nocturns of three psalms in each of them; but of these festivals must be excepted Easter and Whit Sunday, and their respective octaves, when there is but one nocturn of three psalms each day at matins.

On those saints' days whose festivals were kept with only three lessons at matins, a difference existed between Sarum (123) and Rome. By the rubrics of the latter, a saint's feast, with three lessons only, has the twelve psalms at matins, in the psalter, on that day of the week it may chance to fall. Such however was not the Salisbury rule, except for a short period of the year; and at other times there were said with the three lessons those nine psalms which formed the three nocturns in the office of similar saints whose feasts were kept with nine lessons. This explains St. Osmund's mention of a saint's office with three lessons and nine psalms.

In like manner the *Dirige*, or matin office for the dead, was said when the corpse was not present, with three lessons, and nine, not three psalms, as in the Roman breviary, which directs but one nocturn to be sung on such occasions. After the closing, sometimes of one, sometimes of several psalms, comes an anthem; and at the end of the last of such anthems, follows a verse with its response; and of these the same may be said on the resemblance which they bear to the corresponding parts of the Roman breviary.

The same wish to follow ecclesiastical usage which was shown by St. Osmund in ordaining the weekly repetition, among his clergy, of the psalter, was exhibited by his arrangement of the lessons at matins, in such a way that within the year some portion out of almost every book in the old and new Testament should be read in the divine office.

Though chosen from the same books of Holy Writ, according to the season or the festival, the lessons in the Sarum matins were much shorter than those now read in the Roman breviary; often, too, the commentaries accompanying them were extracted out of other writings and homilies of the holy fathers An additional lesson, called "the genealogy," was sung at the end of matins on Christmas morning and the Epiphany, from the rood-loft, with (124) much solemnity, by the deacon, robed in his dalmatic, and attended by incense, lights, a cross, and a subdeacon. There were several festivals during the year, on which the lessons of the third nocturn were from the saint's legend, and not an exposition of some part of the gospel with a verse or two of it at the beginning of the seventh lesson, as is the custom in the Roman breviary.

Before the lessons at the first nocturn, the Lord's Prayer and the Apostles' Creed were said in silence, at the end of which were repeated aloud these last two petitions from the Lord's prayer, *Et ne nos inducas in tentationem; sed libera nos a malo.* No absolution was pronounced at any of the nocturns: the same blessings however as those in the Roman breviary, along with a variety of others, were asked and given When any part of the prophecies was read, the lesson always finished with—*Hæc dicit Dominus. convertimini ad me, et salvi eritis;* but at all other times it closed with the common ending — *Tu, autem, Domine, miserere nostri.* These lessons were parted one from the other by responses and versicles, varying with the time or with the festival. Some of these responses were, in the Sarum rite, denominated " histories," because they echoed, as it were, the feelings, and spoke the meaning, of those passages from Holy Writ, chanted during that especial season, or at that particular feast.

With the exception of Advent time, and of the interval between Septuagesima and Easter Sundays, and of a few especial feasts of the year, the hymn *Te Deum* was sung, not in place of, but immediately after, the response to the last lesson of matins.

On St. Nicholas' day, that of St. Stephen, of St. John the Evangelist, and of Holy Innocents', immediately after the ninth lesson and its response, and—as it would seem, instead of the *Te Deum*—was solemnly chanted, and with

(125) a peculiar ceremony, what was called a "prose," in honour of the occurring feast.

Just before lauds came a short versicle, with its response; and this particular versicle was known under the name of the "priest's versicle," from being chanted by the celebrant, and not by one of the singing-boys, like all the other versicles.

At lauds themselves we find two distinctions, which, though small, are nevertheless characteristic. Immediately after the canticle, *Benedictus*, there was sung, in the Sunday's office, Ps. cxxii. [cxxiii.], *Ad Te levavi*. The recital of this was, however, looked upon by many as a thing binding only upon the clergy of Salisbury choir itself, and hence it was not done in some other cathedrals. Immediately after the collect for the day, the first *Benedicamus Domino* was said. Then came the "memories," if any, or, as we now call them, "commemorations," and the suffrages. At the close of these was intoned a second *Benedicamus Domino*, a ritual practice unknown to the Roman breviary.

Upon Christmas morning, along with the first *Benedicamus*, there were chanted, by four clergy chosen from among the upper row of canons, two anthems, with a response and versicle, in honour of the mystery of the Incarnation.

Another peculiarity of the Sarum rite is to be found in the way in which the service at lauds finishes on each of the three nights before Easter, in what we now call "Tenebræ."

On all the higher holy days throughout the year, the altar was incensed by a canon vested in a silk cope, at the second lesson of each nocturn, and afterwards the thurifer incensed the choir [52] Those who read the lessons of the (126) third nocturn wore silk copes.[53] At lauds the altar was incensed by the officiating priest on all days that were not ferial.[54]

At the hour of prime there occurred but few, and those unimportant, variations between the Sarum form and that of Rome. Of these, we ought, perhaps, to point out the following two. Before and after the creed attributed to St. Athanasius, there was an anthem ; and whenever the cxxii. [cxxiii.] Psalm, *Ad Te levavi*, was said at lauds, then at prime was recited Ps. cxx. [cxxi.], *Ad te levavi oculos meos*,—the saying of which, strictly speaking, was confined, like the other psalm, to Salisbury choir itself.

In every cathedral and collegiate church, at the end of prime-song, all the clergy went in procession from the choir to the chapter-house, where each one took that seat which by right belonged to him. The bishop, if there, sat in the first place; in his absence, the dean: on either hand came, in due order, the dignitaries ;

---

[52] *Use of Sarum*, lii (54), vol 1 pp 114, 121, and liv (56), p 126
[53] *Ibid*, lii (54), p 118   [54] *Ibid*, xliii (51), p 97.

then the canons; in a lower row, the minor canons. The boys stood on the floor, ranged at each side of the pulpit. One of these youths, whose week for such a duty it chanced to be, got up in this pulpit, and read the martyrology, and afterwards gave out the " obits," or remembrance to pray for the souls of those who had once been members of, or benefactors to, that church, and whose deaths had happened that day of the year; and the officiating priest, when the boy had gone through these names, said: "May their souls and the souls of all the faithful departed through the mercy of God rest in peace." [55] Then came a lection out of some pious writer; for which purpose clergymen sometimes bequeathed books to a church.[56] According to Clement Maydeston, the writings of Haymo, or Aimo, one of our Alcuin's scholars, used to be, where the Sarum ritual prevailed, always read the year through, with the exception of a very few days.[57]

If any one had been slothful in coming to

---

[55] Animæ eorum et animæ omnium fidelium defunctorum per Dei misericordiam requiescant in pace See *Use of Sarum* xxxii. (30) p 51.

[56] Thus John Newton did Do et lego capitulo ecclesiæ metropolicæ Ebor (127) librum vocatum Speculum Moralium, cum aliis tractatibus Alcuini, quondam canonici Ebor ecclesiæ, et Hugonis de Claustro Animæ, atque Maurici de Sancta Salome, in uno volumine, pro lectura in capitulo —*Testamenta Ebor* , 365, ed Surtees Society

[57] De lectione in capitulo

Quotidie per totum annum, nisi duobus diebus ante Pascha, post

church for his duties, he had here to ask the
forgiveness of his brethren and the dean.   After
this, if it were Sunday, or a holyday, the same
youth read the "board"; that is, he told the
names of those among the canons who had to
rule the choir, to read the lessons, and chant
the responses at matins, to sing the high mass,
or minister as deacon and subdeacon;—among
the smaller boys, who was to read at chapter,
who had to carry the candles, or the holy water,
or the book;—and among the elder ones, who
was to read the long lessons in the chapter-
house, who to bear the thurible, or be acolyte,
—that is, bring in, at high mass, the chalice
with the corporal cloths,[58] during all the week,
or while the octave of the occurring festival
lasted.[59]   To choose out and set down the names
of these several officials, was the work of the
precentor; and the list itself got called the
" table," or (128) " board," because written upon
wax spread over a thin piece of wood, which was
afterwards left hanging up in the chapter-house,
within easy sight of all.

Preciosa est legatur in capitulo vna lectio de Sancto Haymone et
semper cum ista benedictione tam duplicibus quam pro festis diebus . . . Nunquam legatur lectio alia in capitulo nisi de Sancto
Haymone preter quam per octavas Assumptionis et Nativitatis
beate Marie —*Crede Michi* [Wordsworth, *Tracts of C. Maydeston*
(H B S), p 41]

[58] *Use of Sarum,* xxxix (92) vol 1 p. 69
[59] *Ibid.,* xxv (31) p 41.

Not only before, but very long after, paper became known, the use of such tablets, which we may call

The Wax-brede,

was kept on here, as well as abroad, for things of small note, or but a temporary service, and, in particular, for ritual purposes. In early days, St. Aldhelm spoke of it thus:

DE PUGILLARIBUS.

Melligeris apibus mea prima processit origo,
Sed pars exterior crescebat cætera silvis :
Calceamenta mihi tradebant tergora dura
Nunc ferri stimulus faciem proscindit amœnam,
Flexibus et sulcos obliquat ad instar aratri :
Sed semen segeti de cœlo ducitur almum,
Quod largos generat millena fruge maniplos
Heu tam sancta seges diris extinguitur armis.[60]

In the Anglo-Saxon translation of St. Benet's "Rule,"[61] it is called by the name we have given it, "wax-brede"; and the rich library of the ancient and venerable St. Gall's, Switzerland, still has—Sex ligneæ tabulæ cera obductæ (olim pugillares Scotticæ dictæ) quæ ratiocinia œconomica referunt.[62] The shape of these tablets, and the way used by the Anglo-Saxons of writing on them, can be seen in one of the illuminations in Æthelwold's Benedictional.[63]

That the wax-brede continued to be employed

---

[60] S Aldhelm, *Epist ad Acircium*, v [*P L*, lxxxix 193]
[61] Wanley, *Catal*, p 122, Nasmith, *Catal* c c, Cantab [See Logeman's Edition for E E T S, p 93.]
[62] Appendix, A to P, Cooper's *Report*, 84   [63] p 103

for (129) church purposes after the coming hither of the Normans, we gather from several quarters.[64] How St. Anselm used to make a rough draft of his literary works, first upon these wax tables, and write them out afterwards upon vellum, we read in Eadmer's life of that holy archbishop.[65]

The account rolls of Winchester college, during a portion of Richard II.'s reign, not only furnish a proof that the wax-brede still continued in ritual use for the chapel there, but tell us that the wax employed for the purpose was coloured green: *Custos capelle.* In j tabula ceranda cum viridi cera pro intitulatione capellanorum et clericorum capelle ad missas et alia psallenda, viii*d*.

Horman informs us that "tables be made of leves of yvory, boxe, cyprus, and other stouffe, daubed with waxe, to wrytte on";[66] and that the stilus, or graphium, was called a pointel: "poyntyllis of yron, and poyntyllis of sylver, brass, boone, or stoone, havynge a pynne at the ende."[67]

---

[64] Joceline, the monk of Furness (in his life of St Waltheof, who died, A D. 1160, abbot of Melrose), tells us: Hæc autem hujus scripta verba fuerunt, quæ ex seniorum industria sacra pluribus diebus in cera tabulæ capitularis exarata legere gliscentibus patuerunt.—*A A. SS. Augusti,* 1 267.

[65] Reparat Anselmus aliud de eadem materia dictamen in aliis tabulis. . Ille in secretiore parte lectuli sui tabulas reponit, et sequenti die nil sinistri suspicatus easdem in pavimento sparsas ante lectum reperit, cera, quæ in ipsis erat hac illac frustratim dispersa Levantur tabulæ, cera colligitur, et pariter Anselmo reportantur adunat ipse ceram, et licet vix scripturam recuperat. Veritus autem, ne qua incuria penitus perditum eat, eam in nomine Domini pergameno jubet tradi —*A A. SS Aprilis,* 11. 872

[66] *Vulgaria,* fo 81, Pynson, London.   [67] *Ibid*, fo. 81.

From an old manuscript *Ordinarium*, drawn up
for St. (130) Lo's collegiate church at Rouen,[68]
we find that this wax-brede was used also there.[69]
From what De Moleon says, while speaking of
this custom at this church, we learn that the
same usage was once followed by other churches
in France : Ils avoient, comme à l'église cathédrale,
une table enduite de cire, sur laquelle ils écrivoient
avec un poinçon les noms de ceux qui devoient
faire quelque office ou fonction. Quoiqu'ils y
fussent écrits, et qu'elle fût exposée en un lieu
évident, on ne lassoit pas de la lire à la fin du
chapitre après la petite Leçon.[70] And he remarked the same thing done at the church of
St. Martin, at Tours : Les officiers pour l'office
divin étoient inscrits dans un tableau enduit de
cire, comme à Rouen.[71]

The other hours of the day, called Tierce, Sext,
and None, show no difference from the Roman
model of the Sarum rite.

But even-song exhibits a few trifling variations.

---

[68] Qui ad missam lectiones vel tractus dicturi sunt, in tabula
cerea scripti primitus recitentur, quœ tabula, ita debet fieri.

Hodie ad missam
Primam lectionem, talis, &c.

—Johannis Abricensis, *Lib. De Off. Ecc*, ed. Prevotio, 261 [*P.L.*,
cxlvii 159].

[69] Feria sexta, hœc tabula in cera in capitulo recitetur :

Hodie i. lectionem frater talis, &c.

—*Ibid.*, 302 [173]

[70] *Voyages liturgiques de France*, 392.

[71] *Ibid.*, 122.

Upon all high festivals, and every Sunday of the year, betwixt the little chapter, as it is called, and the hymn, there was inserted a response with its versicle, both of which, at the more solemn feasts, were sung by the precentor of the church himself, attended by two others of the upper canons, all three vested in rich silk copes. Moreover, like (131) lauds, even-song had its second *Benedicamus Domino.* On some festivals, too, a prose, instead of at matins, but with the same ceremonial, was chanted at even-song, either just after the response, between the little chapter and hymn, or while walking in procession from the chancel to the altar of the saint whose "memory," or commemoration, was to be made, which was done by the celebrant on having reached and censed the altar which bore the saint's name.

The ritual for even-song, upon Sundays and the lower holy days, though not so majestic as that for festivals of the highest rank, was not without a certain amount of ceremony. In cathedral and collegiate churches, each canon had on his cassock, surplice, black choir-cope, and furred almuce; the boys, their surplices; the rulers of the choir were the only people who walked from the vestry arrayed in silken, embroidered copes. All, including the officiating priest, sat in the choir. After the third psalm had been chanted, three boys, at the bidding of the first ruler of the choir,

went into the vestry to change their surplices foi
amices and girdled albs: two of them to serve as
acolytes, and bear the candles; the third, the
thurible. The officiating priest stopped at his
stall, but turned himself, clad merely in his
canon's dress, towards the altar, while he read
the little chapter. Two canons now put on silken
copes, and sang the response at the foot of the
steps leading from the choir up to the presbytery.
Toward the end of the hymn, the priest came down
from his stall, and had put on him a silken cope;
and the acolytes with their lighted candles, and the
thurifer, came forth to meet him at the foot of the
presbytery steps, where he blessed the incense,
and, going thence up to the high altar, made his
genuflexion. He then incensed the altar, the
image of the B. V. Mary, which always stood
on the (132) north side, and the shrine; or, where
there was none, the relics. Having bowed to
the altar, and with the acolytes and their candles
going before him, he went to the easternmost of
the sedilia, or canopied seats, in the south wall
of the presbytery, and was there incensed by the
thurifer, who afterwards incensed the rulers of the
choir, then the dean and all the higher canons
on the same side, then the precentor and all on
his side, and afterwards the minor canons on
both sides; making, before he did so, a bow
to each one. In the meanwhile was sung the
Magnificat; and, as soon as its antiphon had

also been chanted again at the end, the priest, accompanied by the acolytes, came down to the steps, took his book from the boy who had to carry it, and sang the prayer of the day. After the first *Benedicamus*, a procession of the whole choir went through some part of the church,— at Easter time, to visit the newly-hallowed waters of the baptismal font,—at other seasons, to make the commemoration of the saint whose eve it was, at his altar. Both in going and coming back, they chanted anthems; one, on their return, in honour of the B. V. Mary. On reaching the west door of the choir or chancel, they stopped; that is, held a station there, below the rood, to sing versicle, and antiphon, and collect, in reverence of the cross.[72]

Upon the higher festivals, the incensing at even-song was much more solemn. As soon as the hymn was begun, there were brought to the celebrant two silken copes, of which he put on one, and sent the second to whomsoever among the priests he liked; and thus arrayed, and followed by two thurifers, both walked up together and incensed the high altar This done, they separated: one going to incense all the altars at the eastern, the other, those at the (133) western part of the church; and meeting again by the south door of the presbytery, incensed the bishop, and then one another.[73]

---

[72] *Use of Sarum*, lxxvii (82) p 157.
[73] *Ibid*, lii (54) pp. 115, 116

At St. Paul's, London, this was performed somewhat differently. The two priests went first, and
said a prayer before St. Ethelburga's altar, in the
vestry, and then incensed and kissed it; afterwards
they went, and having knelt and played at St.
Erconwald's shrine, incensed it all round; next
they went to the altar of the B. V. Mary, to the
baptistery, and to the other altars, and incensed
each in its turn. After the *Magnificat* they went,
and kneeling by the tomb of Bishop Roger, said
the anthem, *Corpora Sanctorum*, and incensed,
having kissed it. Going thence to the lowest
step of the high altar, they knelt, and recited
the anthem, *Gloriosi Principes*, and arising, incensed it.[74]

Of all the seven canonical hours of prayer,
complin is the only one which, in its construction,
somewhat differs, in the Salisbury breviary, from
the Roman form, with which it has, after all, much
in common. In the Roman breviary, complin
changes little or nothing during the whole year;
not so in that of Salisbury, which shows a varia-
tion for all the greater movable festivals.

None of the four anthems in honour of our
Blessed Lady are found in the Sarum use, either
at the end of complin, or of any other hour; nor
was there in it either the prayer, *Aperi, Domine*,
before, or that of *Sacrosanctæ et individuæ Trini-
tati*, after the recital of the divine office.

---

[74] Sparrow Simpson, *Registrum*, 80, 81

Though their portous did not in its rubrics bid
our clergy to say any of those anthems in honour
of the B. V. Mary, at the end of the day's service,
so warm was this country's love for the mother of
Christ, that lay-folks linked themselves together
into guilds, and churchmen of (134) their own
devotion chose, to go and sing every evening,
before the lighted image of our dear Lady, one or
other of those anthems in her praise. For this
many an endowment was made;[75] and, by the statutes drawn up for his college at Cambridge, and
his school at Eton, Henry VI. gave special orders
for devotions of this kind before the image of the
Blessed Virgin.[76]

By the usages of Catholic England, not only
the clerk who had been admitted into holy orders,
but each one who enjoyed a benefice, was bound
to say the seven canonical hours of prayer every
day; and he was taught to begin that holy work
by rehearsing the *Pater noster* and the *Ave
Maria*, at the end of which he made upon himself
the sign of the cross. The *Pater noster* concluded

---

[75] See Vol iii pp 224, 225

[76] Statuentes præterea quod omnibus et singulis diebus per
annum ad vesperam tempore congruentiori . omnes cho-
rustæ nostri regalis collegii præsentes una cum informatore in
cantu intrent in ecclesiam, pulsata ad hoc campana, præterquam
in Cœna Domini et in die Parascues, in quibus campana pulsari
non debet, ibidemque coram imagine Beatæ Virginis, accensis
luminaribus, superpellicus induti decantent solenniter et meliori
modo quo sciverint unam antiphonam de Beata Virgine, cum versiculo, *Ave, Maria*, &c, cum oratione, *Meritis et precibus*, &c —
King's Coll. and Eton Statutes, 107, 108

with these words, *Sed libera nos a malo   Amen.*
The latter prayer consisted of nothing more than
the words of the archangel Gabriel and of St.
Elizabeth, and ran thus: *Ave, Maria, gracia
plena, Dominus tecum; benedicta tu in mulieribus;
et benedictus fructus ventris tui, Jesus.   Amen.*
This we have noticed before.[77]

From *The Myroure of oure Ladye*, we learn how
our Catholic forefathers were taught to make (135)
the sign of the cross; for it says: "Then after these
prayers (sc. *Our Father*, and *Hail Mary*) ye aryse
and turne you to the aulter and enclyne, in token
that ye entende to say that holy seruyce to the
onely worshyp and praysynge of oure Lorde, and
of hys gloryous mother, oure Lady.   ¶ And then
ye blysse you wyth the sygne of the holy crosse,
to chase a waye the fende with all hys dysceytes.
For as Crisostome sayth (*Super Math. Omelia*, iv.
[liv. § 4]), where euer the fendes se the sygne of
the crosse they flye away dredyng yt as a staffe
that they are beten wyth all.   And in thys
blyssynge ye begynne wyth youre honde at the
hedde downewarde, and then to the lyfte syde,
and after to the righte syde, in token and byleue
that oure lorde Iesu cryste came downe from the
hed, that is, from the father in to erthe, by his
holy incarnacion, and from the erthe in to the lyfte
syde that is hel, by hys bytter passyon, and from
thense vnto his fathers ryght syde by his glorous

ascencion.   And after this, ye bryng your hande
to your breste, in token that ye ar come to thanke
hym, and prayse hym, in the enderest of youre
harte for tho benefytes." [78]

In part to direct, but more especially to shed
brighter splendours around the Church's cele-
brations, the principal services, on the Sunday
and the festival, were led by those who used to
be called

The Rulers of the Choir.

To the precentor belonged the duty of regulating
all those things which concerned the singing of
the Divine service.   He it was who wrote down
on the board, or wax-brede,—which was read out
in the chapter-house, after prime-song on Sunday
mornings and on high festivals,—the names of
(136) such as should undertake the different choir-
offices, or serve at the altar for the next week,
or through the octave of the occurring festival.
As his deputies for leading the choir-service, the
precentor chose, for all Sundays and feast-days of
the second class, two canons of the lower form ;
for high festivals, and those of the first class, four
canons,—two from the upper, two from the lower
form ; and these were called the "rulers of the
choir" : hence, to say that the choir was "ruled" on
any day, meant that it was a feast of one or other

---

[78] *The Myroure of oure Ladye*, Pt 11., ed. J H Blunt [E.E T S],
p 80

MONKS IN CHOIR.

From Brit. Mus., Domit. A. xvii. 121ᵛ.

class; and that there were not three, but nine
lessons read at matins.[79]

How the rulers of the choir, or, as they are now
called, "chanters," were arrayed in silken copes
and furred almuces, and bore each one a staff of
beautiful workmanship in his hand, we have
already said. It was for the first ruler always
to ask, at the beginning of even-song, from the
precentor, in what tones the psalms were to be
chanted, and by whom, among the upper canons,
the antiphons were to be intoned.

On a bench, or else stools, ranged from north
to south, and overspread with stuffs of price, sat
the four rulers of the choir, so that they could
read from the antiphoner on the eagle to the east
of them. As each psalm had to be given out,
those two on the south end of the seats arose,
and, with their staves in their hands, walked together towards that dignitary who had been named
for singing the antiphon. Stopping on the spot
in front of his stall, they made him a low bow, and
intoned the words, which this canon, arising to
them, took up and repeated after them in the same
notes. Getting again to the lectern, they and their
other two companions gave out the psalm. The
next antiphon was announced in this same way,
by the (137) other two rulers, unto some personage
on their north side; and thus did they alternately
go, in pairs, to announce the antiphons, before

[79] *Use of Sarum*, xxi (21), vol. 1 pp 30 and ff

the psalms, to their respective sides of the choir at matins, and lauds, and even-song, upon high festivals. When there were but two rulers, as on Sundays and lower saints' days, each took his own side of the choir for the intonement of the antiphons.

The first ruler, it was, who began the hymn, as well as the *Magnificat*, at even-song: all sang the antiphons for the commemorations or memories.

At matins, the rulers led the choir in singing the invitatory and the *Venite;* they intoned the psalms, and signified by whom the lessons were to be read. At lauds they did as they had done at even-song.

At mass, they chanted the introit, or, as the Sarum rite calls it, the " office," the *Kyrie,* the sequence, the *Sanctus,* and the *Agnus Dei.*[80] Before the celebrant gave out the *Gloria in excelsis,*[81] it was always intoned to him by the first ruler, as among the Anglo-Saxons; and when the bishop pontificated, this was done by the precentor [82] Besides controlling the singing, these rulers had to look after and watch over the boys, that they did not misbehave themselves, nor go out of the choir without leave.

Few Englishmen of these our times know that Richard of the lion - heart used, on principal festivals, to take upon himself a part, at least,

---

[80] *Ibid*, xxiii (23) p 38   [81] *Ibid.,* 39

[82] *Ibid* , iii. (3) p 3.

of the duties belonging to a ruler of the choir.
That hand of his which had just before been
lightening death-strokes upon its foes,—Richard,
the very next holy day uplifted in the choir of his
castle, as a sign for his chaplains to sing matins
or even-song louder; and the voice which had but
lately roared, thunder-like, above the battle-din, now
arose, in sweet, peaceful strength, to (138) lead the
chanting of hymns, and psalms, and antiphons.[83]

In monasteries, the rule always was to arise
at night and sing matins, so that lauds might
begin by day-break: in collegiate and cathedral
churches, served by the secular clergy, this same
practice continued, for many years after St.
Osmund's time, to be followed.[84] The people, too,

---

[83] Circa divinum officium in præcipuis solemnitatibus plurimum
delectabatur, vestibusque pretiosis capellam suam sollicite adorna-
bat, clericosque sonora voce modulantes donis et precibus ad can-
tandum festivius exstimulabat, atque per chorum huc illucque
deambulando voce et manu, ut altius concreparent, excitabat —
Ralph, abbot of Coggeshall, *Chron. Anglicanum*, ed Martene, *Vet.
Scrip. et Mon. Amp Coll*, v. 857.

[84] Et quia canonicæ horæ secundum temporum interstitia, in
ecclesiis parochialibus, sicut in cathedralibus et collegiatis ne-
queunt decantari, præcipimus ut presbyteri parochiales ab ecclesiis suis recedere non præsumant donec festis diebus ante missam
vel post, canonicas horas decantaverint, vel saltem legerint absque
cantu cum dies fuerit feriandus.—*Synod. Exonien* (A D 1287), in
Wilkins, *Concil*, ii. 144

Hoc in collegio (de Tonge) volumus et præcipimus temporibus
perpetuis observari, quod singulis diebus, exceptis tribus diebus
proximis ante Pascha, et quando matutinæ præmissariæ ibidem
dicuntur, tempestive saltem ad tardius in aurora diei, vel statim
post solis ortum prout tempori convenerit   pulsetur ad matutinas . . . et extunc pulsationibus more loci, prout solempnitati
diei convenerit debite factis, conveniant omnes presbyteri dicti

(139) loved to go and hear the canonical hours;
and thus, in all our parish churches, matins and

INTERIOR OF FRIARS' CHURCH
From Brit. Mus. MSS. Add. 28962, f. 263.

collegii ad matutinas et ad alias horas diei secundum usum Sarum,
&c.—Dugdale, *Mon. Anglic.*, viii. 1407.

In telling us of a miracle that happened in London, to one
Bricstam, who had been thrown into prison during the reign of

lauds were sung every day at early morn.[85]   What
our English fathers thought but an act of volun-
tary devotion upon week-days, they deemed more
or less binding upon them for the hallowing of
the Lord's day and His saints' festivals ; and, as
the Sunday's observances began on Saturday afternoon,[86] (140) even-song that day, as well as

William Rufus, the English monk Ordericus Vitalis says :—
Nocte quadam cum signa per urbem (Lundoniam) ad nocturnas
lauds pulsarentur, &c —*Hist Eccl*, 630

Of an old pious woman, who had given her the duty of ringing
the bells for day and night service, in a church at Mechlin, in
Flanders, we are told that she kept a cock to awaken her at
night —Mulier matricularia eadem et nonna Geilindis nomine,
pia devotione ecclesiæ ejus (S Rumoldi) adhæserat   sonandarum
campanarum officium habebat.   Hæc prosequendarum horarum,
die solem, noctu gallum sibi nutrnerat monitorem —*AA. SS.
Julii*, 1 245.

[85] During the times of Advent and Lent, Margaret, queen of
Scotland (c A D 1093), used to get out of bed and go to church
at night for matins and lauds —Qualiter ante Dominicum Natale
quadraginta dies, et totum Quadragesimæ tempus, solita fuerit
ducere breviter tentabo dicere   Cum principio noctis paululum
requievisset, ecclesiam ingressa primum matutinas de Sancta
Trinitate, deinde de Sancta Cruce, postmodum de Sancta Maria
ipsa sola complevit   .   Celebrantibus hora congrua presbyteris laudes matutinas, interim ipsa psalterium finivit . .   His
peractis quieti se ac sopori contulit   Cum vero mane facto lecto
surrexisset precibus et psalmis diu insistebat, &c —*AA. SS.
Junii*, 11 333

In the statutes for Whittington College and Hospital, London
(A D 1424), it is ordained —quod idem magister et capellani, devote, distincte et aperte ad audientiam parochianorum, et aliorum
illuc confluentium dicant adinvicem matutinas, vesperas, et alias
horas suas canonicas de die, &c —Dugdale, *Mon Angl*, vii 740

[86] In primis sacrum diem Dominicum ab hora diei sabbati
vespertina inchoandum non ante horam ipsam præveniendum, ne
Judaicæ professionis participes videamur   Quod etiam in festis
quæ suas habent vigilias, observetur   *Constitutio Simonis Islepe
Archiep Cantuar   De Festis Sanct Obser*, ed Lyndwood, 57, ad
finem tomi   Our old writers of the saints' lives afford us more

matins before mass on the (141) Sunday, were
looked upon as part of the Christian's duty,[87]

---

than one example to show how a saint's festival, like the Sunday,
began to be kept just after nonetide, on its eve   Reginald, the
Durham monk, for instance, tells us —Instante igitur Beati
Laurentii martyris Deo preciosi vigilia sollempni, puella quoddam
de fusticotincto indumentum studio sibi sagaci consuit, jamque
hora diei prima præterit   Ad quam mater, filiam instruens, ait,
Filia mea, opus quod præ manibus citius accelera, ut omnino
consummatum sit opus quod agressa es, antequam nos præveniat
hujus diei hora nona   Exstat quidem hodie Sancti Laurentii   ..
veneranda vigilia .   nam feriantes citra horæ nonæ terminum
jam propiantem sæpius gravi ultione perplectere consuevit, &c —
Lib de B Cuthberti Virtut , 243

Dives asks *Pauper*   " How longe ought the holy day to be kept
and halowed ? "   *Pauper* answers, " From even to even · never the
lesse some begynne sooner to halowe after that the feaste is, and
after use of the countreye.   But that men use in the Satyrdayes
and vygylles to ryng holy even at mydday compelleth not men
anone to halowe, but warneth them of the holy daye folowyng, that
they shuld thynke theron and spede them, and so dyspose them
and theyr occupacions, that they myght halowe in dewe tyme "
(*Dives and Pauper*, xiii , ed Berthelet, A D 1536, fol. 122, b)
Again *Pauper* says —" whan evensonge is done at after none in
the Soneday, yet is it not leful for to werke then   And also whan
that evensonge is sayde in the Satyrdaye at after none, yet is it
lefull for to werke tyll the sonne go down."—*Ibid.*, xvi.

Mulier apud Kilingeham nata nebat die Sabbati, vespero jam
in occiduum declivi.   Ammonita a considentibus ut, reverentiam
Dominicæ diei habens, ferias faceret, non solum non paruit, sed
etiam illas arrogantiæ notavit quod se necessariis inservientem
arguerent, &c —Wil Malmes, *Gesta Pontif* , v 276 [*R S* , lii 439]

[87] Not only the hearing of mass, but also of matins, was taught
as needful for hallowing the Sunday, thus Pauper, speaking of
such as may follow their calling or trade upon the Lord's day,
says —" also messangers, pylgrymes, and wayfarynge men, that
may not well reste withoute greatto harme, ben excused, so that
they doo their dilygence to here masse and matyns, if they canne "
—*Dives and Pauper*, cap xv , fol 124   In another place, talking
of the ungodly, he says —" they have leaver to go to the taverne
than to holye church   Lever to here a songe of Robynhode, of
some ribaudry, than for to here masse or matynes," &c —*Ibid* ,
cap.li , fol 69, b

which nothing but sickness should hinder.
Speaking, under these feelings, of his own times,
Langland says .

> " For holy churche hoteþ alle manere puple
> Vnder obedience to bee · and buxum to þe lawe · · ·
> Lewede men to laborie , [and] lordes to honte
> And vp-on sonedays to cesse godes seruyce to huyre,
> Boþe matyns and messe · and, after mete, in churches
> To huyre here eucsong, euery man ouhte
> Thus it by-longeþ for lorde · for lered, and lewede,
> Eche halyday to huyre hollyche þe seruice." [88]

While blaming the idleness of some, the same poet
asks :

> " Wher see we hem on sonedays · þe scruyse to huyre,
> As matyns by þe morwe ? · tyl masse by-gynne,
> Oþer sonedays at euesonge " [89]

And, in another place, he makes the sorrowing
sinner plight a promise for the better keeping of
the Lord's day, thus : (142)

> " þanne sat sleuthe vp · and seynede hym ofte,
> And made a-vowe by-for god for hus foule sleuthe,
> 'Shal no soneday þis seuene ȝer be bote sycknesse hit make,
> þat ich ne shal do me or daye to þe dere churche,
> And huyre matyns and masse · as ich a monke were ·
> Shal no Ale after mete · holde me þennes,
> Til ich haue hurd euesong ich by-hote to þe rode ! ' " &c. [90]

This old English custom of every one's going to
the parish church and hearing matins there

---

88 *Piers Ploughman*, Passus x 219–231 [ed Skeat, 170]
89 *Ibid* , 242–244 [171]
90 *Ibid* , Passus viii. 63–69 [ed. Skeat, 124]

before eating breakfast, is furthermore noticed thus by Sir Thomas More : "Some of us lay men thinke it a payne ones in a weeke to ryse so soone fro sleepe, and some to taiye so longe fasting, as on the Sonday to com and heare out theyr matins. And yet is not the matins in every parishe, neyther, all thyng so early begonne, nor fullye so longe in doyng, as it is in the Charterhouse, ye wot wel." That this part of the divine service might be well performed, it was moie than once enacted in our national synods, that all such priests as held the benefice of a chantry should not meiely say their mass in their respective chapels, but be present in the chancel of the church, and help in singing there all the canonical hours.[91]

(143) Not only clerks, but some lay folks, and those of high degree, used to carry about with them a portous, out of which their daily wont was to read matins and even-song. While saying his matins on horseback, as he rode all alone, and half-a-mile ahead of his retainers, was

---

[91] Præcipimus ut omnes capellani qui in una parochia commorantur, simul intersint et conveniant matutinis et vesperis, et aliis horis canonicis, in ecclesiis celebrandis, &c *Constit IV de Cantilupo Wigorn. epis* (A D 1240), ed Wilkins, *Concil ,* i 668 In a constitution sent forth by Archbishop Robert Winchelsey (A D 1305), in the synod of Merton, to regulate the services of stipendiary priests in parish churches, it is ruled thus —jurent prædicti presbyteri, quod debeant interesse cancello matutinis, vesperis et aliis divinis officiis, horis debitis, induti superpelliciis canentes, legentes, et psalmodizantes, piout eis Deus scientiam dederit.—Wilkins, *Concil.,* ii 281. Of this custom we have already spoken, vol. iii 102

it that one of the Treshams fell, run through by the spear of a foeman : "In tymes paste, one William Tresham, owner of these landes, cumming from Northampton to Siwelle, and saying his matens, was cruelly slayne by one Salisbyri and Glin of Wales, with their route, servantes to the Lorde Gray of Ruthyne. This William had a route of servantes, cumming by chaunce half a myle behind him," &c.[92] Richard, Lord Scrope, one of the leading men of his own times, bequeathed to his son Roger the codex which he himself had often employed for such a purpose [93]

The ringing for these canonical hours let the world know the time, by day and by night; and in those large churches, where such a custom was followed, the several bells, as well as the different ways in which they were rung for the purpose, told that precise service which was then about to be chanted [94]

---

[92] Leland, *Itin*, vi 33 That many of our old catholic countrymen were in the daily habit of saying, not only matins and evensong, but the other canonical hours also, seems clear from the Life of St Brandon :—

This fowles song ek her matyns wel right tho it was time,
And of the sauter sede vers and seithe also prime,
And undarne seithe, and midday, and afterward seith non,
And ech tyde of the day songe as Cristenemen scholde done

Quoted by Hearne in his Glossary to Langtoft's *Chronicle*, ii 670.

[93] Item Rogero filio meo predicto melius meum spiceplate, et secundum missale meum, cum porteus meo quo usus fui ad dicendum matutinas meas et vesperas —*Testamenta Eborac*, 278

[94] Of the many writers from (144) whom we might gather this,

If all the while England was Catholic, her children's household words were borrowed from the rites and pious usages set forth by the Church of Christ, in which they so steadfastly believed; this was strongly exemplified by that form of speech in which, throughout those ages, the time of day was spoken of Prime, undern, none and even-song were the terms in every man's mouth, high or low, to tell how the moments had sped and were speeding, or the period when a thing had happened: "The seventh day of Juny," says Peter Langtoft, "died that lady bituex undron and prime."[95] In speaking the praises of Christ's beloved mother while yet a girl, the preacher told how "every daye, from morow to underen, she was in her prayer-es; and from underen tyll none, she occupyed her craft of weving of clothes in the temple; and at none the methe and the drinke that was broughte to her, she gaaf to powie peple," &c.[96] Of his Ploughman, William Langland tells, that

"Atte hye pryme peers · let þe plouh stonde,"[97]

Reginald the Durham monk is one, and he says In ecclesia Beati Cuthberti plura sunt signa ad divini operis ministeria pro officiosa diversitatis immutatione pernecessaria Nam pro immutatione diversitatum distinguendo discernunt alternantium tempora vicissitudinum Unde ex signo pulsante dinoscitur cujus horae terminus, tam nocturnis quam diurnis momentis, ex ipsorum variata immutatione celebietur —De S Cuthbeiti Virtut, 189

[95] Chronicle, ed Hearne, ii 243. [Not in R S, xlvii]
[96] Liber Festivalis, fol cxliii b.
[97] Passus ix 119 [ed Skeat, 145]

And Chaucer, too, makes his " Clerke " notice how (145)

"The tyme of undern of the same day
Approcheth, that this wedding sholde be." [98]

As matins and even-song were held to be a portion at least of the divine service which each one ought to hear for the hallowing of the Lord's day and the festivals, a part of the parishioners' obligations was to find the wax tapers that were kept burning at the high altar of their church during those offices, as well as mass.[99] That while being thought of, he might be prayed for by those who came to church, the dying man often bequeathed lands and money to find lights to stand over his burial-place in his chantry chapel, all through those public services, every Sunday, during a certain length of time. Thus, Nicholas de Beaupie willed " ii. candlesticks of laton, with ii. wax candles of ii. pound, to be set upon his grave, to burn every Sunday and holy-day, at matins, hey mass, and even-song, for the space of a yere." [1] With a like wish was it, that books which had in them these canonical hours, were sometimes left, by will, to be fastened to a desk or reading-stand nigh some altar, that those who wished might say or sing their matins and even-song out of them · for such an end did

---

[98] Student's Chaucer [ed Skeat, 599].

[99] Parochiani tenentur invenire cereum paschalem et alios cereos in cancello ; et lumen sufficiens per totum annum, tam ad matutinas quam ad vespertinas et ad missam, &c —Wilkins, Concil ,i 714

[1] Blomefield, Norfolk, vii 459

John Norys bequeath "his portous of paper rial to be chayned in the chapel of our lady" in the church of South Lynn, where he had been vicar.[2]

Besides being, at best, but a shrunken shadow of the old matins, the morning prayer, in the Book of Common Prayer, is said too late in the day by some hours, and (146) made to take up that place in the public offices which was once filled by a higher, because a holier service—the Eucharistic sacrifice. Anciently, matins were said in every church throughout this land, at early morn, and before breakfast, as a preparation for mass, now, the Establishment's Morning Prayer is said after breakfast-time, and instead of mass. Oddly enough, however, in many a country parish, the Establishment keeps up, without meaning it, some faint traces of the olden usage, by tolling a particular bell at eight o'clock on Sunday mornings; this serves no liturgical purpose now, but it used to be, in Catholic times, for matins : another bell, still rung at nine o'clock, was to call the people to undern and mass. But at the present day, though Protestants go on thus ringing, their morning service, for which they toll again, begins at eleven o'clock; and, if asked, they cannot tell why they use the earlier ringing.

The Holy Sacrifice was, however, as it had always been among the Anglo-Saxons, the great object of our Anglo-Norman people. But

---

[2] Blomefield, *Norfolk*, VIII 547

THE MASS, ACCORDING TO THE SARUM RITE,

had in it some slight variations by which it differed both from the Anglo-Saxon and our present Roman form.

After having sung or said the matins, prime, and undern or tierce of the day, the parish priest offered up the holy sacrifice.[3] While putting on his vestments, he (147) recited the hymn *Veni Creator Spiritus*, besides the collect *Deus cui omne cor;* the psalm *Judica me, Deus*, with the anthem *Introibo ad altare Dei*, before and after; then *Kyrie eleison*, &c., *Pater noster*, and *Ave Maria*. On reaching the foot of the altar from the vestry, the priest began mass by saying up aloud: *Et ne nos inducas in tentationem. Sed libera nos a malo. Confitemini Domino quoniam bonus Quoniam in secula misericordia ejus:* and then the *Confiteor Deo, beatæ Mariæ, omnibus sanctis et vobis; quia peccavi nimis cogitatione, locutione, et opere, mea culpa · precor sanctam Mariam, omnes sanctos*

---

[3] Nullus sacerdos parochialis præsumat missam celebrare, antequam matutinale persolvat officium, et Primam ac Tertiam de die. —*Constit editæ in Concil. Oxon.* (A D 1322), in Wilkins, *Concil*, II. 512

Whilst the priest was vesting himself, the sacristan gave three strokes to a small bell, got ready the wine and water in the cruets, lighted the candles and strewed the altar cloths smooth upon the altar Vir Dei exsurgens funem corripuit, et sicut mos est missam dicturis, ter signum pulsare cœpit, aquam haustam ampulla et urceolo protulit, et lumine accenso quæque linteamina, missarum solemniis convenientia, circa altare composuit —Reginald, *Lib de Vita S. Godrici*, 227 (ed. Stevenson, for the Surtees Society).

Dei et vos orare pro me. Such, and not our present, was the form for the "Confiteor" then in use in this country. Going up the three steps to the altar and kissing it, he made the sign of the cross upon himself as he uttered the words *In nomine Patris,* &c. What we now call the "introit," formerly went under the name of "office"; and, upon high festivals, used to be said or sung by the celebrant and his acolyte, alternately, at every mass. This we learn from a passage in the life of St. Bartholomew, once an ankret on Farne Island.[4] The holy virgin Wiborada, in the tenth century, once helped the priest to sing the tract in the mass on the first Sunday of Lent, at St Gall's, in Switzerland.[5]

When the *Gloria in excelsis* had to be said, the priest went and began it at the middle of the altar, but came back to recite the remainder at the south, or epistle end.

---

[4] Celebrata namque in salutem fidelium Missa, in nocte solenni, quodam die Nativitatis Dominicæ, laudibusque matutinis in laudem Dei completis, post modicum temporis intervallum egressus est vir Domini Bartholomæus, videre an adhuc dies ille sacer in auroram albesceret, quatenus secunda (148) celebratio fieri potuisset. Et reversus vidit cereos accensos et venerandi vultus sacerdotem coram sancto altari, sacerdotalibus indutum assistere. Cumque nullus ad ministrandum apparuit, ipso accessit, dictaque alterutrum confessione, canebant officium "*Lux fulgebat*" cum ceteris, in voce jubilationis et lætitiæ . Cumque hoc aliquando fratri Willelmo aperuit, inquisitus est ab eo, utrum inter sacræ celebrationis obsequia osculum pacis ei dederit; quod licet confiteri noluerit, dubium non est quin id exhibuerit, qui debitum et devotum in ceteris ministerium impendit —*Vita S Bartholomæi eremitæ Farnensis,* auctore monacho coævo, A.D. 1182, in *AA. SS Junii* iv 840.

[5] *AA SS Maji* i. 285.

As in the Anglo-Saxon, so in the Sarum rite, the custom was to intermix,—both along with the *Kyrie* and the *Gloria in excelsis, Sanctus,* and *Agnus Dei,*—certain sentences, or, as the rubric calls them, "proses," adapted to the seasons and higher festivals of the year. In this shape, these parts of the service were described as being "cum farsura."[6] Of these "kyries," one there was, cherished very much, and looked upon as having been bequeathed to this land by St. Dunstan, to whom angels had taught the music and the words, as John of Brompton (149) tells us;[7] and which had, half a century before his times, been said by William of Malmesbury.[8] When the youth, or whosoever the person might be, who served at mass, knew Latin well enough, he, instead of the priest, read the epistle.[9]

Immediately after the gradual came the sequence.

---

[6] *Directorium Sacerdotum* (H B S), 1 28

[7] Beatus eciam Dunstanus semel soporatus audivit spiritus angelicos cum suavi nota, *Kyriel, Kyriel,* psallentes, cujus modulos armoniæ adhuc continet tropus ille apud Anglos famosus, *Kirie Rex splendens,* qui in sanctorum cantari majoribus solet festis — *Chron,* ed Twysden, 1. 879

[8] Et credo equidem, nec vana fides, quod etiam angelorum cantum audierit (Beatus Dunstanus) kirrieleison psallentium, quod nunc libenter ecclesiæ discunt et docent Anglorum —*Gesta Pontif Anglor.,* 1 19 [*R S,* lii 31]

[9] Induto tandem sacerdote, et jam missa circa epistolæ legendæ terminum properante, vir Dei statim accedens ad juvenem innuendo multoties præcepit ut epistolam, arrepto libro, legeret, et opere perficiendo jam non se ulterius laicum sed potius litteratum, cunctis ostenderet timidus tamen accessit (juvenis) et epistolam coram cunctis perlegit.—Reginald of Durham, *Vita S Godrici heremitæ de Finchale,* 227.

These sequences, or, as St. Osmund calls them, "proses," were sung or said on the Sundays during Advent and Paschal time; on the Sunday within the octave of Christmas; on all the movable feasts, and on all great saints' days, as well as in the masses in honour of the B V. Mary. Of these sequences we have already spoken at some length just now (pp 23, 24).

After having said the anthem called the "offertory," and received the gifts of the faithful, if any chose to bring an offering,[10] the priest put the paten, with the host on it, (150) before him, at the middle of the altar; and, uplifting the chalice, into which wine, mingled with a very little water, had been poured (sometimes beforehand in the vestry), he pronounced, with boweddown head, instead of the *Suscipe, sancte Pater*, of the Roman missal, this one prayer: Suscipe, sancta Trinitas, hanc oblationem quam ego in-

---

[10] The ritual custom of each one's bringing his gift for the offertory at mass is noticed in many of our old documents thus of Edmund Ironside's granddaughter Margaret, queen of Scotland, her confessor, Theodoric the monk of Durham, tells us —Nam quoniam ipse (Malcolmus rex) ad mandatum suum in cœna Domini, et ad missarum solennia nummos aureos offerre consueverat, ex his aliquos ipsa (Margareta) sæpius pie furari et pauperi qui eam inclamaverat solita erat largiri Et sæpe quidem cum rex ipse sciret, nescire tamen se simulans, hujusmodi furto plurimum delectabatur. — *AA. SS. Junii* ii 332 The order, too, in which Margaret made her children go up to the altar with their offering, is also noticed by the same writer of her life —Unde et inter missarum solemnia, cum post parentes ad offerendum procederent, junior majorem prævenire nullo modo præsumpsit, sed secundum ætatis ordinem major juniorem præcedere consuevit —*Ibid*, 329

dignus peccator offero in honore tuo et beatæ
Mariæ, et omnium sanctorum tuorum, pro peccatis et offensionibus meis, pro salute vivorum
et requie omnium fidelium defunctorum.   In
nomine Patris, &c.[11] Setting down the chalice,
he covered it over, not with the little square
piece of linen we now use, and name the "pall,"
but with the corporal itself, after the manner
which is shown in the pictures on the opposite
page. To answer such a purpose, corporals then
were made much wider than ours are now.
Whilst he washed his hands, the priest did not
say that part of the 25th psalm, *Lavabo*, &c,
but instead, *Munda me, Domine, ab omni in-
quinamento mentis et corporis, ut possim mun-
datus implere opus sanctum Domini.* Often
did he here turn about to the people, and beg
them to join with him (151) in going through
the psalm, *De profundis*, and other prayers, for
the good of those souls of the dead whom he
had named, as we remarked at another place in
this work.[12] Now was it, and not before washing
his fingers, that, bending himself lowly down to
the altar-stone, he recited the prayer, *In Spiritu
humilitatis,* &c ; and then, turning about, uttered

---

[11] Neither the prayer *Deus qui humanæ salutis,* &c , nor that
other of the Roman missal *Offerimus tibi, Domine, calicem,* &c , are
in the Sarum missal

[12] Vol iii p 106   John Baret writes, "I wille Seynt Marie
preest sey a messe of oure Lady at Seynt Marie auter is ende
and reherse John Barettys name opynly, seying *De profundis* for
me," &c — *Bury Wills,* 18, 21.

the usual call unto the people, in these words, *Orate, fratres et sorores*, &c. The Preface said, as well as the *Sanctus* after it, and ere beginning

the Canon, many, if not all, our English priests used to kiss the figure of Christ our Lord, in the illumination which is to be found just before the canon in almost all hand-written, and engraved in every printed, missal. This is ordered in a rubric just before the canon of the mass, in a Sarum manual,—a manuscript of the middle of the fifteenth century, now in my hands.[12a]   That the same use prevailed in France, we learn from Durand, who says that some books had, besides the crucifix, a picture of the Father in majesty: and that some priests were accustomed to kiss the feet of that figure as well as of the crucified Lord.[13]   This "majesty" was the Father Almighty,

---

[12a] Inmediate ante *Sc's*, elevet manus et paulatim eas dimittendo et iungendo cum dicit *Benedictus*, suam signet faciem   Deinde osculetur pedes crucifixi, vel librum.   Deinde inclinet se toto corpore dicens, *Adoramus te, Christe, et benedicimus tibi quia per crucem tuam redemisti mundum, miserere nostri qui passus es pro nobis*

[13] In quibusdam tamen codicibus et majestatis patris, et etiam imago depingitur crucifixi, ut sacerdos quasi præsentem videat quem invocat, et quem alloquitur, dicens, *Te igitur*, &c, et passio quæ hic repræsentatur, cordis oculis ingeratur   Sacerdos autem osculatur pedes ipsius majestatis, et se signat in fronte   innuens quod reverenter ad mysterium passionis accedit   Quidam (152) tamen prius osculantur pedes majestatis, et postea pedes crucifixi, secundum seriem canonis   Alii contra quia per filium pervenitur ad patrem —*Rationale Divin. Offic*, iv 35, 153

On the leaf facing the beginning of the canon of the mass in a Salisbury manual of mine (written *circa* A D 1445), there is an illumination of the crucifixion, the full size of the MS., which is nine inches and a half in height, and six inches and a half in breadth   The face of our Divine Redeemer in this illumination is much smeared, evidently by having been so often kissed   Just such another unmistakable mark is also left, not on the face, but feet of the engraving, upon vellum, and inserted at the same part of the mass, just before another engraving of the "magesty," in a tall and beautiful copy of the folio Salisbury missal, printed (A.D 1555) at Paris, by J Amazeur, for W Merlin,—I rejoice to say, in my hands. This book is doubly dear to me, as I find it belonged, during catholic times, to the church of Buckland—the

represented, like the prophet Daniel's (153)
"Ancient of Days," as an awe-awakening old
man, arrayed in alb, stole, and cope, and crowned
with the papal tiara. In his left hand he held
the mound, or globe of empire; and, with his
outstretched right, he bestowed his benediction.
Such is the form of the "majesty" in a folio
Sarum missal, printed by Amazeur (Paris, 1555),
in my possession. Fanaticism seems to have felt
much spite against this engraving, as it is to be

---

very parish in which I am now living   I learn this fact from an
original entry which stands at the beginning of it, and runs thus
—"Of yor charyte pray for the sowle of dame Elyzabethe ffety-
place some tyme relygious in Amesburye & also for me Elynor
fiety-place her sust^r relygious in Syon, at whose charge thys boke
was bought & geven to thys churche of Bockland   Anno dn'j,
1556" These ladies' family lived in the next parish, viz Pusey
To kiss the painting of Christ's figure was one of the ways
which our forefathers employed for telling their belief in our
Lord   thus St Godrick the ankret drew from his bosom what
was very likely a missal, which had the crucifixion limned just
before the canon, and kissed the illumination —libello de sinu
sibi protracto, imaginem Salvatoris cum Beatæ Mariæ imaginis
similitudine, et Sancti Johannis pictura honeste in folio depicta,
protulit, et cum impetu festinationis ad os ejus apposuit.
"Ecce," inquit, "si in Christo credis, his reverentiam adhibe,
et Christum profitens, ista adorando deosculare"—Reginald, Lib
de Vita S Godrici, 109
Nicholas de Plove lets us know that the same practice obtained
in Germany, when he wrote (c 1490) —Et fit circa canonem
imago crucifixi ut tanto melius imprimatur memoria Christi
passionis in cruce ipsi celebranti. Accedens autem sacerdos post
ablutionem, primo benedicit se, secundo compositis manibus
osculatur imaginem crucifixi, inclinando se humiliter .   Alii
autem osculantur altare   Deinde incipit dicens Te igitur
—Expositio (quarte partis) Misse, sig K b Impres Argentine,
A D M CCCC XC

very rarely found now in Salisbury missals, copies
of which become more precious from having it.

If not during St. Osmund's days, soon after,
at least, the custom was, as the priest said the
Sanctus, &c., to toll three strokes on a bell. For
hanging it so that it might be heard outside,

RINGING THE SACRING BELL BEFORE THE ALTAR

as well as within the church, a little bell-cote
often may yet be found built on the peak of
the gable, between the chancel and the nave,
that the rope might fall at a short distance from
the spot where knelt the youth or person who
served at mass. From the first part of its use,
this bell got the name of the " Saints," " Sanctys,"

or " Sanctus," bell ; and many notices concerning it are to be met with in old accompts. At the other masses in the chantry chapels, and at the different altars about the (154) church, a small hand-bell was employed for this, among other liturgical uses.[14]

At the beginning of the canon, the priest prayed —by name, but within himself—for the then pope, the bishop of the diocese, and for the king, besides his own friends, and all there present ; and among those other saints whose memory is venerated there, he enumerated that one whose body lay enshrined in the church wherein he was then offering up the holy sacrifice. Of this latter rite, we are told by Matthew Paris, in his life of Abbot William, who got this privilege from Pope Innocent III. in the council of Lateran.[15]

---

[14] In some, very likely in most, places there were two distinct bells, one for the " sanctus," the other for the elevation thus, in the inventory of the goods, plate, &c , gathered together for king Edward VI 's use in the county of Durham, we find, very often, such an entry as this —thre bells in the stopell, a lyttell sauce bell, a sacring bell, and a hand bell —*Eccl Proceedings of Bishop Barnes* (Surt. Soc , vol xxii), lii   The council of Exeter (A D 1287) decreed that in every church there should be —campanella deferenda ad infirmos, et ad elevationem corporis Christi —Wilkins, *Concil*, ii 139

[15] Abbas (S Albani), erectus in medio, satis modeste et eleganter exorsus est, coram Papa et toto Concilio, suam sic in propatulo quæstionem —" Sancte Pater, nos qui alicujus Sancti corpus in ecclesiis habere dinoscimur, licetne nobis in Secreto Missæ, inter alios quos invocamus Suffragatores, nomen ipsius recitare ? Desideramus super hoc certificari   " Ad quod, in audientia omnium, respondens Papa ` . . dixit; " Videtur mihi dignum, jurique consonum, ut devote in Secreto Missæ (videlicet, in serie primo nominatorum), Sanctus, cujus corpore aliqua gratulatui

(155) On getting to the *Hanc igitur oblationem,* &c., instead of spreading his hands over the chalice, as we now do, he laid them upon the corporal; and, looking down at the host, said the above prayer.[16]

All through the Anglo-Saxon period there was not, as now, any elevation immediately after the consecration, although our fathers of those ages believed as strongly in transubstantiation, and worshipped with just as much love and awe the very body and blood of Christ in the mass, as we do This has been shown at full length in another part of the present work.[17] To' make the liturgy speak out her true teaching, and thus withstand those new, and therefore false, doctrines of Berenger against the holy Eucharist, the Church in France, where that heretic had scattered about his bad seed, bethought herself, towards the end of the eleventh, or the beginning of the twelfth, century, of the Elevation. This beautiful and becoming ceremonial spread slowly from France all through Latin Christendom; but we have no grounds for thinking that it had reached so far as Normandy during William I.'s

ecclesia, nomen, eiusque suffragium in loco suo proprio merito postuletur.'—*Vitæ S Albani Abb*, 76 [*R S*, xxviii 1 261, 262]

[16] Cum autem venerit (sacerdos) ad *Hanc igitur oblationem*, &c, submittens manus super altare ex utraque parte corporalium respiciat hostiam donec dicat *Quæsumus Domine*, &c , tunc elevans in pristinum statum, modesto respiciat sursum, et cætera prosequendo —Manuale ad Usum Sarum, MS , in my possession

[17] Vol 1 p 18

reign : certain is it, that neither in the valuable
work of John of Avranches (*Liber de Officiis
Ecclesiasticis*), nor in the *Tractatus* on the same
subject by St. Osmund, can be found the slightest
traces of it The precise time when the elevation
just after the consecration got into use in England,
is not known ; we learn, however, from various
(156) sources, that the thirteenth century is, most
likely, the period which saw its first adoption
here. In a synod held under Archbishop Stephen
Langton, at Oxford (A.D. 1222), it was decreed that
the laity should be continually urged to genuflect
when the Blessed Sacrament was carried by, and
also at the elevation of the host in the consecration of the mass · [18] and Hugh Patshull, bishop
of Lichfield (A D 1240), gave similar directions,
in one of his statutes for his cathedral.[19] Whether,
at that period, the chalice also used to be ele-
vated, as well as the host, is not quite clear ;
and, from the wording of the two quotations just
cited, it would seem it was not. Though perhaps, at its first introduction, this rite may not
have been accompanied by the tolling of any

---

[18] Frequenter moneantur laici, ut ubicunque videant Corpus
Domini deferri, statim genua flectant tanquam Creatori et Re-
demptori suo, et junctis manibus, quousque transierit, orent
humiliter, et hoc maxime fiat tempore consecrationis in elevatione
hostiæ, quum panis in verum corpus Christi transformatur, et id,
quod est in calice, in sui sanguinem mystica benedictione transformatur —Wilkins, *Concil*, 1 594

[19] Quando elevatur corpus Christi adoret stando, quo dimisso
prosternat se chorus —Dugdale, *Mon. Anglic.*, viii 1259

bell, the practice soon after was to ring at the elevation. This was particularly required in one of the statutes drawn up (A D 1240) by William de Cantilupe, for his diocese of Worcester.[20] A few years afterwards, John Peckham, archbishop of Canterbury, sent forth (A.D. 1281) a series of *Constitutiones*, one of which (*De custodia Eucharistiæ*) not only required a bell to be rung at such a part of the mass, but that all who might hear it, whether at home or abroad in the fields, should kneel down and pray [21]

For this ringing at the parish mass, so that the toll might be heard both within and far beyond the church itself, the "Sanctus" bell, of which we have already spoken [p. 153], was no doubt used; but for the elevation at all other masses, little hand‑bells, sometimes made of silver and called the "sacring" bell, were employed: may be, too, a small bell used to be hung somewhere nigh the altar, for liturgical purposes. "In the church of Hawsted, Suffolk," says Cullum, "there still hangs a little bell on the rood-loft It is about six inches diameter." [22]

---

[20] Cum autem in celebratione missæ corpus Domini per manus sacerdotum in altum erigitur, campanella pulsetur, ut per hoc devotio torpentium excitetur, ac aliorum charitas fortius inflammetur —Wilkins, *Concil*, 1 667.

[21] In elevatione vero ipsius corporis Domini pulsetur campana in (157) uno latere, ut populares, quibus celebrationi Missarum non vacat quotidie interesse, ubicunque fuerint, seu in agris seu in domibus, flectant genua, indulgentias concessas a pluribus episcopis habituri.—*Ibid*, 11 52, see also 132

[22] *Hist and Antiquit of Hawsted*, 34.

On hearing the sacring bells first tinkle, those in church who were not already on their knees knelt down, and, with upraised hands, worshipped their Maker in the holy housel lifted on high before them.

When he got to the *Supplices te rogamus*, instead of joining his hands as we do, the priest folded his arms cross-wise—*cancellatis manibus*—upon his breast, and bowed him down very lowly before the altar the while he said that prayer. At the *Libera nos*, after taking up and kissing the paten, he put it first to his left then to his right eye, before he made the sign of the cross upon himself. When he broke the host into three parts, instead of laying the two larger ones on the paten, he held them both in his left hand, as, having the small particle in his right hand, he made the sign of the cross three times with it over the chalice whilst he said *Pax Domini sit semper nobiscum* He then said the *Agnus Dei* thrice; but, as he still kept holding the small particle between the (158) forefinger and thumb of his right hand, he could not, as we do, strike his breast each time at those words; and at the *dona nobis pacem*, ending the last *Agnus Dei*, he dropped that fragment into the chalice.

Throughout a great part of the year, on ferial and lower class saints' days, prayers for the recovery of the holy land, and in behalf of those Christians who were bondsmen there, used to be said at the parochial mass immediately before the *Pax*. These prayers consisted of the three psalms : *Deus venerunt gentes*, &c. (psalm lxxviii.) [lxxix.], *Deus misereatur nostri*, &c (psalm lxvi.) [lxvii.], and *Domine in virtute tua*, &c. (psalm xx.) [xxi.], followed by as many collects ; one beseeching the return to Christian hands of Judæa, the second for the bishop's weal, the third for the king's. Such a service was appointed in the York as well as the Sarum missal, both forms for which are very much alike.[23]

---

[23] The following is the service as appointed in the York Missal —*In omnibus feriis et in omnibus Festis trium lectionum a festo Sanctæ Trinitatis usque ad Vigiliam Nativitatis Domini, et ab Octavis Epiphaniæ usque ad Cenam Domini ac etiam tempore Paschali exceptis Octavis præcipuis, post* Pater noster *dicantur Psalmi sequentes*

Psalmus Deus venerunt gentes, *et cetera, ut in Psalterio, cum singulis versibus* Gloria Patri Sicut erat in principio Kyrie eleyson Christe eleyson Kyrie eleyson. Pater noster. Et ne nos Sed libera. Exsurgat Deus, et dissipentur inimici ejus. Et fugiant Salvum fac populum tuum, Domine Et benedic hæreditati tuæ Oremus pro afflictis et captivis Mitte eis, Domine auxilium, de sancto Esto nobis, Domine, turris fortitudinis Fiat pax in virtute tua Domine, Deus virtutum, converte nos. Domine exaudi orationem meam. Dominus vobiscum Et cum spiritu tuo Oremus *Oratio* Deus, qui admirabili providentia cuncta disponis, te suppliciter exoramus, ut terram quam (159) Unigenitus Filius tuus Dominus noster proprio sanguine consecravit, de manibus inimicorum crucis Christi eripiens, restituas cultui Christiano, vota fidelium ad ejus liberationem instantium misericorditer dirigendo in viam salutis æternæ Per eundem

Quando vero alia Missa ferialiter celebratur eodem die infra ecclesiam sive extra Ecclesiam preces dicuntur in alia Missa hoc modo

Psalmus. Ad Dominum, cum tribularer. Gloria Patri Sicut erat.

Psalmus Levavi oculos Gloria Patri. Sicut erat

Kyrie eleyson. Christe eleyson Kyrie eleyson. Pater noster, &c —*York Missal* (Surtees Soc), i 206, 207.

In the Sarum Missal the same prayers are found among the *Post Missam dicenda.* At these prayers a particular bell was tolled.[24]

Just before the *Pax Domini,* certain prayers were sometimes said for the welfare while they lived, and their soul's good after death, of par-ticular benefactors. Thus did the convent of Durham bargain with king Henry VII, that at every Chapter Mass prayers should be said for him by the clergy at the altar and by the choir.[25]

Keeping up the old usage followed by the Anglo-Saxons, the Salisbury rubric was to send, just before the communion, the *Pax* all about the church. This token of good-will and brotherly love was conveyed from one to another by a kiss upon the cheek. Pressing his lips to the out-side of the chalice, which held the blood of Christ, the sacrificing priest thus took, as it were, the

[24] Pulsatur campana pro terra suncta in celebratione missæ — Wilkins, *Concil.,* 1 625.

[25] Concessimus insuper, et per præsentes concedimus eidem sacratissimæ vestræ majestati, ut in qualibet Missa capitulari ad aliquod altare ecclesiæ prædictæ, per nos vel aliquem nostrum vel successorum nostrorum, aut alium monachum fratrem, sacerdotem, sive ministrum quemcumque, celebranda, statim post fraccionem postea et decantacionem vel leccionem *Per omnia secula seculorum,* et ante inchoacionem *Pax Domini,* quod celebrans ipse una cum sibi assistentibus ministris inter se et chorus prostratus, scilicet inter se, pro salute et incolumitate ac prospero et felici statu majestatis vestræ singulis diebus quoad vixeris, psalmos et suffragia sequencia dicent et (160) legent . . Cum vero ab hac luce migraveritis, extunc in omni supradicta missa, &c —*Hist Dunelm Scriptores Tres,* cccxcii &c

kiss from our Lord himself, and then gave it
either to the individual highest in holy orders
then present, or to the person who served his
mass.   This clerk, in his turn, carried the kiss
from the altar to the people by kissing the chief
personage among the men, who, turning about,
saluted each his neighbour.   Of such a ceremony,
we have more than one interesting evidence amid
our national records.   Happening to go into a
church which stood nigh the spot where he had
but just landed on the English shore, prince—afterwards king—Henry II. had given him immediately
the kiss by the clerk who had that moment received it from the priest.[26]   The way in which
Richard I. once gave the kiss of peace to St. Hugh
of Lincoln, is curiously illustrative of this rite.[27]

(161) Before sending forth the *Pax*, or kiss of
peace, the priest said this prayer : *Domine, sancte
Pater, omnipotens aeterne Deus: da michi hoc
sacrosanctum corpus et sanguinem Filii tui Domini
nostri Jesu Christi ita digne sumere, ut merear
per hoc remissionem omnium peccatorum meorum*

---

[26] Applicuit igitur in Angliam dux Henricus, divertitque in
ecclesiam littori contiguam oraturus   Ingrediensque basilicam
subito obvium habuit ministrum altaris, acceptumque a presbytero celebrante divina misteria, osculum pacis oblatum ab eo
primus omnium ipse accepit —John of Hexham, in Twysden,
1. 278

[27] Et cum pacis osculum sacerdos cuidam dedisset archiepiscopo,
qui regi pacem oblaturus esset, rex ei usque ad gradum obuius
processit, sumptumque pacis accepte signum cum humili reueren-
tia episcopo lincolniensi per oris sui osculum porrexit.—*Vita S
Hugonis*, in Capgrave, *Nova Legenda Anglie*, ed Horstman, ii. 47.

accipere et tuo Sancto Spiritu repleri, et pacem tuam habere. Quia tu es Deus et non est alius praeter te; cujus regnum et imperium gloriosum sine fine permanet in secula seculorum.

About the middle of the thirteenth century, a new way of giving this kiss of peace was followed. Instead of the clerk's cheek, the priest kissed the figure of our Blessed Lord, painted on a small piece of wood, or graven on a plate of copper, set in a frame, with a handle behind, as is shown in this cut. So shaped, it could easily be carried about among the people by the clerk, in his left hand; and, after each kiss bestowed upon it,

·From the original in my possession

wiped with a little napkin which he held for that purpose in his right hand. The earliest mention anywhere of such a ritual appliance, is to be found among this country's ecclesiastical enactments, in which it is called " osculatorium," " asser pacis," " tabula pacis." [28] Its more common name was

[28] Among other sacred things to be found by the parishioners for their church, according to the statutes of Archbishop Walter Gray, for his province of York (A.D. 1250), was " osculatorium." (Wilkins, *Concil.*, i. 698.) In like manner the synod of Exeter

(162) " pax-brede," which at once told its liturgical
purpose, and of what material it happened, at first,
to be generally made.   Afterwards, gold, silver,
ivory, jewels, enamel, and the most beautiful workmanship, were bestowed upon it ; though, for poor
churches, it still continued to be of wood, or, at

GIVING OF PAX

most, of copper gilt.[29]   How the pax-brede used
to stand on the altar all through mass, is shown

(A.D. 1287) decreed there should be " asser ad pacem " (*ibid.*, ii. 139),
and the council of Merton (A.D. 1305), " tabulas pacis ad osculatorium " (*ibid.*, 280).

[29] Jeffrey Baxter and Johne his wyffe gave ij paxbreds of sylver
to the church of Swaffham. (Blomefield, *Norfolk*, vi. 219); and
Thomas Rotherham, Archbishop of York (who died A.D. 1550),
bequeathed to the parish church of his birthplace " unum paxbred deauratum cum ymagine Christi passi venerat. a Sto. Gregorio, pond. v. un'c. di.   Item unum paxbred deauratum, cum uno
birall in medio, pond. 9. un'c. quar't. di.   Item unum paxbred cum
osse Sancti Firmini, pond. x. un'c. et i. quart." — Hearne, *Liber
niger Scaccarii*, ii. 673.

by the accompanying picture. As a kind of public penance from notorious and hardened sinners, the first thing was to withhold, not only the holy bread, but the "pax" also, (163) at the parochial mass on Sundays.[30]

That, at one period, the practice was to send

PAX ON THE ALTAR

The " pax " is standing on the gospel side of the altar, at mass

round the kiss of peace in every low mass, we learn from many documents. It is noticed in the passage we gave just now about the "introit," from the life of St. Bartholomew (p. 171); and when St. Thomas of Canterbury, as he was fleeing from his enemies, stopped at a little village, then called Estere, on the Kentish coast, the pax used to be brought him in his hiding-place, which was

---

[30] Inderdicto eis primo pacis osculo et pane benedicto in ecclesia.—Wilkins, *Concil.*, i. 635.

so close to the chancel of the church, that he could hear mass through a small hole in the wall.[31]

Not only the pax-brede itself, but the book of the gospels especially, when bound in gold or silver, used to be employed, at high mass on holydays, for such a ritual purpose. Thus, at Durham cathedral, "when the monkes went to say or singe the high masse, the gospeller did cairye a marvelous faire booke, which had the epistles and gospells in it, and did lay it on the altar, the which booke had on the outside of the coveringe the picture of our Saviour Christ, all of silver, of goldsmith's worke, all parcell gilt, verye fine to behould; which booke did (164) serve for the pax in the masse." [32]   Most likely the textus—of which we have already spoken (vol. i. p. 249), and now in the British Museum—used to be carried about for the same service

As soon as he had sent forth the pax, the priest took up from off the paten the host in both his hands, and prayed those sublime prayers which, whilst they differ from, are much more beautiful and warmer than those now in the Roman missal at the same place : *Deus Pater fons et origo totius bonitatis qui ductus misericordia unigenitum tuum*

---

[31] Ubi facto in pariete foramine (fuit utique prope ecclesiam), audivit missarum solennia cum plebe id ignorante presbytero etiam sacramenti perceptione perfruente. Clericus quidam hujus rei conscius osculum pacis ad archiepiscopum deferebat —Alan, *Vita S Thomæ*, ed. Giles, 1 352 [*R S*, lxvii ii 335]

[32] *Ancient Monuments, Rites, and Customs within the Monastic Church of Durham*, 7 (ed Surtees Society)

pro nobis ad infima mundi descendere et carnem sumere voluisti Then, as he uttered those words : *Quam ego indignus hic in manibus meis teneo—* which flesh of thine only Son, that I, unworthy man, am here holding in my hands—he bowed to the host; then continuing : *Te adoro, Te glorifico, Te tota mentis ac cordis intentione laudo et precor, ut nos famulos tuos non deseras, sed peccata nostra dimittas quatinus tibi soli vivo ac vero Deo puro corde ac casto corpore servire valeamus. Per eundem Christum Dominum nostrum. Amen.* To this followed, *Domine Jesu Christe,* &c., as in the present Roman missal . then, *Corporis et sanguinis tui, Domine Jesu Christe, sacramentum quod licet indignus accipio non sit michi judicio et condemnationi sed tua prosit pietate corporis mei et animæ saluti. Amen.* Before putting the flesh of Christ into his mouth, it was with these words that he hailed it, bending himself lowly down : *Ave in aeternum sanctissima caro Christi. michi ante omnia et super omnia summa dulcedo. Corpus Domini nostri Jesu Christi sit michi peccatori via et vita. In no✠mine Patris; et Filii; et Spiritus sancti Amen ·* making the sign of the (165) cross upon his mouth with that precious body before receiving it. Ere he drank the sacred blood in the chalice, he spoke to it these feelings of his love : *Ave in eternum celestis potus michi ante omnia super omnia summa dulcedo. Corpus et sanguis Domini nostri Jesu Christi prosint michi peccatori ad remedium sempiternum*

*in vitam eternam   Amen.   In no✠mine Patris;
et Filii; et Spiritus sancti.   Amen.* After
taking the blood the priest bowed himself down,
and made his thanksgiving thus: *Gratias tibi
ago, Domine sancte pater omnipotens eterne Deus:
qui me refecisti de sacratissimo corpore et sanguine
filii tui domini nostri Jesu Christi, et precor ut
hoc sacramentum salutis nostre quod sumpsi indignus peccator non veniat michi ad judicium
neque ad condemnationem pro meritis meis, sed
ad profectum corporis mei et anime saluti in vitam
eternam.   Amen.*

Next, the priest went to the south corner of the
altar, holding the chalice so that the first finger
and the thumb of each hand might be within it,
and thus washed them, as well as the inside of
the chalice, with the wine and water that the
acolyte poured over them. This wine and
water the priest drank. If, however, he had
to offer up another mass that day, this rinsing
of his hands and of the chalice the priest either
poured down the piscina, or into a small cup,
that he might take it along with the last rinsing of
his fingers in the chalice.[32a] Every priest might

[32a] Qua dicta eat sacerdos ad dextrum cornu altaris cum calice
inter manus digitis adhuc conjunctis sicut prius   et accedat sub-
dyaconus et effundat in calicem vinum et aquam, et resinceret
sacerdos manus suas ne alique relique corporis vel sanguinis
remaneant in digitis vel in calice   Cum vero aliquis sacerdos
debet bis celebrare in uno die   tunc ad primam missam non
debet percipere ablutionem ullam, sed ponere in saciario vel in
vase mundo usque in finem (166) alterius, tunc sumatur utraque
ablutio   Such is the rubric in most of the printed and hand-
written missals   [Ed Burntisland, col 627]   In a Sarum Manual,

say more than one mass, not only on Christmas
day but Easter Sunday, and whenever a burial
was to take place in his church. Thus, in the
council of Oxford (A.D 1222), the canon "ne quis
celebret bis in die" lays down this rule.[33] That
before the council of Oxford, the custom with some
priests was to say two masses a day—one mass being
for the dead—is clear from the life of Gundulf,
consecrated bishop of Rochester, A.D. 1077.[34]

(167) After the first washing of his fingers, the
priest said *Quod ore sumpsimus*, &c.; and then
washing them a second time over the chalice
he recited this prayer to himself: *Hec nos communio, Domine, purget a crimine, et celestis
remedii faciat esse consortes.* At the end of

---

a MS of the fifteenth century, belonging to me, it is shorter,
thus Post hæc accedat minister et effundat vinum et aquam in
calicem. Et si necesse fuerit ut sacerdos iterum celebret nichil
de effusione percipiat sed in sacrario ponat. Post primam infu-
sionem, dicit, &c

[33] Districtius inhibentes, ne sacerdos quispiam Missarum solennia celebret bis in die, excepto die Nativitatis et Resurrectionis
Dominicæ, vel in obsequiis defunctorum , viz , cum corpus alicujus
in ecclesia eodem die fuerit tumulandum, et tunc prior Missa de
die, posterior vero pro defuncto celebretur —Wilkins, *Concil* , 1. 586

[34] Of this prelate we are told. Duas denique singulis fere
diebus celebrare solitus erat Missas, quas inter oculum vix sudum
habebat Primam quidem de dominica aut de commemoratione
B Mariæ vel B Andreæ aut alicujus sancti cujus memoriam
specialius recolebat, sive pro familiaribus amicis ; secundam pro
defunctis Cum autem in directum absque cantu usque post
evangelium, quod ipse legebat, eadem Missa diceretur, dicto
Dominus vobiscum, excelsa voce dicebat *Oremus* Statim subse-
quebantur pueri, dulcisona modulatione cantantes offerendam
Domine Jesu Christe, sive *O pie Deus* —Monachus Roff , *Vita
Gundulfi*, in Wharton, *Anglia Sacra*, 11. 282

this prayer came the following rubric in the printed, but not in the older hand-written, copies of the Salisbury missal :—Post perceptionem ablutionum ponat sacerdos calicem super patenam ; ut si quid remanserit in calice stillet : et postea inclinando se dicat orationem sequentem *Adoremus crucis signaculum per quod salutis sump-*

Dat.xxrij.artikel vander miffen es

simus sacramentum.[34a]   The custom, nowhere practised now, of laying the chalice down to drain upon the paten, is well shown in this picture.

The priest then washed his hands,—if not always, at least almost everywhere,—in the piscina : for the rubric in a MS. in my possession is thus : Deinde lavet in sacrario : postea dicat cō et postcō, &c. That the piscina, or sacrarium, served, among

---

[34a] *Sarum Missal,* 628.

other liturgical purposes, for both the washings of
hands at mass, is clear, not only from the foregoing rubric, but also from the words, *Lavate
puras manus*, that are found written either within
or above some of them, in some of our old
churches [35]

(168) Having sipped up any little drop which
might have run down upon the paten, or to the
rim of the chalice, the priest folded the corporals
and put them into the corporas-case, and then
said, as now, the communion and post-com-
munions proper to the day ; and, at the end of
the last of these prayers, drew upon his forehead
the sign of the cross After saluting the people
with *Dominus vobiscum*, with *Ite, missa est*, or
Benedicamus Domino, as it might be, he bowed
him down at the middle of the altar, and, with
hands joined, recited the *Placeat tibi sancta
Trinitas obsequium servitutis meæ*, &c , at the
end of which he raised his head, signed the
cross upon himself, with the words *In nomine
Patris*, &c.; and, having made a low bow to
the altar, without either giving his blessing to
the people or reading a gospel of any kind, he
went back to the vestry, saying, not aloud, but to
himself, St. John's *In principio erat verbum*, &c.

Though not prescribed, the blessing, after some
way or another, of the people by the priest who

---

[35] As in Great Cressingham, Norfolk ; see Blomefield, *Norfolk*,
vi 101.

had just done mass, it is likely, was allowed under
the Sarum use. In that of York, the priest gave
a blessing to those about him, with the empty
chalice and the folded corporals after mass, upon
every festival of the double class.[36]

(169) At Evreux the custom was to bestow
this benediction with the chalice only;[37] and in

Belgium the paten served the purpose, as the
accompanying illustration shows.

---

[36] ¶ *Benedictio generalis, cum calice et corporalibus plicatis, post
missam dicetur omnibus festis duplicibus per annum hoc modo :*—

> Adiutorium nostrum in nomine Domini:
> Qui fecit celum et terram.
> Sit nomen Domini benedictum:
> Ex hoc nunc et usque in seculum.

Benedictio.

Benedicat vos divina maiestas et una deitas ; pater et filius ✠
et spiritus sanctus.—*York Missal* (Surtees Soc.), ii. 196.

[37] Martene, *De Antiq. Ecc. Rit.*, i. 4, art. xii. ordo xxviii.

If not the general, it seems to have been a very common, practice with our old English priests to distribute the Eucharist among the people, not at the communion of the mass, but when the holy sacrifice had been done. After the mass said for his good speed and welfare the day he started, was it, as we already noticed (vol. iii. p. 377), that the pilgrim had given him the housel; and the poet Langland, himself a priest, makes *Do best* thus speak:

> (I) dude me to churche,
> To huyre holliche þe masse   and be housled after [38]

Instead of the acolyte, the communicant, whenever he was scholar enough, said the *Confiteor* for himself.   Thus of Richard II. at his coronation, Walsingham tells us that he did so before his communion; [39] so, too, did Henry VII. and his queen at their coronation, as will be observed hereafter (p. 199).

After communion, lay folks drank, not of the (170) consecrated chalice, but unhallowed wine from out another chalice, to help them to swallow with more ease and readiness the Eucharistic particle.   Such a rubric was especially followed at the general houselings of the people at Easter, Whitsuntide, and Christmas, and the priest was

---

[38] *Piers Ploughman*, Passus, xxii 2, 3, ed Skeat, 399

[39] Percelebrata Missa usque ad Communionem, reductus est Rex ad altare, et genu flexo coram Archiepiscopo, dixit "Confiteor" Quo absoluto, communicatus est, et iterum reductus est ad sedem suam —Ed Camden, 197 [*R S*, xxviii , Walsingham, i. 337]

told to warn his flock, that what they sipped from the chalice was mere wine ; for in the Sacrament, though given them under one kind only, they had the blood as well as the flesh of Christ,—Christ whole and entire, true and alive, with all of himself, flesh and blood, in the Sacrament.[40]

The purchase of wine for such a purpose is often set down in old church accompts thus : In vino empto per annum (1364) pro celebracione et pro communione parochianorum ad Pascam xvs. jd[41] In (171) the *Device for the coronation of Henry VII.*, it is set forth that "the king shall offre (at the high mass, in Westminster Abbey), an obley of bred laid uppon the patent of saynt Edward his chalice, with the which obley after consecrate the king shalbe houselled ; also, he shall offre, in a cruet with wyne, which he shall use in the said chalice after he is housilled, and whiles the said

---

[40] This we learn from Archbishop Peckham, who says · Attendant insuper sacerdotes, quod cum communionem sacram porrigunt simplicibus paschali tempore vel alio, solicite eos instruant sub panis specie simul eis dari corpus et sanguinem Domini, immo Christum integrum, vivum et verum, qui totus est sub specie sacramenti Doceant etiam eosdem illud quod ipsis eisdem temporibus in calice propinatur, sacramentum non esse, sed vinum purum eis hauriendum, traditum, ut facilius sacrum corpus glutiant, quod perceperunt —Wilkins, *Concil*, ii. 53 By the council of Exeter (A D 1287) it was enacted that in every church there must be, among other things, a little cup of silver or tin for taking to the sick, who should drink out of it the water in which the priest had washed the tips of his fingers after he had given them the viaticum —Sit in qualibet ecclesia . . ciphus argenteus vel stanneus pro infirmis, ut postquam Eucharistiam assumpserint, loturam digitorum suorum sacerdos sibi præbeat in eodem —*Ibid*, 139

[41] *Priory of Coldingham*, xliv., ed. Surtees Society.

quere is so synging (the *Agnus Dei*) the chieff bisshopp that afor bare the gospell boke to the king and the quene, shal bring the pax unto them; and when the king and quene have kissed it, thei shall descend, and, susteyned and accustomed as above, they shall goo to the high aulter, and after the cardinall hath commoned his self, he having betwene his hands the same chalice wheruppon the holy sacrement shalbe laide, shall turne hymself to the king and to the quene, and thei lying prostrate before hym shall saye their *Confiteor*, all the prelates answering *Misereatur*, and the cardinall seying absolucion; that doon, the king and the quene shall somwhat arise kneling, and with great humylite and devocion receyve the sacrament by thands of the said cardinall; ij. of the grettest astate then present holding befor the king and the quene a long towell of silke. This so done, the king and the quene shall stand upp and take wyne of the bove rehersed chalice by thandes of thabbot of Westmynster."[42]   Such a draught is indeed, to this day, given to all clerks after they have received the Eucharist at their ordination; and is also prescribed for the people, every time they communicate, by the Roman missal.[43]   Such a rubric, however, like a few otheis, is nowhere observed now.   The old English

---

[42] *Rutland Papers*, ed Camden Society, 21, 22.

[43] Minister autem dextera manu tenens vas cum vino et aqua, sinistra vero mappulam, aliquanto post sacerdotem eis porrigit purificationem et mappulam ad os (172) abstergendum.

had its peculiar ceremonies, especially its blessing, both in the Salisbury and York uses. The sacrament itself of wedlock used always to be gone through at the church door, that so as much of the world as possible should witness it. To afford shelter from bad weather for the priest and those unto whom he had to administer this and other rites of religion, a wide porch was everywhere built before the people's door into church. Hither the king, no less than the beggar-man, brought her whom he was about to make his wife.[44] From the porch the priest led the married couple into church and up to the altar steps, where, begging all present to join with him, he prayed over them, and then, putting them to kneel on the south side of the chancel, he began mass.[45] At the

---

[44] Thus, of Henry I 's marriage with Matilda, one of our old writers tells us —Verum, cum ipsa conjunctio juxta ritum Ecclesiæ fieri firmarique deberet, Pater ipse (Anselmus Archiep Cantuar.) totam regni nobilitatem populumque minorem, pro hoc ipso circumfluentem, necnon pro foribus ecclesiæ regem et illam circumvallantem, sublimius cæteris stans in commune edocuit, &c. (Eadmer, *Hist Novor*, iii. [*P.L*, clix 428]) ; and of Edward I.'s, with Margaret of France Archiepiscopus Cantuariensis Robertus celebravit sponsalia inter prædictum regem Edwardum, et Margaretam sororem regis Franciæ in hostio ecclesiæ Christi Cantuariensis versus claustrum . . . et subsequenter idem archiepiscopus celebravit Missam sponsalium ad altare feretri S Thomæ Martyris — Wharton, *Anglia Sacra*, 1 51

[45] Statuantur vir et (173) mulier ante ostium ecclesie sive in faciem ecclesie coram Deo et sacerdote et populo, &c . . Hic in trent in ecclesiam usque ad gradum altaris, et sacerdos in eundo cum suis ministris dicat ps. *Beati omnes*, &c ; tunc prostratis sponso

"Sanctus," both the bride and bridegroom knelt near the altar's foot; and then, if neither had been married before, over them a pall, or as it used to be called, the "care-cloth," was held at its four corners by as many clerics [46] Whilst glancing at this ceremony, the far-famed Grossetete, Bishop of Lincoln (who died A.D. 1253), brings to our knowledge a curious fact once bound up along with it, viz., that illegitimate children who were legitimised by the subsequent marriage of their parents according to civil law and custom were placed under this canopy at the wedding as a sign of their legitimation.[47] (174) The bride, when a maiden, wore her hair flowing down loose upon her shoulders, and nothing but a wreath of jewels

---

et sponsa ante gradum altaris, roget sacerdos circumstantes orare pro eis, . . Finitis orationibus et introductis illis in presbiterium scilicet inter chorum et altare ex parte ecclesie australi, et statuta muliere ad dexteram viri scilicet inter ipsum et altare incipiatur Missa de Trinitate.—*Missale Sarum*, Ordo Sponsalium. [Burntisland Edition, 830*.] The liturgical and archæological student should notice how the above rubric so clearly sets forth what we are to understand by the "presbytery" of a large church

[46] Post *Sanctus* prosternant se sponsus et sponsa in oratione ad gradum altaris extenso pallio super eos quod teneant quattuor clerici ad quattuor cornua, nisi alter eorum vel ambo prius desponsati fuerint et benedicti quia tunc non habetur pallium super eos, neque sacramentalis benedictio.—[*Ibid*, 839*.]

[47] Sicut notissimum, jura etiam civilia natos ante matrimonium per subsequens matrimonium legitimos decernant et hæredes; et ut seniorum relatione didici, consuetudo etiam in hoc regno antiquitus obtenta et approbata, tales legitimos habuit et hæredes unde in signum legitimationis, nati ante matrimonium consueverunt poni sub pallio super parentes eorum extento in matrimonii solennizatione —*Opuscula Grosseteste episcopi Lincoln,* in Brown, *Fasciculus Rerum Expend*, ii 320.

(called a "paste"),[48] or flowers, about her head:
"Thre ornamentes longe principally to a wyfe:
a rynge on her fynger, a broche on her breste,
and a garlonde on her hede . . . the garlond be-
tokenethe gladnesse and the dignitie of the
sacrament of wedloke," says Pauper.[49] At her
marriage with King James of Scotland, our
Henry VII.'s eldest daughter Margaret, "had
a varey riche coller of gold, of pyerrery and
perles round her neck, and the cronne apon hyr
hed, her hayre hangyng. Betwyx the said cronne
and the hayres was a varey riche coyfe hangyng
down behynde the whole length of the body."[50]

After the *Pater noster*, and just before the
Pax, turning himself about towards the married
couple, the priest bestowed upon them the nuptial
benediction. The care-cloth was then taken away,
the bridegroom arose from his knees, went up
and got the kiss of peace immediately from the
priest, and coming back to his wife, gave it to
her by a kiss upon the cheek. The clerk taking
the *pax* in the ordinary way with the paxbrede
from the celebrant, went and carried it about

---

[48] The blessed Virgin Mary is so figured in all works of mediæval
art Items for making and mending these "pastes" and diadems
are found in old churchwardens' accompts, thus :—paid to Alice
Lewis, a goldsmith's wife of London, for a serclett to marry may-
dens in, iij*l.* A.D. 1540. — *Illustrations, &c*, 11.

Every church was to have, by the decrees of the council of
Exeter (A D 1287), velum nuptiale.—Wilkins, *Concil.*, 11. 139.

[49] Fol 197, b.

[50] Leland, *Collectanea*, IV. 293

as usual to the rest of those there.[51] After mass, bread and wine or other drink were hallowed by the priest, who tasted of them along with the bride and bridegroom and all their friends present in the church.[52] At princess Margaret's marriage "two prelates helde the cloth upon them duryng the remanent of the masse. That and all the ceremonyes accomplysched, ther was brought by the lordes bred and wyn in ryche potts and ryche cuppes." So, also, when Queen Mary wedded Philip in Winchester cathedral, both stayed in the choir "untill mase was don, at which tyme wyne and sopes were hallowed and delivered unto them," &c [53]

In the bridal mass, the York varied somewhat from the Sarum use: only two clerics held the care-cloth, and a blessing was bestowed by the priest with the chalice upon the newly-married folks.[54] This blessing, according to the York

---

[51] Post hec vertat se (175) sacerdos et dicat *Pax Domini* et *Agnus Dei* more solito   Tunc amoto pallio surgant ab oratione sponsus et sponsa, et accipiat sponsus pacem a sacerdote et ferat sponse, osculans eam et neminem alium nec ipse nec ipsa   sed clericus statim a presbitero pacem accipiens proferat aliis sicut solitum est.—*Sarum Missal*, 844 *

[52] Post Missam benedicatur panis et vinum vel aliquod bonum potabile in vasculo et gustent in nomino Domini, &c.—*Ibid.*

[53] Leland, *Collectanea*, 294, 400

[54] *Da propitius pacem*, &c   Hic sacerdos faciat fractiones Eucharistie more solito et dicat *Per omnia secula seculorum*.   Postea dimittat fractiones supra patenam, et calice corporalibus cooperto vertat se sacerdos ad sponsum et sponsam et dicat super eos orationes sequentes illis genu flectentibus sub palio super eos extento quod teneant duo clerici in suppelliciis   Propter solemnitatem huius sacramenti dat sacerdos benedictionem cum calice si

rite with the chalice, like the blessing with the paten abroad, seems to have been given at the end of mass on high festivals.[55]

The Mass for the Dead,

or "soul mass," as our fathers called it, had its ritual peculiarities, but they were very few. Neither the *Gloria in excelsis*, nor *Alleluia* was said; after the gradual *Requiem æternam*, &c., followed the tract *Sicut cervus desiderat ad fontes aquarum*, &c., or *De profundis*, &c. There was no sequence of any kind, and therefore no *Dies iræ*, which is not to be found in any part of the Sarum use.[56] Beautiful, nay, sublime as is that hymn, it (177) is comparatively new even to the

placet et deposita casula antequam exeant, dicat sacerdos super eos hanc orationem *Domine* (176) *sancte pater omnipotens eterne Deus*, &c —*York Missal* (Surt. Soc), ii 192

[54] In the foundation-deed for Carman's Spital, Flixton, Yorkshire, in the reign of Henry VI, it is ordained that Vicarius ecclesiæ de Folketon . . ad quandam capellam, infra hospitale prædictum situatam . singulis annis in festo S Andreæ . . Missam hanc ibidem solempniter, cum benedictione calicis celebrare, ac post Missam illam panem et aquam sanctificare, et inter populum Missam illam audientem dividere et spergere hucusque usitati fuissent, &c —*Mon Angl*, vii 614

[56] That as far back as St Osmund's days, there was known in England a sequence beginning with the words, "Dies illa, dies iræ," we learn from a writer of the twelfth century, the monk of Rochester, who, in the life of Gundulf, one of St Osmund's brother bishops, says of his prelate ·—Aliquando enim cum in ecclesia illud decantari audiret . . *Afflicti pro peccatis nostris assidue cum lacrimis expectamus finem nostrum* . . . vel illud, *Dies illa, dies iræ*, vel aliud simile compunctioni amicum, &c. (*Anglia Sacra*, ii 286) The likelihood is, that our present magnificent hymn is but an expansion of a much older sequence [The sequence is in *Sarum Missal*, col. 884 *]

Roman liturgy ; for the true date of its employment at Rome is not earlier than the end of the
fifteenth century. When we bear in mind that
the very spirit of a prose or sequence is one of
gladness, exultation and thanks,[57] and that *Te
Deum* is left out of lauds, and *Gloria in excelsis*
and *Alleluia* out of mass for the dead, we cannot
be surprised that, magnificent as the *Dies iræ*
is, it came to be inserted so late in the Roman
missal [58] The offertory prayer with its rubrics,
was after this form :—Post ablutionem manuum
incipiat sacerdos junctis manibus in medio altaris
hoc modo. *Hostias et preces tibi Domine offerimus.* Chorus respondeat: *Tu suscipe pro ani-
mabus illis quarum hodie memoriam agimus,
fac eas Domine de morte transire ad vitam.*
Et interim dicat sacerdos privatim *In spiritu
humilitatis* more solito. Deinde dicat similiter
privatim *Orate* (178) *fratres et sorores pro
fidelibus defunctis.* Et chorus respondeat can-

[57] As the *Ordo Romanus* tells us Jubilatio quam sequentiam
vocant—Hittorp, i. 3, and Honorius better still: Alleluia ideo
canimus, quia ad gaudiam Anglorum tendimus Sequentia ideo
jubilamus, quia faciem Domini in jubilo videbimus —*Gemma Animæ,*
i. 96, Hittorp, 1208

[58] Some indeed have objected to its use, thus, Maldonatus
says —Colligo curiositate privata aliquorum sacerdotum fuisse
additam prosam in Missis quæ pro defunctis dicuntur, ut dicant
Dies iræ, dies illa quod fit extra rationem, et antiquissimos mis-
sales libros, qui tantum habent sequentiam in diebus lætis. And
by the Dominicans it was forbidden to be said Dominicani in
notis quas (A D. 1576) Salamanticæ ediderunt in proprii missalis
ordinarium, hanc prosam, utpote quæ contra rubricas sit, statuunt
non esse canendam —*Bona*, ed Sala, iii 143

tando : *Requiem eternam dona eis, Domine, et lux perpetua luceat eis. Quam olim Abrahe promisisti et semini eius.*

The *Agnus Dei* ended, as now, twice with *dona eis requiem*, the third time with *requiem sempiternam.* Though no rubric in the Sarum missal or in St. Osmund's treatise speaks distinctly on the point, we cannot think that the kiss of peace was given at mass for the dead An old English writer, Clement Maydeston, learned in the Sarum rubrics, says in his valuable little book, *Crede michi*, that the priest did not take the pax by kissing either the altar or the rim of the chalice, as in other masses ; presumably therefore he did not give it to others [59]

The difference between the present Roman and the Salisbury form of the mass, the liturgical reader must have already seen let us now find out in what the latter varied from the Anglo-Saxon.

The Sarum, like the Anglo-Saxon rite, taught the priest to begin mass with the *Confiteor.* All through the Anglo-Saxon, as during the earlier times of the Sarum period, no elevation took place immediately after the consecration. As in the Anglo-Saxon, so in the Sarum liturgy, as we shall behold a little further on, the use

---

[59] Sacerdos celebrans pro defunctis non debet post *Agnus Dei* pacem ab altari accipere, nec a calice secundum vsum Sarum — Wordsworth, *Tracts of C. Maydeston* (H. B S), p 37

was for a bishop, whenever he said or sang mass, to give his blessing just before the *Pax*. There was no reservation of a fragment of the Eucharist from one mass to another in the Sarum, such as used to be in the Anglo-Saxon ritual. The Anglo-Saxon priest eat the flesh and (179) drank the blood of Christ in the sacrifice immediately after the third *Agnus Dei*, for none of those three prayers put in the Roman missal, noi any of those others set forth in that of Salisbury to be said between the *Agnus Dei* and the communion, are to be found in our Anglo-Saxon codices: the former of the two missals, bound up together in that very precious codex known as the Leofric Missal at Oxford, gives, at full length, the canon of the mass as it used to be said to our forefathers in the tenth century, and it ends with the *Agnus Dei*.[60] The earliest notice we have of these prayers, is in Theodoric's Life of St. Margaret, Queen of Scotland; and from this Durham monk's words we learn that, when he wrote (A.D. 1093), one of them—*Domine Jesu Christe*—was said not before, but after the priest's communion.[61] The likelihood is that St. Osmund brought this prayer

---

[60] Ed Warren, p. 62

[61] Senserat illa (Margareta) mortem adesse moxque orationem, quæ post perceptionem Domini corporis et sanguinis a sacerdote dici solet incepit *Domine*, inquiens, *Jesu Christe, qui ex voluntate Patris*, &c Cum diceret, *libera me*, liberata vinculis corporis anima, ad veræ libertatis, quem semper dilexerat, auctorem Christum migravit —*AA. SS Junii*, ii 335

into use in this country; and, after his days, the one following—*Perceptio corporis tui*—got to be added to it, and that both were at first said not, as now, before, but after the communion. Very soon they were put to be recited, as a preparation, before the taking of the sacrament, along with those splendid declarations of Catholic belief in transubstantiation in the Sarum missal.

Regarding mass for the dead, or soul-mass, Theodore the sixth, archbishop of Canterbury after St Austin, says that it differs from the ordinary mass in the omission of *Gloria, Alleluia*, and the kiss of peace.[62]

But it was in

THE SERVICE UPON SUNDAYS AND THE GREAT FESTIVALS, ACCORDING TO SARUM USE,

that, besides its splendours, some other peculiarities of our venerable old ritual, as distinguished from the Roman form, might be witnessed.

Every Sunday, before undern-song or tierce, the priest for that week, and who was about to sing the high mass, went through

The Blessing of Holy Water.

To do this, along with him came, unto the steps between the choir and presbytery, a deacon and

---

[62] Missa pro mortuis in hoc differt à consueta missa, quod (180) sine *Gloria*, et *Alleluia*, et pacis osculo cælebratur. — *Liber Pœnitentialis*, cap xlv, in Thorpe's *Ancient Laws*, ii 51.

subdeacon, with the gospel-book; a thurifer with his censer; the two acolytes with their candles; a cross-bearer, with his tall staff, having at top a cross, which, in Lent,—the first Sunday excepted, —was of wood painted red, and without our Lord's image to it; from Easter till Ascension Thursday, of beril, or of rock crystal; at other seasons, of gold, silver, or copper gilt. Each one of these ministers was clad in an apparelled amice and alb; besides such a vesture, the priest had on a silken cope; the boy who held the salt, and afterwards carried the holy water, wore a surplice, as did the other youth, who bore the book or manual.

When he had hallowed the water and the salt, and had mingled them together,—the ceremonies and prayers for which were the same as among the Anglo-Saxons, and in the present Roman ordinal,— the priest went up to the high altar, and sprinkled it all about. While coming down (181) again, he sprinkled his above-named attendants; and, as soon as he had got back to the steps, all the clergy, the highest first, came, each as he went past to be sprinkled with holy water by the cele-brant, who afterwards sprinkled such lay folks as happened to be standing in the presbytery. This done, he said the versicle, *Ostende nobis,* and the prayer, *Exaudi nos.* If the bishop of the diocese was there, he sprinkled the clergy, who, for this purpose, came up in due order to the episcopal throne; and, whenever a festival of the higher class fell upon a Sunday, that morning the water was hallowed, not in the choir, but privately, at some side-altar, and not sprinkled till midday song, or sext, had been chanted. After this, did they alway go round the church with

The Procession,

in which walked, first, the vergers, to make way through the crowd; then came the boys with the holy water; the cross-bearer, followed by the two acolytes abreast, the thurifer, the subdeacon, the deacon, the priest; behind him, the lower canons; then the upper canons, all in their choir array, and though proceeding two and two, yet so wide asunder as to leave a lane, as it were, between them. Whenever he was present, the bishop, in a silk cope, walked the last of all, wearing his mitre, and leaning upon his pastoral staff. This procession, singing all the while, first went out of the presbytery, through its north door, then turning to the right, walked all round it, and going down the south aisle, as far as the baptismal font, nigh the south porch, thence passed over into the nave, up which it marched till it reached the choir's great or western gates, above which always arose the rood, in the loft over what is now called the screen. There they halted, and, drawn up into a body, made a station, during which was (182) said aloud, in English, by the celebrant, the bidding-prayer, in which God's blessings were craved for His

Church in this land, for the king, the archbishops, and bishops, the bishop of the diocese in particular, for the dean . in parish churches, for the parson, for the winning from the Paynim of the holy land, for peace, for the queen and her children, for the souls of the dead,—more especially those who had been, while alive, that church's friends. Whether the bishop was there or not, the celebrant always went at the head of the procession; and upon Sundays that were not holy days as well, sprinkled with holy water each altar which he met upon his road. In obedience to a well-known liturgical principle, the procession, at starting from the north presbytery door, turned to the right,—to the region of warmth, light, and brightness,—so that, while coming back, it might follow the sun's seeming path in the heavens. For like reasons, on occasions of woe or sadness, the usage was to walk the wrong way, to turn to the left, the side of gloom, and cold, and darkness,—to go, not along with, but against, the sun.[63]

On the high feast days, while prime-song was being chanted, six young clerks brought into the

---

[63] Thus the monks of Winchester (A D 1122),—Nescientes igitur quid eis agendum esset, crucium pedes invertunt sursum, et capita deorsum, et processionem nudis pedibus contra solis cursum et morem ecclesiasticum fecerunt, ut sicut episcopus (Willelmus Wintoniensis) contra decreta canonica victus eis necessaria in ecclesia Deo servientibus abstulit, sic ipsi ecclesiæ contra jus et decreta ecclesiastica deservirent.— *Annal Eccl Winton*, in Wharton, *Anglia Sac*, 1 298.

middle of the choir, and strewed upon a carpet
spread out to receive them, silk copes enough for
all the upper canons, who put (183) them on for the
procession.   As soon as midday song, or sext, was
over, this procession formed, and moved down the
middle of the choir, going out by its western or
great gates, beneath the rood-loft; then, turning
to the right, walked outside the choir, by the
processional aisle, and so proceeded on to the
cloisters in this order.   The vergers went first;
then came the youth who had the holy water;
after him, three acolytes abreast,[64] in apparelled
amices, albs, and tunicles, bore as many processional
crosses ; then two acolytes, with their candles, and
vested in amices, albs, and tunicles ;[65] two thurifers, in the same garments ; the subdeacon in his
tunicle, the deacon in his dalmatic, each carrying
a gospel-book ; then followed the priest, in alb
and silk cope ; and behind, all the choir,—the
boys first, then the lower canons, next the upper
canons, in silk copes.   Thus was formed the procession every high feast, with the exception that
on the less solemn ones, instead of three, two
crosses only were borne.   On Ascension day and
Corpus Christi, banners were carried, and two
minor canons, arrayed in silk copes, took on their
shoulders a shrine with relics.   All the way they
went they sang a prose befitting the occasion.

---

[64] See Wordsworth, *Salisbury Processions*, 49 , *Processionale*, ed.
Henderson, 12.

[65] 11 tunicis pro ceroferariis.—Gutch, *Collect Curiosa*, 11 265

Each parish church copied, as near as it might, the rubrics followed at the cathedral; but it is likely that, instead of keeping within, it always, unless hindered by the weather, went beyond its walls, and walked at least all round its own burial-ground, if it did not even go further, in its processions on the Sunday and the festival.

One part of the canonical penance to be undergone by every public sinner, was to walk barefoot and bareheaded, and but scantily clothed, in the Sunday's procession of his (184) parish church, and afterwards to stand the high mass out at the foot of the rood-loft.[66]

The bidding prayer, which in cathedrals the

---

[66] Thus Archbishop Courtney, in Richard II's reign, gave the following order respecting three Lollards,—two men and a woman · Eorum quilibet proxima die dominica post reditum suum ad propria, ante processionem ecclesiæ collegiatæ beatæ Mariæ novi operis prædicti ipsi Willelmus et Rogerus camisiis et braccis, ipsa vero Alicia sola camisia induti, nudis pedibus et capitibus, dictus Willelmus cum imagine sanctæ Catharinæ, præfati vero Rogerus ac Alicia cum imaginibus crucifixi in dextris, et singuli eorum cum singulis cereis ponderis dimidiæ libræ in sinistris procedent, easdem imagines trina vice, in principio processionis hujusmodi, in medio et in fine, ad laudem crucifixi, et memoriam passionis suæ ipsiusque virginis honorem, genuflectendo, devote osculabuntur, et eandem ecclesiam cum processione sic ingressi, coram imagine crucifixi, dum alta missa inibi decantatur, cum imaginibus et cereis prædictis in eorum manibus stabunt . . . et die dominica extunc immediate sequenti, in ecclesia eorum parochiali dictæ villæ stabunt, et facient simili modo. . Et quia propter nimium frigus aeris et temperiei jam instantis, prædicti pœnitentes si tanto tempore nudi starent, corporaliter lædi possent et gravari, rigorem mansuetudine obtemperare volentes, ut post eorum ingressum in ecclesias memoratas dum fuerint in audiendo missas prædictas, vestibus necessariis indui valeant, ita quod nudi pedes et capita licentiam impertimur.—Wilkins, *Concil*, iii 211.

celebrant said before the rood, as the procession halted below it, in parish churches, was read after the gospel, out of the pulpit. The holy loaf or bread, too, was hallowed, as we before showed,[67] in all our parish churches, and afterwards (185) cut up into small pieces, and given to the people, who carried it home.[68] One among the ecclesiastical censures of those times, was to forbid the holy bread and the kiss of peace to such as lived in open sin.[69]

High Mass, according to the Sarum Rite,

was celebrated with a splendour quite unknown in these our days. After the procession, and while the choir was chanting undern-song, or tierce, the priest and his ministers went into the vestry to put on their sacred garments If the bishop was going to sing the mass, he had never less than three deacons and three subdeacons, except upon Good Friday, when he had but one each of those ministers. On Whit Sunday and Maundy Thursday he had seven deacons and

---

[67] See vol 1. p 110

[68] This usage is glanced at by abbot Benedict, in his work on the miracles of St. Thomas of Canterbury Vidimus Balde-winum testificantem se septimanis quinque lecto fuisse affixum, nihil aliud quam aquam se toto illo tempore gustasse, Dominicis duntaxat diebus exceptis, in quibus allatum ab ecclesia, ut moris est, panem benedictum quasi pro communione sumebat.—*Mirac. S Thomæ Cantuar*, iv 9 [*R S*, lxvii ii 188]

[69] Interdicto eis primo pacis osculo et pane benedicto in ecclesia, &c.—*Constit. S. Edmundi*, in Wilkins, *Concil*, i 635.

seven subdeacons; upon all other high festivals, he had five of each For the Sundays during Advent, both deacons and subdeacons wore chasubles like the bishop's or the priest's, but never showed the hands from beneath those vestments, as did the celebrant . hence, as soon as their ministry needed the free use of their arms, their chasubles were either taken off, or rolled up over the shoulder. Besides these ministers at the altar, there were always two, sometimes four, rulers of the choir, in albs (186) and silk copes, with their beautiful and ponderous silver staves in their hands.[70] As soon as they had begun singing the *Gloria Patri* at the end of the introit, the celebrant, with his long array of attendants, came forth from the vestry, and, on reaching the foot of the altar, knelt down in adoration of the Holy Eucharist, hanging in its golden cup, shrouded beneath a little tent-like veil, just over their heads. Arising from the ground, the celebrant went through the *Confiteor*; and, having said the absolution after it, he kissed the deacon, then the subdeacon, which he always did, except at mass for the dead, and during the last three days of Holy Week. In the meanwhile the acolytes put down their candlesticks and burning tapers upon the altar-steps.

---

[70] Among the plate of Cardinal Wolsey was " oone rector cory staffe, of silver and gilt, poiss ccxxiij oz "—Gutch, *Collect. Curiosa,*
ii 322

The celebrant, attended by the deacon and sub-deacon, or, as they were sometimes called, the "gospeller" and "epistoler," now went up to the altar, and, having made his reverence, fumed it all about with incense, and was afterwards himself censed by the deacon. He then kissed the book of the gospels, which the subdeacon had, for that purpose, laid wide open on the middle of the altar. Going with the deacon and subdeacon to the right, or south end of the altar, he read the introit, or "office," which the choir had just sung; and then retracing his steps to the middle of the altar, he heard intoned for him the chant in which he had to give out, which he did, the *Gloria in excelsis.* If the celebrant was a bishop, the precentor—if only a priest, the rulers of the choir—came to the foot of the altar to announce, by singing those words themselves, the tone in which he was afterwards to chant them; (187) having done which, he went to finish saying the rest of that hymn at the south end of the altar. Then he and his ministers walked down to the sedilia, and sat there till the choir had done singing it. When the *Kyrie,* with its proses, happened to be sung, they went thither, and rested until the chanting was over. If the bishop pontificated, he sat, not in one of the sedilia, but in his episcopal seat or throne, and stayed there till the more solemn part of the service. Gervase, the monk of Canterbury, tells us that, in his time, the archbishop, on all great festivals, used to sit upon his primatial chair, which stood full east of the high altar, and arose eight steps above the pavement.[71] St. Thomas of Canterbury used—and the practice was a very old one—to read to himself out of a prayer-book the while he was thus sitting down, that he might keep his thoughts from wandering.[72]

These sedilia were sometimes called, even in smaller churches, the "presbytery"; and, in large churches, the whole of the space in that part of the chancel where they stood, was hence known by that same name. On festivals, all the wall behind and about them used to be hung with tapestry; each niche had its own cushion, and all the (188) ground on which the feet of the priest, deacon, and subdeacon rested as they sat there, was spread with carpeting [73]

After the introit, there was a little procession,

---

[71] Supra prædictum murum in circinatione illa retro altare et ex opposito ejus cathedra erat patriarchatus ex uno lapide facta, in qua sedere solebant archiepiscopi de more ecclesiæ in festis præcipuis inter missarum solennia usque ad sacramenti consecrationem, tunc enim ad altare Christi per gradus octo descendebant —Twysden, ii 1294 [*R S*, lxxiii i 13]

[72] This we learn from one of the many lives of that great and holy man Dum ministri cantabant, ipse libellum orationum in manu consueverat tenere, ne fieret sine devotione cor orantis tanquam terra sine aqua —*Anecdota*, &c, 228, ed Giles, for the Caxton Society

[73] Thus, in the collegiate church of Cobham, Kent, there were. Pannus lineus pictus diversis ymaginibus pro presbyterio, cum iij. pulvinaribus de blodio velvett, et ij de nigro panno aureo .. Item iii. pulvinaria stragulat pro cotidianis pertin presbiterio — Thorpe, *Regist Roffense*, 240

of a kind quite unknown at this present time.
Both of the acolytes went into the vestry, and
soon came out again, bearing along with them,
—one, the obley, or bread, for the Eucharist,
within a silver-covered dish, and two cruets, with
the wine and water,—the other, a basin, with
water and a hand-towel. These things they
carried, in a slow solemn manner, to the sacra-
'rium [74] or piscina, and left the bread and wine
there, upon a little shelf,—often, to this day,
found within such hollows, between the sedilia
and the east end of the south chancel wall. The
dishes set apart for holding the bread are particularly specified in some lists of old church-
plate [75] Having done this, the two acolytes
uplifted their candlesticks, and went and met,
at the presbytery door, a third acolyte, (189) who,
with his hands muffled in the folds of a silken
mantle that hung from about his shoulders, bore
the chalice, upon which lay an offertory veil,
or scarf, for holding the paten at mass, and a
pair of corporals in a corporas case. With the

---

[74] Abbot Benet, in his *Life and Miracles of St Thomas of Canter-bury*, speaks of this part of the altar's architectural adjuncts thus.
Quod in ampullæ fundo pulveri admixtum invenit, in sacrarium
altaris projecit — Benedictus, *Miracula S Thomæ*, &c, ed. Giles,
65 [*R S*, lxvii. 11 53]

[75] Thus, at York minster, there were Una pixis argentea cum
scriptura circa eandem Eligiæ de optimis, pro pane portandum
diebus ferialibus, ponderis decem unciarum et dimid Item una
pixis argentea deaurata cum rotundo nodo pro pane portando ad
summum altare in festis duplicatis, ponderans unam libram —
Dugdale, *Mon Angl*, viii 1205.

two burning tapers carried befoie him, this acolyte solemnly walked unto the sacrarium,—that
is, piscina,—where he left the chalice, but carried
the corporals up to the altar, kissing, before he
left, the holy table In the mean time, the other
two acolytes went and set down their candles
upon the altar-steps again. Foi ordinary Sundays,
and holy days of the second order, all these three
acolytes were vested in amices and albs; for the
high festivals, over those garments they wore each
a tunicle of rich embroidered silk, corresponding
in colour to the day.

From the pulpit on the south side of the choir
was it that in St. Osmund's days the subdeacon
chanted the epistle : when the old ambones fell
into disuse this was done, in small churches,
much nigher the altar, close to the sedilia, wheie
the book with the epistles was rested upon a
lectern, which folded, and so light that it could
be easily carried about · over it was always cast
a pall or covering of some rich stuff, or cloth
shot with gold, and answering in colour to the
vestments.[76] Having ended the epistle the subdeacon went[77] to the sacrarium, where the aco-

---

[76] j pannus rubeus aureus pro lectrino cum ij blodiis pertin.
eidem.—Thorpe, *Regist. Roffense*, 240

[77] In St. Osmund's time, the usage, at least at Canterbury
cathedral, was for the subdeacon to go, if a bishop was the celebrant, and kiss his feet. In telling a dream that he had, as he lay
ill in bed, one of Lanfranc's chaplains says Videbam in visione
beatum Dunstanum, solemnes in ecclesia Salvatoris missas agen-
tem, meque illi in ministerio subdiaconatus servientem. Cumque

lytes (190) awaited him, and held the basin and towel as he washed his hands before he took the obley or bread out of its little silver box or dish and put it upon the paten; and poured first the wine, then a very few drops of water into the chalice.

To sing the *Alleluia* after the gradual, two upper canons, arrayed in silken copes, were led by the rulers of the choir into the southern ambo; and two young clerks went into the north ambo, and over the eagle, upon which the *evangeliarium* or book with the different portions of the gospels for the year was to lie open, cast a splendid pall or hanging. At the *Alleluia*, and just before the choir began to sing the prose or sequence, the deacon, having washed his hands, went up and set out the corporals upon the altar and afterwards fumed it all about with incense; then taking up the *textus* or book of all the four gospels which had been lying there from the beginning of mass, he bent himself before the celebrant and got his blessing. Accompanied by a certain number of attendants did he go thence down the middle of the choir to the pulpit:[78] the two acolytes, with their lighted tapers, headed this procession; after them fol-

---

perlecta a me fuisset epistola, ad pedes illius ex more deosculandos accessi, benedictionem petii, et ita cum ejus benedictione recedens convalui —Osbern, *Vita S. Dunstani*, in *AA SS Man*, iv. 381 [*R S.*, lxiii 153]

[78] Of the pulpit, as it was called, we shall speak further on

lowed the thurifer: next the subdeacon, carrying
the book with the gospels for the year, and out
of which the deacon was about to chant the
gospel for that day; last of all came the deacon
himself, reverently bearing the *textus* or gospel-
book athwart his breast and leant upon his left
arm   Every one arose to the procession as it
came forwards.   When they had reached the
pulpit, the subdeacon put the book, with the gospels open at the gospel for that day, upon the
(191) eagle ; and took from the deacon the *textus*
or gospel-book.   This *textus* the subdeacon held
in both his hands, and leaning upright upon his
breast.   When the *Gloria tibi Domine* was being
sung, each one signed himself with the cross,
bowing the while towards the altar, and then
turned about to the pulpit to hear the gospel.
All the time the deacon was going through it,
the subdeacon, with the *textus*, stood at his left
side ; when the deacon had finished chanting,
the subdeacon went round to his right, and
stretched out to him the *textus* or gospel-book
to be kissed.   This procession then went back
in the same array, but the subdeacon, and not
as before the deacon, bore the *textus*, which he
did in a way different from the deacon's, carrying
it, as he did in the pulpit, not across, but straight-
wise upon his breast.   At a later period the
custom was to have permanently set up on the
north side of the presbytery or chancel, a large

tall beautifully-wrought lectern, made of brass, with the book-desk itself shaped like an eagle spreading out its wings. Such an one stood once in Durham cathedral, " with a gilt pellican on the height of it finely gilded, pullinge hir bloud out hir breast to hir young ones, and winges spread abroade. It was thought to bee the good-lyest letteron of brasse that was in all this countrye."[79]   Moveable, though much smaller lecterns, were fashioned after somewhat the same manner, as can be seen in our picture (vol. ii. p 392). In Chipping Warden Church they con-trived, for the singing of the gospel at high mass, a curious stone lectern, still there : it stands out of the wall on the north side of the chancel, and rests upon a bracket of a man's head crowned ; on the topmost part runs a sunken moulding purfled with flowers.

Not until the celebrant had entoned the *Credo* was he (192) censed by the deacon, and had brought to him by the subdeacon the *textus* to be kissed.[80] The liturgical student should note how two distinct codices were here employed ; one, with the whole of the four gospels all at full length, and called the *textus;* the other, with merely those parts or "gospels" read at some time or another through the year at mass. The book of the gospels, or

---

[79] *Ancient Monuments, &c , of Durham,* 11

[80] Honorius of Autun (A D 1130) says of this rite   Liber Evangelii infra *Credo in unum* osculatur, quia pax per Christum reddita declaratur —*Gemma Animæ,* 1 119 [Hittorp, 1214]

textus, had, in general, a binding of solid gold, studded with gems, and especially pearls, and was used for being kissed ; the other, the gospel-book, which served for reading out of, was often as richly adorned   Followed by the subdeacon with the book of the gospels, the thurifer went down into the choir and there censed the canons, each of whom kissed that *textus* which the subdeacon, immediately after the incensing, held up to his lips for the purpose.   The creed was sung by all the choir together, in signification of one unbroken belief throughout God's true church.

In parochial service, after the gospel, the bidding prayer was said, and the sermon preached. As soon as the *Credo* was done, the offering, if the day happened to be one of those upon which it had to be given, was made by all the people, each of whom walked up to the foot of the altar to leave their gift, or, as it used to be called, "the mass-penny," in the basin held by a clerk, or upon the celebrant's own hand, covered with the broad end of his stole.

After the *Credo*, from the third acolyte, who stood at the sacrarium, the paten with the obley on it first, then the chalice with the wine and a few drops of water, went up through the subdeacon's and deacon's into the (193) celebrant's hands, which the deacon kissed both times. When the obley and the chalice had been duly placed upon the corporal, they were fumed in proper form with

incense by the priest, who afterwards washed his
hands with the help of the subdeacon and other
ministers, while the deacon was censing the north
end of the altar, the shrine, and what relics lay
around the presbytery. The deacon then put himself on his own or middle step, behind the priest,
who faced the centre of the altar, the subdeacon,
in like manner, on the lowest of those three steps
leading up to the holy table. From this ritual
observance of position, the middle step soon came
to be known as the deacon's ; the third, or bottom
one, as the subdeacon's step ; and the sedilia were,
not unoften, accordingly so arranged that the first,
the priest's, was the highest seat ; the second, the
deacon's, higher than the last, the subdeacon's.
Whenever the celebrant had to turn about and
salute the people, the deacon and subdeacon likewise turned themselves along with him ; but to
the latter of these ministers particularly belonged
the duty of watching that the priest's chasuble was
no hindrance to the outstretching of his hands
whenever he had to upraise them.[81] If the bishop
pontificated, his seven deacons all stood in a line
upon the deacon's step, and the seven subdeacons,
in like manner, on the subdeacon's The principal deacon, and subdeacon, each occupied the
middle place of his respective row. Both grades
followed the movements of its own chief; but to

---

[81] *Use of Sarum,* xxxix. (92) vol 1 67.

the head subdeacon was it reserved to minister
unto the bishop and settle the folds of his wide
majestic chasuble about his arms as that prelate
turned himself round to salute the people.

When the celebrant began the *Per omnia sæcula*
before (194) the preface, the deacon took from off
the altar the paten and offertory-cloth, and handed
them to the subdeacon: he wrapped up the paten
in that thin silken towel, and gave it, so shrouded,
to the third acolyte, who held it up before his face
till the *Pater Noster*, standing the while behind
the subdeacon. This offertory-cloth was not as now
cast about the shoulders of the "patener," for so
he was called, but folded round the paten itself,
with both its ends falling loose upon the bearer's
wrists, as may be seen in the picture at p. 175 of
this volume. At the same part of the mass was it,
that, for many years after St. Osmund's time, the
deacon used to take into his hands the liturgical
fan, and with it keep away the flies from the host
after consecration. Here too both the acolytes left
the burning tapers to stand upon the ground nigh
the altar, and retired themselves into the choir, till
just before the *pax* was given, when they went and
waited on the deacon, as he washed his hands, in
the same way as in the Anglo-Saxon ritual. Immediately, also, before the *pax*, the bishop, if he
it was who celebrated, bestowed his benediction
after a very solemn manner. Having had brought
to him, by its bearer, the pastoral staff, and hold-

ing it with its crook towards himself, the deacon cried out in a loud voice, "Bow yourselves down for the blessing." The bishop turned about, and taking in his left hand this staff, so that its crook might point outwards to the people, he read the blessing-prayers for that day, made with his right hand the sign of the cross over his flock there present, and so gave his episcopal benediction after the self-same way that his forerunners, the Anglo-Saxon bishops, bestowed it in their times. What the precise words were for each Sunday and festival, may be seen in the Benedictional, sent forth, after revision, by the Archbishop of Canterbury, John Peckham,[82] A.D. 1279–1292. By such a (195) blessing was granted to the worthy receiver an indulgence, or pardon, of forty days.[83] If the Archbishop happened to be at church, he gave his blessing as well as the celebrating prelate, but at the end of mass.[84] This rite of giving the pontifical blessing just before the *Agnus Dei* lasted in

---

[82] *Exeter Pontifical*, 152–208

[83] Reginald of Durham, speaking of a high mass sung by the bishop in that cathedral one Whit Sunday, says —Siquidem et ibi pontificale benedictionis absolutio, et quadragenaria dierum pœnitentiæ indulta remissio, &c —*De Adm S Cuthberhti Virt*, 202

[84] Thus of the opening of the synod held in London (A D 1309) we read —episcopus Norwicensis, astante archiepiscopo in sede pontificale London episcopi, episcopis vero et aliis prælatis juxta magnum altare commorantibus in ecclesia S Pauli, missam de Spiritu Sancto solenniter celebravit ad magnum altare In fine vero missæ, ante *Agnus Dei*, prædictus episcopus Norwyc de præcepto et licentia speciali Cantuar archiepiscopi solennem benedictionem super populum fecit Expleta missa archiepiscopus benedictionem populo dedit —Wilkins, *Concil*, ii 312

England as long as the use of Sarum was followed;
and is thus noticed in the "Device for the coronation of Henry VII." :—The masse this wise to be
said unto the tyme the cardinall have song thise
words, *Per omnia secula seculorum*, next afore
Agnus; which songen, the cardynall, pontifically
arraied, shall turne hym to the kyng and to the
peple, blessyng them, with thise orisons, *Omnipotens Deus carismatum;* that endid, and the quere
answeryng *Amen, Agnus Dei* shal be songen, &c.[85]

To have the kiss of peace from the celebrant,
the deacon and subdeacon went up and stood
both of them at his (196) right hand, the deacon
next the priest, and the subdeacon next the
deacon. Having got this so-called kiss, the
deacon gave it first to the subdeacon, and then
going down to the further end of the presbytery,
took it unto the two chief rulers of the choir who
were waiting there. They, in their turn, carried
each to his own side of the stalls In the meanwhile, the subdeacon brought the pax-brede to
the celebrant, who bestowed upon it the kiss that
was afterwards to be taken to the people. At
the high mass, at which our kings were crowned,
"the chieff bisshopp, that afor bare the gospell
boke to the king and the quene, shal bring the
pax unto them, and when the king and quene
have kissed it," &c.[85] Among the clergy a kind
of half embrace no doubt was, as it yet is, the

---

[85] *Rutland Papers,* 22

method for expressing the conveyance of this
kiss of peace; but among the people, the pax-
brede of which we have just now spoken, was
carried about and really kissed by each individual.

After the priest had received the holy communion, and washed his hands, the deacon folded
up the two corporals, and put them into their
case,[86] which he laid, together with the offertory-
cloth and paten, upon the chalice. This sacred
vessel he gave into the hands of the third acolyte,
or patener, who, with a solemnity like that in
which he had brought it out of the vestry, carried
it back thither. After the *Ite, missa est*, all went
away in the same order they had followed while
coming to the altar, and thus ended the high
mass.

(197) In his comparison of the two forms of
liturgy, the reader will have found that the difference between the Anglo-Saxon and the Salisbury
ritual for the celebration of mass, was very small.
As, however, in both uses, there were some few
things which are no longer to be seen in any
part of Latin Christendom, it may not be amiss
to say here a word or two upon them. Of these

---

[86] In the Royal Chapel there was "a corporace case of golde,
garnyssed with ij course saphures, twoo course balaces, and x
course perles, weyinge clxix oz di"—Palgrave, *Ancient Kalendars
and Inventories, &c.,* ii 275

The Fan

is not the least curious. That such a liturgical appliance was employed among the Anglo-Saxons, there can be but little doubt, since, in their times, its use was general throughout the rest of western Europe, at the holy sacrifice. In summer-time, one part of the deacon's office, at high mass, was to carry in his hand a fan, and with it drive away any flies that might come to hover about the holy sacrifice, or teazed, by their creeping upon, the person of the celebrant.

In the oriental liturgies, the use of the fan may not only be traced down to the earliest antiquity, but be still witnessed, as it is yet kept up in all of them. At his ordination the Greek deacon has given him, to this day, the ἅγιον ῥιπίδιον, or holy fan,[87] which is made in the likeness of a cherub's winged face, as may be seen from our woodcut. The form of fan, with a hoop of little bells, is employed by the Maronites and other orientals, and is generally wrought of silver or brass. The third is the head of one of those two fans, composed of ostrich and peacock feathers, and carried upon long staves on each side the pope whenever he goes in state, borne seated on a throne aloft on men's shoulders to and from the altar on high festivals.

---

[87] Morin, *De Ordinationibus*, 69, 217

(198) Among the sacred ornaments found belonging to the church of St. Riquier-en-Ponthieu, A.D. 813, occurs "flabellum argenteum j";[88] and

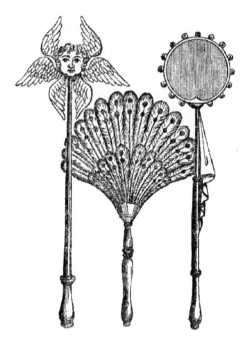

in the chapel of Everard, a nobleman, who began the monastery of Cisoin, near Lisle (A.D. 937), was there also a silver fan.[89] When Martene wrote his valuable *Voyage Littéraire*, A.D. 1777, the church of Tournus could show an old fan: it had an ivory handle some two feet long and beautifully carved, and upon the two sides of the head were graven several saints' figures, and all about ran the following among other verses :—

---

[88] *Chron. Centul.*, iii. 3 [*P.L.*, clxxiv. 1257].
[89] See vol. ii. 102 of this work.

Virgo parens Christi voto celebraris eodem
  Hic coleris pariter, tu Philiberte sacer.
(199)   Sunt duo quæ modicum confert æstate flabellum,
  Infestas abicit muscas et mitigat æstum
  Hoc decus eximium, pulchro moderamine gestum
  Concedet in sacro semper adesse loco :

upon one of the knobs in the handle was this
line :—

Johel me sanctæ fecit in honore Mariæ

At a Dominican convent in the diocese of Toulouse,
Martene saw just such another liturgical fan.[90]

The ritual purposes of this sacred appliance
are often set forth either directly by the rubrics
followed during those times, or glanced at indirectly by writers who make a symbolic reference
to it. Thus, in the Cluniac customs (A.D. 1110),
it was laid down that the fan-bearer is to keep
off the flies from the celebrant, the altar, and
the sacrifice.[91] In getting ready what was wanted
for high mass, the clerks of the pope's chapel
were warned by the "Ordo Romanus," drawn
up, as it would seem, by cardinal Gaietano (c.
A.D. 1298), not to forget this fan [92] : and the
deacon's office was to stand by the pope and
drive the flies away from him [93] · this service was

[90] *Voy Litt* , i 231, 232
[91] Unus autem ministrorum stans cum flabello prope sacerdotem,
ex quo muscarum infestatio exurgere incipit donec finiatur, eas
arcere a sacrificio et ab altari seu ab ipso sacerdote non negligit —
Antiq Consuet , ii. 30 [*P L* , calix. 719]
[92] Deferant quoque æstivo tempore flabella ad abigendum muscas
a ministerio —Ed Mabillon, *Mus Italic* , ii 289
[93] Stans juxta pontificem, et flabellum tenens abigat ab eo
muscas.—*Ibid* , 297 Gori observed (*Thes. Diptych* , iii 164), that

sometimes done by a lower clerk in his place.[94]
Along with his gift to the Archbishop of Canterbury, of one of these fans, the Bishop of Le
Mans, Hildebert, sent a letter, in which, speaking
of its symbolism, he compares the driving away
of the flies to the banishing of temptation.[95] Our
own Herbert de Bosham, in the same bent of
thought, makes a similar reference to the emblematic fan.[96]

Our John Garland, of whom we have spoken
before (vol. i. pp. 303, 304), in his chapter, *De
ornatis ecclesiæ*, says : Nec careat ecclesia acerra
et flabello, &c ; and, in fact, none of our churches,
nor even our chantries, were ever, at one period,
wanting in such an instrument, for we find it
always set down among those articles which be-

---

among those sacred instruments figured on the spandrels of the
arches in the nave of St Sabina's church, at Rome, the fan is to
be seen

[94] Juxta ipsum diaconum stare potest in parte dextra is qui
mitram servat , et, si tempus requirit, teneat flabellum—(200) ad
abigendum muscas —Mabillon, *Mus. Ital*, 303

[95] Flabellum tibi misi, congruum scilicet propulsandis muscis
instrumentum. .   Dum igitur destinato tibi flabello descen-
dentes super sacrificia muscas abegeris, a sacrificantis mente super-
venientium incursus tentationum —Hildebert, *Epist*, i. 2 [*P L*,
clxxi 143]

[96] Et ibi præsertim, ubi sacerdotii exhibent (sacerdotes Christi)
officium et sacrificii peragunt ritum   Ea hora potissimum quotidie
vagas has et vanas fluxas et fluidas, fluentes et refluentes cogita-
tiones immittens quæ tanquam muscæ tabidæ in tam suave olenti
sacrificio totum perdant mox tantæ suavitatis odorem; hora præsertim sacrificii glomeratim irruentes, nisi confestim per sacrificii
ostiariam fidam circumspectam videlicet devotionem, et promptam
Spiritus Sancti flabello repellantur —*Opp*. ed Giles, i. 51   Durand
makes the same remark, *Rationale, &c*, lib iv cap xxxv. 153.

longed, in the thirteenth century, and even later, to the altars in small places, not to speak of our great cathedrals. The inventory taken (A.D. 1222) of the ornaments at Salisbury, enumerates the " flauellum vnum argenteum," besides the " duo flabella de fusto et pargameno "; and, for the service at the smaller altars, there seems to have been provided a (201) fan. Thus St. Peter's altar, in the same church, had, among its other particular appurtenances, " flabellum unum "; so had that of All Hallows.[97] The fan in St. Faith's, in the undercroft, or " croudes," of St. Paul's cathedral, London, was made of peacock's feathers, " unum muscatorium de pennis pavonum." [98] York cathedral's inventory mentions " unum manubrium flabelli argenteum deauratum ex ejusdem (magistri Johannis Newton) thesaurarii, cum ymagine episcopi in fine enamelyd, ponderis quinque unciarum "; [99] and Hamo, Bishop of Rochester, gave to his church (A.D. 1346) " unum flabellum de serico cum virga eburnea." [1] The shape of this liturgical ornament, and how the deacon held it at mass, are well seen in those three instances from illuminated manuscripts, which form the subject of our picture at p 175.

More interesting still is the way in which

[97] Wordsworth, *Salisbury Ceremonies and Processions*, 170, 177 180

[98] Dugdale, *Hist of St Paul's*, 336.

[99] *Mon. Angl*, viii 1205.

[1] Thorpe, *Regist Roffense*, 554

The Eucharist used to be kept hanging up over the High Altar,

in every church throughout this land, from the earliest times to the very latest hour of Henry VIII.'s sad reign. If we had nothing more than the instructions given for the first acts of worship to be made on going into church, we should see that the custom was to have, even in small chapels, the Blessed Sacrament hanging up. Thus, in his "Rule for Nuns," written about the middle of the thirteenth century, by Simon de Ghent, afterwards [A.D. 1297–1315] bishop of Salisbury, he tells them, in the English of the time, but the spelling of which we have somewhat changed :—(202) "Sprinkleth you with holy-water, that ye shoulen ever have with you, and thinketh o Godes flesh and on his blod, that is over the high altar (heie weovede), and falleth each one theretoward with this greeting : *Ave, principium nostræ creationis. Ave, precium nostræ redemptionis. Ave, viaticum nostræ peregrinationis. Ave, premium nostræ expectationis. Tu esto nostrum gaudium, &c.*" [2]

Of such a ritual practice, and of the golden doves employed for it, in other parts of Christendom, both east and west, we have already spoken in another work.

---

[2] *The Ancren Riwle,* 16 (C S 1853), Cotton MS, *Nero,* A xiv. fol 4.

In the history of our own country and our kings, may we find illustrations as curious as they are interesting, of this liturgical usage, as it was observed here after the fall of Anglo-Saxon rule. While Stephen was hearing mass, one Candlemas day, at Lincoln [1141], the chain by which the Eucharist hung above the altar, snapped in two, and the pix fell down.[3] Henry II.'s eldest son, when warring against his own sire, broke into a monastery, and had the wickedness to steal the very golden dove for the Eucharist, which his father had given to that church.[4]

Though abroad, the vessel for holding the pix, with the adorable Eucharist, was fashioned like a dove, here, in England, it (203) seems to have oftener been a cup, which was either of gold, silver, ivory, or of copper gilt, and enamelled;[5] and around it hung a narrow corona, or hoop, often of silver or gold, and gemmed with precious stones.[6] Salisbury, however, had its silver dove

---

[3] Cum autem de more cereum rege dignum Deo offerens (rex Stephanus) manibus Alexandri episcopi imponeret, confractus est Hoc fuit regi signum contritionis Cecidit etiam super altare pixis, cui Corpus Domini inerat, abrupto vinculo, præsente episcopo. —Roger Hoveden, Chron, ed Savile, fol. 278 [R S, li i 201]

[4] Interim rex puer de cœnobio Grandimontensi thesaurum violenter accepit, et quod auditu horrendum est, non pepercit columbæ aureæ in qua Dominicum corpus habebatur, quam pater ejus dederat olim —AA SS Junii, v 571

[5] Wilkins, Concil, i 666.

[6] In his lives of the abbots of St Alban's, Matthew Paris tells that one of them, Robert, who died A D. 1166,—Eucharistiam vase pretioso et corona argentea collocavit [R.S, xxviii., Gesta Abbat, i. 179]; and how another, Simon,—Fecit praeterea per manum

for the Eucharist.[7] As the reader may have noticed, there generally were two vessels: the smaller one, or the pix, that held the particles of the blessed Euchaiist; the larger cup, or dove, within which the other was shut up.

Afterwards, as it would seem, rich silken stuffs got to be cast about the chains of the corona, and thus formed what used to be called the canopy of the pix. That (204) cone-like tabernacle, hanging just over the altar, may be seen in one of the Peterborough seals,[8] and in the frontispiece to our second volume, but is still better shown in the woodcut opposite, taken though it be from a very late example. Of this canopy, mention is often made in our old documents. In some of our small country churches, the custom once was to keep, as the Greeks still do, the blessed Sacrament in a little flat purse, or pocket.

---

ejusdem Baldewyni (aurifabri) unum vasculum speciali admiratione dignum, ex auro obryzo et fulvo, adaptatis et decenter collocatis in ipso gemmis impretiabilibus diversi generis, in quo etiam "Materiam superabat opus,"—ad reponendam Eucharistiam, supra majus altare Martyris suspendendum Quod cum Regi Henrico Secundo innotuit, unam cuppam nobilissimam ac pretiosissimam, in qua reponeretur et ipsa theca immediate continens Corpus Christi, Ecclesiæ Sancti Albani gratanter ac devote transmisit [R S, ibid, 190] A like gift was made to Peterborough by one of its abbots, Godfrey de Croyland, c. A D. 1299 Dedit etiam magno altari unam coupam de argento et deauratam, cum tribus argenteis cathenis et circulo argenteo et deaurato, et intro capsulam argenteam et deauratam pro corpore Christi reponendo — Sparke, Hist, 170

[7] Corona una argentea cum cathenis iij argent cum columba argent ad eukaristiam —Wordsworth, Salisb Cerem., 171.

[8] Mon. Angl., plate v. of seals, fig. 1

At the visitation (A.D. 1220) of the church of Hill Deverell, in the diocese of Salisbury, William, the dean of that cathedral, reported that this was being done.[9] To forbid such a practice was it, no doubt, that Archbishop John Peckham sent

St. Martin saying Mass. (Taken from the tapestry of Montpezat)

forth (A.D. 1280) his constitution : *De Eucharistia* (205) *custodienda*, ordering the use of a pyx lined with linen and covered with a rich covering.[10]

---

[9] Non est ibi pixis continens Eucharistiam, sed deponitur Eucharistia in quadam bursa serica.—*Osmund Reg.* (R.S.), i. 312.

[10] Dignissimum Eucharistiæ sacramentum præcipimus de cætero taliter custodiri, ut videlicet in bursa vel loculo propter comminutionis periculum nullatenus collocetur, sed in pixide pulcherrima intrinsecus lino candidissimo adornata, in qua ipsum corpus Domini repositum in aliquo cooperticulo de serico, purpura, vel lino purissimo operiri præcipimus, ita quod sine comminutionis periculo possit inde faciliter extrahi et apponi.—Wilkins, *Concil.*, ii. 48.

A year afterwards, the same archbishop decreed
that each church should have a tabernacle to hold
the pyx under lock and key.[11] How the whole
of such a sacred appliance was made, may be well
seen in the following description of the splendid
one which belonged (A D. 1385) to St. George's
chapel, Windsor. It was made of ivory with
silver-gilt ornaments, and cover garnished with
jewels and surmounted by a crucifix.[12] Besides
this, the royal chapel had a copper pyx with two
canopies.[13] Those silken hoods thrown upon the
chains of the *corona*, or hoop, so as to form the
tabernacle of which Archbishop Peckham speaks,
and that was afterwards called the canopy, used,
it seems, to be changed, according to the season.[14]
But over the cup itself was cast the Sacrament
cloth, or piece of thin, cloud-like muslin,—pannus

---

[11] Ut in qualibet ecclesia parochiali fiat tabernaculum cum
clausura decens et honestum, secundum curæ magnitudinem et
ecclesiæ facultates, in quo ipsum corpus Domini in pyxide pulcherrima et lineis tegumentis . . collocetur.—Wilkins, *Concil*, ii 48.

[12] Una pixis nobilis eburnea, garnita cum laminibus argenteis
deauratis, cum pede pleno leopardis et lapidibus pretiosis, habens
coopertorium argenteum deauratum cum bordura de saphyris, in
cujus summitate stat figura crucifixi cum Maria et Johanne,
garnita cum perlis, cum tribus cathenis in pomello argenteo
deaurato, et una longa cathena argentea, per quam dependet, et
extat longitudinis trium virgarum.—*Mon Angl*, viii 1365

[13] Una pixis de cupro pro corpore Christi imponendo cum cathena
de eadem secta cum duabus canapis, viz majore et minore —*Ibid.*

[14] This is shown, not only from the mention last (206) made of
two canopies, but in the notice of the same ornaments for the
collegiate church at Cobham, Kent Item ij. panni seric palleat.
pro canopeo, cum ij pannis nebulatis pertin eidem —Thorpe,
Regist Roffense, 240

nebulatus,—as this woodcut, from an illumination in the manuscript life of St. Edmund, martyr, lets us see.[15] This sacrament-cloth used to be wrought with beautiful needlework, as we learn from the *Ancient Monuments, Rites, and Customs of the Church of Durham:* for " within the said quire, over the high altar, did hang a rich and

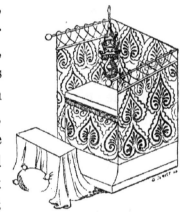

most sumptuous CANAPIE, for the BLESSED SACRA- MENT to hang within it, which had two irons fastened in the French peere, very finely gilt, which held the canapie over the midst of the said high altar (that the pix did hang in it, that it could not move nor stir), whereon did stand a PELICCAN, all of silver, uppon the height of the said canopie, verye finely gilded, givinge hir bloud to hir younge ones, in token that Christ did give his bloud for the sinns of the world; and it was goodly to behould, for the blessed Sacrament to hange in; and a marveilous faire PIX, that the holy Sacrament did hange in, which was of most pure, fine gold, most curiously wrought of gold- smith work. And the white cloth that hung over the pix was of very fine lawne, all embroydered and wrought about with gold and (207) red silke, and

---

four great and round knopes of gold, marvelous
and cunningly wrought, with great tassells of
gold and redd silke hanginge at them, and at
the four corners of the white lawne cloth; and
the crooke that hung within the cloth that the
pix did hang on, was of gold; and the cords
that did draw it upp and downe, was made of
fine white, strong silke."[16]   Among other things
bought (A.D. 1486) for a church, were: "A
pyx clothe for the hight aulter, of sipers frenged
with golde, with knoppes of golde, and sylke of
Spayneshe makyng."   "A canape for the pyx,
of whyte baudekyn."[17]

How from out the reredos of the Durham high
altar sprang the iron branch with the canopy and
pix, may be seen in the woodcut opposite, after an
engraving in *L'Histoire de* (208) *l'abbaye de Saint
Denys*, which shows us the method by which,
until barely sixty years ago, the Blessed Sacrament used to be kept hanging over the altars of
France.   There was a something sublime in the
idea of such a very old ritual observance; for
while it told that Christ is always coming down
from above, to dwell upon his altars, and among
men, it said how the earth was not worthy of
being touched by such a heavenly gift.   Better
able to call unto itself the eye and heart of the
worshipper, than our present tabernacles, were

---

[16] *Rites of Durham*, 7.
[17] *Illustrations, &c*, 114.

this old usage helped by our modern contrivances
and mechanism, it might be brought back again
most advantageously, and made to hinder some,
at least, of those horrible profanations perpetrated
against the Holy of Holies in the Eucharist; for
hardly does a year go by, but we are pained at
hearing that a tabernacle has been broken open

by thieves, in some part or other of this country.
The canopy, with the pix, could be hung so high
as to be far above reach; and the hidden chain,
which let it down, so linked with a bell outside
the church, that it might ring each time it was
drawn up or down.

The first wooden or stone tabernacle resting on

the altar, seen in this land, was put up in Queen Mary's reign.[18]

About St. Osmund's time,—perhaps even somewhat earlier,—some few changes took place in our old Anglo-Saxon ritual architecture, and

A new way of building the Altar and Choir

was followed. The ciborium, or dome, just over the holy table ceased to overshadow it ; but its two eastern columns were left, and across them ran a broad thick beam for saints' images and relics to stand upon : immediately from the altar-table itself, and beneath the beam, arose the crucifix. The bishop's chair was still left in its high place ; in cathedrals, some way from, and to the east of, (209) the altar.[19] In smaller churches, it was upon this " beam " that the crucifix between St. Mary and St. John was fixed ; and there, too, were put the holy water,

---

[18] [For the elaborate tabernacle which survives at Milton Abbas see *S. Paul's Eccles Soc. Trans*, iv 80]

[19] In his description of the choir at Canterbury as rebuilt by Prior Conrade, full thirty years after St Osmund's death, Gervase says Ad cornua altaris orientalia erant duæ columpnæ ligneæ auro et argento decenter ornatæ, quæ trabem magnam sustentabant, cujus trabis capita duorum pilariorum capitellis insidebant. Quæ per transversum ecclesiæ desuper altare trajecta, auro decorata, majestatem Domini, imaginem Sancti Dunstani et Sancti Ælfegi, septem quoque scrinia auro et argento cooperta, et multorum sanctorum reliquiis referta sustentabat   Inter columpnas crux stabat deaurata   in medio chori dependebat corona deaurata, viginti quatuor sustinens cereos This gilt corona, with its four-and-twenty wax lights, hanging down, in the middle of the choir, must have been beautiful —Twysden, ii. 1295 [*R S*, lxxiii. i 13]

the box with the altar breads, the wine and water,
with other things required for divine service.[20] Of
the " beam " itself, and the difference between it
and the " perch," we have already spoken ;[21] and
an example of it is shown in the illumination of
the high altar in the church of St Austin's abbey,
given in vol. iii. p 316. Upon this " beam " there
stood, at Salisbury, six lights. At that cathedral,
too, a corona for lights hung (210) down in the
presbytery; there was a seven-branched bronze
candlestick standing on the pavement, as at
Canterbury,[22] and upon the pulpit wall four
tapers burned on high feasts. Only two lights
seem ever to have been placed upon the altar
itself, though for holy days many were put about
and near to it.

With regard to the choir, the walls which shut
it in were left about seven feet high ;[23] and those

----

[20] This we gather from various passages in the life of the ankret,
St. Godric, by Reginald, who in one place tells us Postea cum
aqua urceolum, et deindo quicquid supra lignum steterat, quo
de more infixum fuerat crucis sacrosanctæ vexillum . . et lignum in quo crux infixa fuerat cum omni suppellectili reliquo, ex
ulterutro pariete evulsit, &c.—*Vita*, 94

[21] Vol iii pp 388, 389

[22] Among the beautiful things which Conrade, chosen prior of
Christchurch, A D 1108, bestowed upon that primatial church, was
Candelabrum miræ magnitudinis de aurichalco fabricatum, habens
tres hinc et tres inde ramos ex medio proprio prodeuntes stipite
unde septem recipit cereos.—*Anglia Sacra*, 1 137

[23] They could have been no higher, for at Canterbury the
primatial throne, which rested on the top of the marble skirting
about the choir and presbytery, was ascended from the floor
whereon the altar stood, by a flight of eight steps , a flight of
three steps led from the choir to the presbytery , and another,
of the same number, from the presbytery to the pavement about

two ambones (211) that had hitherto stood,—one
on the north side, for the singing of the gospel,
the other on the south, for the epistle,—were
carried down, and thrown into one low kind of
lobby, which served for those same ritual purposes, the while it made the western bound of
the choir, with a doorway through the middle,
into the nave below. This new erection, which
brought together two old appliances that had for
ages stood so wide asunder, soon got called the
pulpit. Above it, like as at the altar, went a
great beam, from out the centre of which, and
over the doorway, arose a tall crucifix, besides
other images ; and beneath, within the pulpit
itself, often was there a small altar of the holy
cross.[24] The eagle-shaped lectern for the *evange-*

---

the altar Ad bases pilariorum murus erat tabulis marmoreis
compositus, qui, chorum cingens et presbiterium, corpus ecclesiæ
a suis lateribus quæ alæ vocantur dividebat Continebat hic
murus monachorum chorum, presbiterium, altare magnum in
nomine Jesu Christi dedicatum, altare Sancti Dunstani, et altare
sancti Ælfegi cum sanctis eorum corporibus. Supra prædictum
murum in circinatione illa retro altare et ex opposito ejus cathedra
erat patriarchatus ex uno lapide facta, in qua sedere solebant
archiepiscopi . tunc enim ad altare Christi per gradus octo
descendebant. De choro ad presbiterium tres erant gradus De
pavimento presbiterii usque ad altare gradus tres Ad sedem vero
patriarchatus gradus octo. (Gervase, *Chron*, ed Twysden, ii 1294)
[*R.S*, lxxiii i. i3] Allowing six inches in height to each of these
fourteen steps between the level of the choir and the foot of
the throne, we shall find that this wall must have been seven
feet high

[24] Turris ergo in medio ecclesiæ maximis subnixa pilariis posita
est . pulpitum vero turrem prædictam a navi quodammodo
separabat, et ex parte navis in medio sui altare Sanctæ Crucis
habebat Supra pulpitum trabes erat, per transversum ecclesiæ

liarium stood in the northern division of this pulpit; and hither came, from the altar, that solemn procession for the singing of the gospel at high mass. As the choir's enclosure uplifted itself on high, so did the pulpit, till at last it grew up into that comely feature of our old church - building, which, in our cathedrals, is known as the "screen," but in parish churches, the "roof-loft."

The Service-books after Sarum Use,

were the same in their contents as those required in the (212) Anglo-Saxon ritual; and, if any difference exists between them, it is to be found in this fact, that the earlier volumes were afterwards broken into smaller codices, the names of which tell the specific part of the service that they were meant for. The *Legend* contained all the lessons out of Holy Writ, and the works of the fathers, read at matins; the *Passional*, or *Passionary*, had in it the lives of martyrs and saints, and was used for some of the lessons at matins, on saints' days. The *Martyrology* was read at the end of prime-song, and contained a short notice of all the saints and martyrs throughout the world, commemorated each day of the year. The *Antiphoner*, or "Lyggar," was always a large codex,

posita, quæ crucem grandem et duo cherubin et imagines Sanctæ Mariæ et Sancti Johannis apostoli sustentabat —Gervase of Canterbury, *Chron*, ed Twysden, ii 1293 [*R.S*, lxxiii 1. 9, 10].

having in it not merely the words, but the music and the tones, for all the invitatories, the hymns, responses, versicles, collects, and little chapters, besides whatever else belonged to the solemn chanting of matins and lauds, as well as the smaller canonical hours The *Psalter* had the psalms of David usually distributed over the days of the week, together with litanies. The *Portous*, or Breviary, contained whatever was to be said by all beneficed clerks, and those in holy orders, either in choir, or privately by themselves, as they recited their daily canonical hours : no musical notation was put into these books. The *Missal* contained all the various masses for the year : and when a " full missal,"—that is, with all the services at length, and the notation given under the words of the more solemn ones,—this codex was very large and thick. In the *Graduale*, or *Grail*, was put whatever the choir took any part in singing, on Sundays or festivals, at high mass ; and therefore in it might be found the office for hallowing and sprinkling holy water, the different introits, the Kyries, Glorias, the Sanctuses, the Agnus Dei's,— each with its own various proses or verses mingled along with it ; and, besides this, the graduals, the tracts, the (213) sequences, the offertories, the Credo,—all with their musical notation. The *Troper*, after Sarum use, was, in its contents, like the Anglo-Saxon one which we have already spoken of. The *Processional* contained the hymns, the litany, the proses, sung by the clergy as they walked at any time in procession. The *Verritary* [*Venitare*] was a small book, in which the "Venite, exultemus Domino," sung at the beginning of matins, with the appropriate invitatorium, or strophe, repeated at intervals between the verses of the above named 94th psalm, was written out, and the notation for the chant put above the words. On high feast days, the "Venite" used to be sung with great solemnity, by the rulers of the choir. The Sarum, like the Anglo-Saxon *Benedictional,* contained the forms for blessing the people, by the bishop, at high mass, just before the *Pax.* The *Manual* had in it all the services that a parish priest has to perform, with the musical notation where needed, and the full rubrics for the administration of the Sacraments. The *Ordinal* was a directory, or perpetual calendar, so drawn up that it told how each day's service, the year through, might easily be found. For the use of the singing boys often were provided little horn-books, with the responses and their music duly set forth. Among the things which one of the Coventry monks had written out for the use of the church there, we find: Tabulam responsoriorum corneam quam fecit cum magno labore.[25]

---

[25] Hearne, *Hist of Gluston*, p 291

THE RITUAL YEAR, AFTER SALISBURY USE,

was identical with that which we have seen followed among our Anglo-Saxon forefathers; and,
whensoever any difference shows itself, it is always
slight and unimportant.   On (214)

Christmas Day,

St. Matthew's genealogy of our Lord used to be
sung at the end of matins, with all the ritual's
magnificence, accompanied by the acolytes, carrying their tapers, and the thurifer and crossbearer,
all in apparelled albs and tunicles; the deacon,
vested in his dalmatic, went in solemn procession
up into the pulpit, or rood-loft, where he sang
this portion of the gospel. If the bishop were
present, he himself sang it; thus of St. Thomas
of Canterbury we read that: Nocte Dominicæ
Nativitatis legit evangelicam lectionem, *Liber
generationis*, et missam noctis celebravit.[26] The
candlestick held to light the bishop on this
occasion, was sometimes a work of art, made for
this purpose.   Anthony Beck, Bishop of Durham,
among other things, bequeathed to his cathedral:
Unum candelabrum argenteum et deauratum, in
cujus fundo est ymago Sanctæ Mariæ cum filio
suo jacens in puerperio quod vocatur præsepe, pro

---

[26] Wm. Fitz-Stephen, *Vita*, § 129 [*R S*, lxvii. iii. 130]

nocte Natalis Domini.[27] Then, as before, and now, every priest might say three masses upon this festival

St. Stephen's Day

was marked, as of old, by the leading part which the deacons of every large church took in its celebration, for the protomartyr was their especial patron saint. After the first *Benedicamus Domino*, at the even-song on Christmas Day, all the deacons, arrayed in silken copes, and holding each a lighted taper in his hand, walked in procession, and singing, to St. Stephen's altar, where they made a commemoration of him, and the officiating priest incensed his image, after which they went back into the (215) choir, chanting an anthem in praise of the B. V. Mary.[28] On the morrow—the day of the saint's feast—the deacons, vested in silken copes, led the choir in various parts of the service.

St. John the Evangelist's Day

was observed with like solemnities by all the priests, to whom a holy tradition has assigned the well-beloved, youthful apostle, as their immediate patron. Next to this festival came the solemnity of

[27] *Wills, &c , of the Northern Counties,* p 12
[28] [*Use of Sarum,* lu. (54), vol. 1 p 124]

Holy Innocents, or Childermas,

which was marked by what our forefathers loved
to see so much,—the ceremonial of

The Boy-Bishop,

waited on by his youthful ministers.

St. Nicholas was deemed the patron of children
in general, but much more particularly of all
schoolboys, amongst whom the 6th of December
(the saint's festival) used to be a very great holy
day, for more than one reason. In those bygone
times all little boys either sang, or served, about
the altar, at church; and the first thing they
did upon the eve of their patron's festival, was
to elect from among themselves, in every parish
church, cathedral, and nobleman's chapel, a bishop
and his officials, or, as they were then called,
"a Nicholas and his clerks." This boy-bishop
and his ministers afterwards sang the first vespers
of their saint; and, in the evening, arrayed in
their appropriate vestments, walked all about
the parish. All were glad to see them, and those
who could afford it, asked them into their houses,
to bestow a gift of money, sweetmeats, or (216)
food upon them.[29] What was the custom in the

---

[29] One of the items in Edward I's expenses for the year 1299,
is · Septimo die Decembris cuidam episcopo puerorum dicenti
vesperas de Sancto Nicholao coram rege in capella sua apud Heton
juxta Novum Castrum super Tynam, et quibusdam pueris
venientibus et cantantibus cum episcopo predicto, &c, xls —
Liber Quotidian, 25

houses of our nobles, we may learn from the
Northumberland Household Book, which tells
us that—" My Loid useth and accustomyth to
gyfe yerly, upon Saynt Nicolas-even, if he kepe
chapell for Saynt Nicolas, to the master of his
childeren of his chapell, for one of the childeren
of his chapell, yerely, vis. viii*d*. ; and if Saynt
Nicolas com owt of the towne wher my lord
lyeth, and my lord kepe no chapell, than to have
yerely iiis. iiij*d*." [30]   At Eton college, it was on
St. Nicholas's day, and not on Childermas, that
the boy-bishop officiated, which he did, not only
at even-song, but at mass, which he began and
went on with up to the more solemn part at the
offertory [31]

It was upon this festival that some wealthy
man or another of the parish, would make an
entertainment on the occasion for his own household, and invite his neighbours' children to come
and partake of it; and, of course, Nicholas and
his clerks sat in the highest places. The *Golden
Legend* tells how " a man, for the love of his sone
that wente to scole for to lerne, halowed every
year the feest of saynt Nycholas moche solemply.
On a tyme it happed that the fader had doo make
redy the dyner, and called (217) many clerkes to

---

[30] *Liber Quotidian*, 343

[31] In festo Sancti Nicholai, in quo, et nullatenus in festo
sanctorum Innocentium, divina officia præter missæ secreta
exequi et dici permittimus per episcopum puerorum scholarum,
ad hoc de eisdem annis singulis eligendum —*Statutes*, &c, 560

this diner." [32] Individuals sometimes bequeathed money to find a yearly dinner on St. Nicholas's day, for as many as a hundred scholars, who were, after meat, to pray for the soul of the founder of the feast. In our large schools and universities, the festival was kept with public sports and games. But it was at Holy Innocents, or Childermas' tide, that Nicholas and his clerks came forth in all their glory. The boy-bishop had a set of pontificals provided for him St. Paul's, London, had its "una mitra alba cum flosculis breudatis . . ad opus episcopi parvulorum . . baculus ad usum episcopi parvulorum" [33] York minster, too, its "una capa de tissue pro episcopo puerorum"; [34] Lincoln cathedral, "a cope of red velvet—ordained for the barn-bishop"; [35] All Souls' college, Oxford, "j. chem. (ches.?) j cap. et mitra pro episcopo Nicholao"; St. Mary's church, Sandwich, "a lytyll chesebyll for seynt Nicholas bysschop." [36] For the boy-bishop's attendants, copes were also made; and York had no fewer than "novem capæ pio pueris." [37]

Towards the end of even-song, on St. John's day, the little Nicholas and his clerks, arrayed in their copes, and having burning tapers in their hands, and singing those words of the Apocalypse

[32] Impress a Wynkyn de Worde, fol xlvii, London, 1527
[33] Dugdale's *Hist of St Paul's*, 315, 316
[34] *Mon Angl*, viii 1208   [35] *Ibid*, 1282
[36] Boys, *Hist.*, 376   [37] *Mon Angl*, viii. 1207.

(c. xiv), "*Centum quadraginta*," walked processionally from the choir to the altar of the Blessed Trinity, which the boy-bishop incensed; afterwards, they all sang the anthem, and he recited the prayer commemorative of the Holy Innocents. Going back into the choir, these boys took possession of upper canons' stalls, and those dignitaries themselves had to serve in the boys' (218) place, and carry the candles, the thurible, the book, like acolytes, thurifers, and lower clerks. Standing on high, wearing his mitre, and holding his pastoral staff in his left hand, the boy-bishop gave a solemn benediction to all present; and, while making the sign of the cross over the kneeling crowd, he said,—

> Crucis signo vos consigno; vestra sit tuitio.
> Quos nos emit et redemit suæ carnis pretio

The next day, the feast itself of Holy Innocents, the boy-bishop preached a sermon, which of course had been written for him · and one from the pen of Erasmus, "Concio de puero Iesu," spoken by a boy of St. Paul's school, London, is still extant; and Dean Colet, the founder of that seminary, in his statutes for it, ordained that "all these children shall, every Childermas daye, come to Paulis churche, and hear the childe bishop sermon; and after be at the hygh masse, and each of them offer a *id*. to the childe bysshop, and with them the maisters

and serveyors of the scole." [38]   At even-song,
bishop Nicholas and his clerks officiated as on
the day before, and, until Archbishop Peckham's
times, used to take some conspicuous part in the
services of the church during the whole octave
of Childermas tide.   About A.D. 1279, that
primate decreed, however, that the children's
solemnities should be confined to the day.[39]   This
festival, like St. Nicholas's day, had its good
things; and then, as now, was marked by a
better dinner in nunneries, wherein the little
boys who served at the altars of the nuns'
churches were not forgotten, as we see by the
expenses of St. Mary de Prees: "Paid for (219)
makyng of the dyner to the susters upon Childermas day, iiis. iiijd.   It' paid for brede and ale
for Saint Nicholas clerks, iiid." [40]   How the
people loved to look upon, and came in crowds
to witness, this procession, may be gathered from
a statute, issued by a bishop of Salisbury in order
to regulate the ceremonies.   He forbade any
feasting or visits outside to any one other than
canons: and in order to check the damage done
by the crowd at the procession, he pronounced
a sentence of excommunication against any who

---

[38] Knight, Colet's Life, p 308

[39] Puerilia autem solennia, quæ in festo solent fieri Innocentum,
post vesperas S Johannis tantum inchoari permittimus, et in
crastino in ipsa die Innocentum totaliter terminentur.—Wilkins,
Concil, ii 38

[40] Mon Angl, iii 360

hustled or hindered the boys as they did their ceremonies.[40a]

If schoolboys had the patron St. Nicholas, little girls had their patroness, too, St. Catherine, who, by her learning, overthrew the cavillings of many heathen philosophers, and won some of them to Christianity. On this holy martyr's festival, therefore, did the girls walk about the towns in their procession. All this was looked upon with a scowl by those who pulled down the church of God in this land: hence Cranmer, towards the end of Henry VIII's reign, forbade these and other like processions · (220) "Whereas heretofore dyverse and many superstitious and childysshe observations have been used, and yet to this day are observed and kept in many and sondry parties of this realm, as upon sainte Nicolas, sainte

---

[40a] Electus autem puer chorista in episcopum modo solito puerili, officium in ecclesia prout fieri consuevit licenter exequatur, convivium aliquod de cetero vel visitationem exterius seu interius nullatenus faciendo, sed in domo communi cum sociis conversetur nisi cum ut choristam ad domum canonici causa solatii ad mensam contigerit evocari ecclesiam et scholas cum ceteris choristis statim post festum Innocentium frequentando Et quia in processione qua ad altare Sanctæ Trinitatis faciunt annuatim pueri supradicti, per concurrentium pressuras et alias dissolutiones multiplices nonnulla damna personis et ecclesiæ gravia intelleximus priscis temporibus pervenisse, ex parte Dei omnipotentis et sub pœna majoris excommunicationis quam contravenientes ut pote libertates dictæ ecclesiæ nostræ infringentes et illius pacem et quietem temerarie perturbantes declaramus incurrere ipso facto inhibeamus ne quis pueros illos in præfata processione vel alias in suo ministerio premat vel impediat quoquo modo — [*Constitutions of Roger de Mortival* (1319) in *Statutes of Sarum*, ed Daymen & Jones, p. 75]

Catheryne, sainte Clement, the holy Innocentes,
and such like; children be strangelye decked
and apparelid to counterfaite priestes, byshoppes,
and women; and so ledde with songes and
daunces from house to house, bleassing the
people, and gatherynge of monye; and boyes
doo singe masse and preache in the pulpitt . . .
the kyng's majestie willith and commaundeth
that from henceforth all suche superstitions be
loste and clyerlye extinguished," &c.[41]   Queen
Mary restored these harmless rites, and the people
were glad to see this, along with other of their
old religious usages, given back to them; and
an eye-witness tells us that, in A.D. 1556, "the
v day of December was Sant Necolas evyn, and
Sant Necolas whentt a-brod in most partt in
London, syngyng after the old fassyon, and was
reseyvyd with mony good pepulle into their
howses, and had myche good chere as ever they
had, in mony plasses."[42]   On

The Epiphany, or Twelfthtide,

our kings, whose especial festival it was that
day, made an offering, at mass, of gold, frank-
incense, and myrrh, in imitation of the three
wise men.[43]   Some of our princes used to go in

---

[41] Wilkins, *Concil*, iii 860   [42] Machyn, *Diary*, p 121.

[43] In an accompt of Edward I's alms for the year 1300, we find
set down· vi die Januarii in oblacionibus regis, in capella sua in
honore trium Regum, die Epiphanie, viis   . Eodem die in
oblatione regis in pretio unius florini auri per eundem oblati cum
thure et mirra —*Liber Quotidian.*, p. 27.

great state to sing their matins and afterwards
to (221) hear mass that morning, clad in their
royal robes and crowned. In a description of
the way in which Henry VII. once kept his
Christmas at Greenwich, we are told that, " On
the xiith even the king went to the evensong
in his surcoot outward, with tabert sleves, the
cappe of astate on his hede . . and on the
morowe at matens tyme, al other astats and
barons had ther surcots outward, with ther hodys;
and in the procession tyme they were all in their
roobes of astate. The king and the quene wer
corouned," &c.[44]

Candlemas and Ash Wednesday varied nothing
in their ceremonial from the olden forms of the
Anglo-Saxons; but

Lent

brought along with it certain ritual peculiarities.
From the evening before the first Sunday of that
season of fasting till the Thursday before Easter

The Lenten Curtain

hung down between the people and holy of holies.
In cathedials, it parted the presbytery from the
choir, in parish churches, the chancel from the
nave. It was only at the Gospel that it was
pulled aside, and so remained till the *Orate
fratres*, except on festivals of the double class,

---

[44] Leland, *Collectanea*, iv 235

when it was withdrawn for the whole day. Upon the first Monday in Lent all the crucifixes, as well as the large tall one in the rood-loft, images of every kind, the reliquaries, and even the cup with the Blessed Eucharist hanging over the high altar, were all covered up. The little wooden shutters by the side of those canopied tabernacles, within which so often stood the figure of a saint, well served, and were meant, for such a purpose This (222) and other ritual observances are clearly set before our eyes in the following passage out of the *Historie of the Arrivall of Edward IV. in England*—"The kynge, with all his hooste, cam to a towne called Daventre, where the kynge, with greate devocion, hard all divine service upon the morne, Palme Sonday, in the parishe churche, wher God and Seint Anne shewyd a fayre miracle . . afore that tyme, the kynge, being out of his realme in great trouble, prayed to God, our Lady, and Seint George, and amonges othar saynts, he specially prayed Seint Anne to helpe hym, where that he promysed, that at the next tyme that it shuld hape hym to se any ymage of Seint Anne, he shuld thereto make his prayers and gyve his offeringe, in honor and woishipe of that blessyd saynt. So it fell, that the same Palme Sonday the kynge went in procession, and all the people aftar, in goode devotion, as the service of that daye askethe, and whan the processyon was comen into the churche, and by ordar

of the service were comen to that place where
the vale shul be drawne up afore the Roode,
that all the people shall honor the Roode, with
the anthem, *Ave*, three tymes begon. In a pillar
of the chuiche, directly aforne the place where
kynge knelyd and devowtly honory d the Roode,
was a lytle ymage of Seint Anne, made of alle-
blaster, standynge fixed to the piller, closed and
clasped togethars with four bordes, small, payntyd,
and growynge rownd abowt the image, in manar
of a compas, lyke as it is to see comonly and all
abowt, where as suche ymages be wont to be
made for to be solde, and set up in churches,
chapells, crosses, and oratories, in many placis.
And this ymage was thus shett, closed, and
clasped, accordynge to the rulles that in all the
churchis of England be observyd, all ymages to
be hid from Ashe Wednesday to Easter-day in
the mornynge. And so the said ymage had
bene from Ashwensday to (223) that tyme. And
sodaynly, at that season of the service, the bords
compassynge the ymage about gave a great crak,
and a little openyd, which the kynge well per-
ceyved," &c [45] Not only the large rood with St.
Mary and St. John in the rood loft, but most
other crucifixes, and not a few of the images
about our old churches, had to be muffled up in
cloths, which, like the wide curtain at the chancel
arch, were either of white linen or silk, and

---

[45] Leland, *Collectanea*, pp 13, 14

marked all of them with a red cross. Of such Lenten veils often do we find mention in wills and inventories: St. Frideswide's, Oxford, had, at its suppression by Henry VIII., "a veall of new whitt sercenett for Lentt xxs., itm. hangings for the highe alter, for above and benethe of new whit sercenett wth redd crosses, called alter-clothes, for Lent, xs." [46] Durham Priory had (A D. 1446): Duo panni albi pro Quadragecima, cum crucibus rubeis superconsutis; [47] All Souls' College, Oxford: j. velum de serico, et j. de panno lineo, j. descloth cum rubea cruce pro XL. [48]—"Velum unum de serico quadragesimale," was among the ornaments of Salisbury, A.D. 1220. [49] The finding of the large curtain, that hung between the people and the chancel during Lent, or the "velum quadragesimale," belonged to the parishioners. [50]

Outside this large chancel veil, and in the sight of every one, was it that, all through shrift-time, or Lent, confessions—of women especially—used to be heard; and when one of our old canons says,—Confessiones mulierum extra velum audiantur; [51] the veil about which the statute speaks (224) is not to be understood of the article of dress worn by women, as some Protestant writers

---

[46] *Mon Angl*, ii 167
[47] *Wills, &c, of the Northern Counties,* p 91.
[48] Gutch, *Collect. Curiosa,* ii 264.
[49] Wordsworth, *Salisbury Ceremonies and Processions,* 173
[50] Wilkins, *Concil.,* ii 49   [51] *Ibid ,* i 689

have oddly enough mistaken it, but of the veil of
the sanctuary. The accompanying woodcut, after
an illumination in a manuscript Flemish book of
Hours, will help to show us how the inside of

one of our own old English churches must have
looked in Lent. A white curtain hangs between
the chancel and the nave; the rood, with St. Mary
and St. John, is wrapped up in white cloths,
marked with red crosses; the reredos is covered
with a like cloth; the priest, with his furred

amice on, is hearing confession, in open view of
everybody, seated on a bench, and not enclosed
in anything like (225) a modern confessional,
which is of very late introduction. To signify
his full faculties in all cases, the little escocheon
charged with the Peter-keys and Pope's tiara,
is nailed behind, above him; and, with a long
outstretched wand, at once the emblem of the
rod of discipline, and the staff of authority, he is
touching the head, while his upraised right hand
is blessing the man who, in going by, kneels,
beyond earshot, to crave it, as is to this day done
at St. Peter's, Rome. The use of York [52] was, on
this point, exactly like that of Salisbury.

All through Lent, on Wednesdays and Fridays,
as well as every Sunday, there was made, between
undern-song tide and high mass, a procession
about the church. The clergy stopped before

---

[52] Feria iiij in capite ieiunii, post sextam prelatus cum ministris
in albis, sacris indutus vestibus et capatus, sermonem de diei pro-
prietate, scilicet qualiter rei se in tempore illo contineant, in
ambone seu in pulpito, cruce erecta, faciat, et post sermonem
huiusmodi presente cruce et ceroferariis ante gradum altaris benedicat cineres —*York Missal*, i 43

Ab hac dominica (prima Quadragesime) velum suspensum
habeatur inter sancta sanctorum et clerum usque ad Cenam
Domini , nec abstrahatur nisi dum legitur Evangelium, et ad
elevationem hostie, et ad processionem Feria quarta et sexta,
et in obitibus ad commendationem, et ad missam tantum, et in
dominicis, et in aliis festis novem lectionum , sed in festis sanctorum novem lectionum apponatur velum ad missam de feria ; et
tantum amoveatur ad Evangelium et ad elevationem hostie sicut
in aliis feriis. In presentia tamen prelati amoveatur velum ad
Confiteor.—*Ibid.*, i. 53, Feria secunda quadragesime. [*Cf.* Feasey,
Ancient English Holy Week Ceremonial.]

some altar to pray and prostrate themselves
Having kissed the ground, they arose and went
back to the choir, singing the litany. No cross
was borne before them. Excepting some few
devotional or solemn occasions,

(226) *The Processional Cross carried about in
Lent, was always of Wood painted red,*

according to Sarum use ; and there was no figure
of our Lord upon it. This we are told by the
priest Clement Maydeston in his curious work on
the Salisbury ritual, *Crede Michi.*[53] Sir Thomas
More walked to the block " carrying in his hands
a red cross," as his great grandson, Cresacre More,
tells us.[54] Belonging to the Chapel Royal of
Scotland, A.D. 1505, there was : Una crux lignea
rubri coloris habens hastam longam. Langland,
as he glances at the church service on Easter
morn, does not forget the reference made by the
blood-red cross, to the throes of our Lord upon
it, in the following lines .

> " Ich fel eft-sones a slepe   and sodeynliche me mette,
>   That peers the plouhman   was peynted al blody,

---

[53] ¶ De ij dominica Quadragesime et de Cruce lignea —Dominica secunda et in omnibus dominicis per xl. Excepta prima
dominica deferatur crux lignea   rubei coloris depicta sine ymagine
Crucifixi   Sed in alijs processionibus festiuis in Quadragesima
contingentibus, causa deuotionis vel causa venerationis, vt contra
Aichiepiscopum legatum, proprium episcopum, regem vel reginam,
vel mortuum suscipiendum, ordinetur crux sicut in alijs temporibus anni —Wordsworth, *Tracts of Maydeston* (H B. S), p 49

[54] *Life*, ed Hunter, 284

And cam yn with a croys . . .

' Is this ihesus þe Iouster ? ' quaþ ich · ' þat Iuwes duden to
    deþe,

Oþer is hit peers plouhman ? ho peynted hym so rede '

Quaþ conscience, and kneolede þo · ' þes aren cristes armes,

Hus colours and hus cote-armure · and he þat comeþ so
    blody,

Hit is crist with his crois   conquerour of crystine,' " &c [55]

(227) *Palm Sunday,*

as of old, had its blessing of flowers, and so-
called palms, which were afterwards given to the
clergy and people, who carried them in their hands
in a procession made all about the church-yard.
Some ceremonies for this day, in the Sarum, differed
from those of the Anglo-Saxon ritual.   In many
parts of this country, a large and splendidly ornamented tent [56] was set up at the furthermost end

---

[55] *Piers Ploughman*, Passus xxii 5–14 [ed Skeat, 399, 400]

[56] The beauty and the costliness of some of those shrines in
which the body of our Lord used to be carried in this procession,
and the feelings which wrought upon Englishmen of old, to bestow
so many of their thoughts, so much of their gold, upon those
works of handicraft, may be seen in the following description of
one of them which St Alban's Abbey once possessed —Nec
praetereundum   quod idem Abbas Simon unum vas mirificum,
per modum scrinii compositum (cujus arcam schema quadrat
venustissimum ; culmen vero per modum feretri surgendo coar-
tatur, et undique circulis elevatis orbiculatur, in quibus historia
Dominicae Passionis imaginibus fusilibus figuratur, et per totum
laminis ductilibus solidae spissitudinis, ita, scilicet, quod basibus
vel sustentaculis ligneis non indiget), Deo et Ecclesiae Sancti
Martyris Albani, ad perpetuum ipsius ecclesiae honorem et
decorem, contulit fabricatum   Et . . . constituit ut in Dominica
Palmarum Corpus Dominicum in ipso scrinio veneranter reponeretur, et ab aliquo fratrum moribus et aetate venerabili, in
ucasla alba usque ad papilionem in Coemiterio, de pretiosissimis

of the close or burial-ground; and thither, early
in service-time, was carried by two priests, accompanied with lights, a sort of beautiful shrine, of
open work, within which hung the Blessed Sacrament, enclosed in a rich cup or pix. The long-
drawn procession, gay and gladsome, with its
palms and flowers,[57] went forth, and halted every
now and then, as it winded round the outside of
the church, to make a station. While they were
going from the north side towards the east, and
had just ended the gospel read at the first of these
stations, the shrine with the Sacrament, surrounded with lights in lanterns and streaming
banners and preceded by a silver cross, and a
thurifer with incense, was borne forwards so that
they might meet it as it were; and our Lord was
hailed by the singers chanting *En rex venit man-
suetus* Kneeling lowly down and kissing the
ground, they saluted the Sacrament again and

---

pallus compositum, nisi inclementia aurae impediatur, et tunc in
Capitulum deportaretur, duobus fratribus, in cappis, brachia
bajulantis dictum vas sustentantibus. Et eodem modo, sequente
processione, ad ecclesiam venerantissime reportaretur, ut videant
fideles quanto honore dignum sit sacrosanctum Corpus Dominicum, quod ipso tempore se exposuit flagellandum, crucifigendum,
et sepeliendum —Matt Paris, *Vitæ Abb S Albani*, p 61 [*R S*,
xxviii, *Gesta Abbatum*, i 191, 192]. Gervase of Canterbury speaks
of the tent as of common use tentorium quod (apud ecclesiae
Cantuariae) pro consuetudine et solennitate diei (dominicae Palmarum) erectum est.

[57] Items for the purchase of these appear in churchwardens'
old accompts thus "For palme, boxfloures, etc, A D 1510, iiijd,
for box and palme on Palmesonday, is." &c —*Illustrations*, &c.,
270, 94

again, in many appropriate sentences out of holy writ; and the red wooden cross withdrew from the presence of the silver crucifix. The whole procession now moved to the south side of the close, or church yard, where, in cathedrals a temporary erection was made for the boys who sang the (228) *Gloria, laus et honor tibi sit, rex Christe redemptor*, as a halt was made for a second station. Here was it that sometimes, in parish churches especially,

The Church-yard Cross

was the spot at which they stopped. Falling down on the ground, they yielded their worship to Him who chose to die on the rough hard rood for the love He bore mankind. All about they strewed flowers and green boughs; and after the Passion had been recited at Mass, blessed Palms were brought and this cross was wreathed and decked with them to symbolize Christ's victory over death and sin　References to such a ritual practice are not wanting among our records; and our forefathers liked to think of it; thus Henry Bunn, by his will (A.D. 1501), orders a cross to be set up in Hadley church-yard 'pro palmis in die ramis palmarum offerendis.'[58] This ceremony at the Palm-cross—so it was sometimes called—used to be performed in the churches of France and Germany,

---

[58] Blomefield, *Norfolk*, x. 141

with great effect.[59] In France they sometimes heard a sermon at this church-yard cross.[60]

From the stone cross on the southern side of the church-yard, still to be found in so many places, the procession went next to the western doorway, if the church had one, otherwise to the south porch, and there paused to make its third station. The door itself was shut, but after a while flew wide open. The priests who bore the shrine with the Blessed Sacrament and relics, stepped forwards with the heavenly burden, and held it up on high at the doorway, so that all who went in, had to go under this shrine; and

---

[59] An old 'Ordo Romanus,' seemingly drawn up for some church in Germany, gives the following rubrics —Ut autem peruenerint cum Psalmis, vbi statio est sanctae Crucis, clerus populusque reuerenter stent per turmas in ordine suo cum baiolis, et reliquo ornatu, et infantes paraphonistae in loco competenti subsistentes imponant antiphonam . . Tunc scolastici e regione crucis, lento gradu veniant ante eam, et cum omni reverentia casulas vel cappas in terram jactantes, proni adorent crucifixum, clero interim cantante antiphonam *Pueri Hebræorum vestimenta prosternebant in via, &c*, His recedentibus, continuo veniant ex latere pueri laici *Kyrie eleison* cantantes et sequendo vexillum quod ante eos portatur, veniant ante crucem et   jactent ramos palmarum in terram, proni adorando Crucifixum, et clerus (229) interim canat antiphonam *Pueri Hebræorum tollentes ramos oliuarum obuiauerunt Domino, &c.* . . His finitis, incipit schola cum baiolis antiphonam : *Omnes collaudent nomen tuum et dicant, Benedictus qui venit in nomine Domini.* . . Et tunc prosternit omnis populus hincinde flores seu frondes   . veniat episcopus vel sacerdos ante crucem et prostratus in terram cum omni populo, adoret Crucifixum, clero interim cantante antiphonam, *Scriptum est enim, percutiam pastorem, &c* —Hittorp, 50, 51

[60] Duo latrones in dominica Ramis Palmarum clamore facto post sermonem in cimiterio praefatae ecclesiæ B. Mariæ, ubi tunc ad crucem buxatam monachi venerant —Martene, *Vet. Script. Collect*, v 1123.

thus the procession came back into church, each
one bowing his head as he passed beneath the
sacrament. Walking up the nave till they reached
the rood-loft, they knelt down there and made the
fourth and last station. That large curtain which,
throughout Lent, had been hanging at the chancel-
arch so as to hide from the people's sight the
crucifix there, was now drawn away; and, on
beholding the rood, the celebrant and choir hailed
it thrice with *Ave rex noster fili David redemptor*,
and each time knelt down and kissed the floor,
and afterwards passed into the chancel. (230)
This ceremony is noticed in the extract given just
now from the *Arrivall of Edward IV. in England*, and is still further attested by friar Parker,
while he affords us the truly Catholic explanation
of it in these words ·—On Palme Sondaye (says
DIVES) at procession the priest drawith up the
veyle before the rode, and falleth down to the
ground with al the people, and saith thiise : *Ave
rex noster*, hayle be thou our kyng, and so he
worshippeth that image as king. PAUPER. *Absit*.
God forbede. He speketh not to the image, that
the carpentar hath made, and the peinter peinted,
but if the prest be a fole, for that stock or stone
was never king, but he speakethe to hym that died
on the cross for us all, to him that is kynge of all
thynge.[61] After even-song on Palm-Sunday, the
rood was hidden once more by the curtain.

---

[61] *Dives and Pauper*, fol xv. b.

York and Sarum agreed in the main outline of
the ceremonies for Palm-Sunday.[62]

---

[62] Clement Maydeston, the great rubrician of his time, sets forth
the whole ceremonial thus —

¶ De Dominica in Ramis palmarum.

Hac dominica ante benedictionem florum et frondium legatur
lectio deinde sequatur evangelium *Turba multa* et legatur super
lectrinam vbi ad missam leguntur euangelia in diebus ferialibus
(diacono ad orientem conuerso) non ad lectrinam more simplicis
festi   ¶ Finito euangelio et stante executore officij in gradu
tercio ab altari in dextera parte eiusdem altaris ad orientem conuerso, . . . positis prius palmis cum floribus supra altare pro
clericis, pro alijs vero super gradus altaris in parte australi,
sequatur benedictio et cetera   Post distributionem palmarum
exeat processio cum cruce lignea sicut in alijs dominicis quadragesime vsque ad primam stationem.   Deinde lecto euangelio
Cum appropuinquasset Jesus, feretrum cum reliquijs preparetur,
in quo corpus Christi in pixide dependeat obuiam veniente cum
cruce argentea, cum ymagine (232) Crucifixi precedente cum
duobus vexillis et cetera
Statim vero visa cruce argentea recedat crux lignea.   Deinde
dicat executor officij *Salue quem Jesu*   ¶ Sciendum est quod ante
missam super Crucem non imponuntur flores vel frondes in die
Palmarum apud Sarum, ne videantur parari crucem Saluatori suo
Nam si talis crucis adornatio post passionem lectam esset facta,
videretur satis congrue fieri   Nam ex lecto passionis auditu, constat nobis ex cruore Saluatoris nostri ipsam crucem esse sanctifi-
catam   ¶ Si quis opponendo dicat, quare adoramus denudatum
crucem in introitu ecclesie ante passionem ,   ¶ respondendum est
quod non crucem sed ipsum Crucifixum adoramus dicendo *A ue rex
noster*
Finita tercio statione cantore incipiente ℞ *Ingrediente Domino,*
aperiatur ostium ecclesie et intret processio per idem ostium in
ecclesiam sub feretro, et capsula reliquiarum ex transuerso ostij
eleuatur.
¶ Erubescant sacerdotes parrochiales qui percutiunt ostium cum
cruce in introitu ecclesie, expresse contra Ordinale —*Crede Michi*
[Wordsworth, *Tracts of C Maydeston* (H B. S), pp 50, 51]
   The York rubrics are as follows ·—Deinde cum ante tentorium
processio ordinata fuerit diaconus accepta benedictione a prelato
cum presbitero et subdiacono et crucifero et ceroferariis in medio

(233) The office of

Tenebræ,

or matins and lauds for Thursday, Friday, and
Saturday in the last week in Lent, was the
same in form, especially at the end of lauds, as
among the Anglo-Saxons ; and the same number
of twenty-four lights [63] were set upon a triangular
candlestick, known by the English by the name
of the tenebræ or Lenten " hearse "—hert(ium)
quadragesimale,[64] hercia ad tenebras, — one of
which had to be found by the inhabitants of
every parish for their church.[65]   Of the "Tene-

stans legat evangelium sec^m M xxi., " In illo tempore   cum
appropinquasset Iesus Hierosolimis," &c   Et postea sacerdos
flexis genibus dicat ter   " Dignus es, Domine, accipere gloriam
et honorem "   Adorans corpus Christi quod tenet presbiter in
tentorio, et similiter chorus adoret ter, dicens, " Dignus es," etc.
Tunc redeat sacerdos cum corpore Domini et ministri eius in ecclesiam per eandem viam per quam venerunt —*York Missal*, i 86

Cum autem ad portas urbis vel ostium occidentale ecclesie
perventum fuerit, ibi ordinata processione, incipiat cantor   R
" Collegerunt pontifices," &c   Finito reingressu, pueri in altum
supra ostium ecclesie canant versum, " Gloria, laus," &c   Chorus
cum genuflexione dicat   " Gloria, laus, et honor tibi sit," &c —
Ibid, 87

In ingressu processionis prelatus ter flexis genibus ante crucem
discoopertam adoret dicens cantando, " Ave, Rex noster ", et
chorus idem repetat.   .   Postea vero quattuor vel sex vicarii in
pulpito incipiant R " Circumdederunt me "   Reincepto ab eisdem
R intret processio in chorum et sequatur versiculus sacerdotalis.
—*Ibid*, 88   The liturgical student should notice that the temporary erection over the church door, for the boys to sing the
" Gloria, laus," &c , is specified in the above York rubric

[63] *Use of Sarum*, lxvii (102), vol. i. 142

[64] *Hist of St Paul's*, 336

[65] Wilkins, *Concil.*, ii. 139.

biæ " and the symbolic meaning of that service,
the *Liber Festivalis* speaks thus :—" Good friends,
ye shall understand that holy church useth these
three days, and sayeth service in the even-tide,
that is meekness, wherefore we call it tenebre,
but holy church calleth it tenebris. Then why
this service is thus done in meekness holy fathers
tellen for three causes One is, the night before
that our Lord Ihesu Christe was taken, he went
unto the mountain of Olivete and prayed thus .
(Pater mi (234) si possibile est; transeat a me
calix iste), my Father, if it be possible that this
bitter passion may pass from me, if it were the
Father's will, and else not. And for dread and
fear of that bitter passion that he felt in spirit, he
swet both blood and water. And another cause
is this, that anone, after midnight, came Judas
with fifty knights and much other people to take
Christ, and, for it was dark and they could not
well know him from Saint James he was so like
Christ. Therefore Judas said, (Quem osculatus
fuero tenete eum), ' Forsooth,' quoth he, ' him
that I shall kiss it is, take ye him,' for Saint
James was so like Christ, that much people called
him Christ's brother. And thus Judas betrayed
his master, and thus was Christ taken in meekness, with all the spite they could do to him,
beating him and spitting in his face. The third
cause is, when Christ was naked on the cross,
feet and hands, hanging iii hours from underne

till none.   Then the sun withdrew her light, and was dark through all the world, showing that the maker of light was at that time pained to death. For these three causes, the service of the night is done in darkness, the which service maketh mind how Judas betrayed Christ, and how the Jews came as prively as they could for dread of the common people, wherefore (at) the service is no bell rung, but a sound made of tree whereby all Christian people may have knowledge to come to this service prively without making of any noise, and all that the people should speak of, coming and going, should sound of the tree, that is, the cross that our Lord was done on."

As in the Anglo-Saxon, so in the Sarum rite, on

Maundy Thursday,

or, as it used then to be called,

(235) *Sheer Thursday,*[66]

exactly the same services were celebrated, and almost all of them with a like ceremonial; the

---

[66] The meaning of this old English term we gather from the following remarks in the *Liber Festivalis* "First, if a man asked why Sherethursday is called so, ye may say that, in Holy Church it is called 'Cena Domini,' our Lord's Supper day; for that day he supped with his disciples openly, and after supper he gave them his flesh and his blood to eat and to drink, and said thus (Accipite et manducate, hoc est corpus meum), 'Take ye this, and eat it, for it is mine own body', and anon, after he washed his own disciples' feet, showing what meekness that was in him, and for the great love that he had to them It is also in English called Sherethursday, for in old fathers' days the people would

oils were hallowed ;[67] every altar in a church was washed; there was the maundy, too, or washing of feet; and a reservation of the Blessed Sacrament under one kind consecrated that day, not merely for the morrow's celebration, but to be kept after a particular way, till Easter morning.

(236) *The washing of all the Altars*

in a church, and not of the high altar only, is set forth by St. Osmund's rubric, and continued to be done to the very last, as Maydeston tells us.[68]

that day sheer their heads, and clip their beards, and poll their heads, and so make them honest against Easterday For on Goodfriday they do their bodies no case, but suffer penance, in mind of him that that day suffered his passion for all mankind. On Eastereven it is time to hear their service, and, after service, make holy day On Sherethursday, a man should do poll his hair and clip his beard, and a priest should shave his crown, so that there should nothing be between God and him , for hairs come of superfluity of veins, and humours of the stomach , and they should pare their nails of hands and feet, that comen of superfluity of filth without forth, and shrive him, and make him clean his soul as without , and thus make him clean both within and without '— Fol xxxii. b

[67] *Use of Sarum*, cxiv. (103), vol 1 201.

[68] ¶ In cœna [Domini] ante mandatum omnia altaria sunt abluenda.

Ita quod inprimis benedicatur aqua more dominicali extra chorum priuatim

Postquam vero executor officij dixerit y̌ et orationem de Sancto de quo altare est dedicatum, tam ipse quam omnes clerici priusquam recedant, humiliter et deuote osculentur altare et eodem modo omnia altaria —*Crede Muhi*, in Wordsworth, *Tracts of C Maydeston* (H. B S.), p 51

The Maundy or washing of Feet,

by our kings, queens, bishops, and noblemen, was a thing most particularly kept up. The number of poor chosen for the occasion was usually thirteen, in remembrance of our Lord and his twelve Apostles, and after the ceremony, they were fed by the same illustrious personages who had washed their feet, and had often either money or clothing—sometimes both—given them ere they went away.[69] The devotion with which Roger, archbishop of York, always went about this ceremonial, and his custom of paying the expenses, is specially recorded by an old writer.[70] Robert Betun, bishop of Hereford, was still more exemplary; for William of Wicumb writes of him, that he twice performed this humble office on Maundy Thursday.[71] The *Household Book* of

---

[69] Of Edward I's queen, we read of her having done this.—Et pro denariis datis per preceptum reginæ xiii puperibus, die Parasceves, quorum eadem regina lavit pedes, cuilibet eorum iijs. Et pro denariis datis quinque pauperibus die Veneris sequente cuilibet vid.—*Liber Quotid*, 45 Elizabeth of York used to bestow "on xxxvij pore women every woman iijs jd, for hir maundy upon Shire Thursday"—*Privy Purse Expenses*, 1

[70] Statuit idem archiepiscopus (Rogerus) . ut sacrista ea quæ ad canonicos spectant in die Cœnæ Dominicæ tam in epulis (237) quam in vino, cervisia et vasis et aqua calida ad ablutionem pedum ipsorum canonicorum, et clericorum, et pauperum, et xs argenti lx pauperibus post ablutionem pedum suorum distribuendos, et victualia quæ secundum consuetudinem matricis ecclesiæ solebant ipso die pauperibus post ablutionem pedem ministrari, sumptibus suis propriis inveniret.—[Stubbs, *Actus Pontif Ebor*, in] Twysden, ii 1723

[71] In Cœna Domini quotannis cum sacramenta diurna peregisset, et pauperibus Christi propriis manibus necessaria ministrasset;

the Earls of Northumberland, we may well believe, shews not merely the home and inward life of that, but of every other like great family in this kingdom during those Catholic times when that document was written. From the above-named valuable work then, we learn that, "My Lorde useth and accustomyth yerely uppon Maundy Thursday when his Lordship is at home, to gyf yerly as manny gownnes to as manny poor men as my Lorde is yeres of aige with hoodes to them, and one for the yere of my Lordes aige to come of russet cloth, &c. Item: as manny sherts of lynnon cloth to as manny poure men. Item: as many tren (wooden) platers after ob. the pece with a cast of brede and a certain meat in it. Item · as manny eshen cuppis with wyne in them. Item: as manny pursses of lether, with as manny penys in every purse, &c. Item: My Lord useth to cause to be bought uj yerdis and iij quarters of brode violett cloth for a gowne for his (238) Lordshipe to doo service in, or for them that schall doo service in his Lordshypes absence, after iiis. viiid. the yerde, and to be furrede with blake lamb, which gowne my Lorde werith all the tyme his Lordship doith service, and after doith gyf to the pourest man Item: for my Lady, as

---

facto vespere Salvatoris exemplum in abluendis pedibus discipulorum in choro reverenter exhibebat Deinde domi præparatis pauperibus aliis, idem humilitatis exemplum repetebat, addens caritatis opus in eleemosynis consolatoriis, &c.—*Anglia Sacra*, ii 310.

manny groits to as manny poure men as hir
Ladyshipe is yeres of aige. Item: for my Lordes
eldest sone, as manny pens of ij pens to as manny
poure men as (he) is yeres of aige; for every of
my yonge maisters, my Lordis yonger sonnes, as
manny penns to as manny poore men as every
of my said maisters is yeres of aige," &c.[72]

How the kings of England used to this, we
are told by Sir Thomas More, who says:—"Then-
sample of Christ in weshyng the Apostles' feete,
with his exhortacion unto them by his ensample
to do the lyke, byndeth no men to folow the
literall fashion thereof in weshyng of folkes feete,
as for a rite or ceremony or a sacrament of the
churche. Howbeit much it hath ben ever synce,
and yet in every country of Christendome in
places of religion used it is, and noble prynces
and great estates use that godly ceremony veri
religiously. And none, I suppose, no where more
godly than our soveraygne lorde the kynges
grace here of this realm, both in humble maner
wesshing and wyping and kyssyng also many
poore folkes fete after the noumber of the yeares
of hys age, and with right liberal and princely
almes therewith."[73]

---

[72] P 354, &c

[73] *Works*, 1319 The whole of the Maundy Thursday's cere-
monials are thus set forth by the rubrics of the York Missal:
Prelatus vero in revestiario festive paratus cum duodecim presbyteris casulatis et septem diaconibus et totidem subdiaconibus
cum dalmaticis et tunicis festive indutis, et thuriferariis et ceroferariis ad altare secundum quod ordinatum erit, incepto " Gloria

(239) In this day's mass, besides the host which he himself had to receive, the sacrificing priest consecrated other two (240) hosts that were put into a pix, and, at the end of mass, carried privately unto some becoming place in the sacristy. Of these two reserved hosts, one was taken on the morrow—

Patri," introeat   Et dicto "Kyrie eleyson," prelatus incipiat, "Gloria in excelsis," quod dum canitur classicum pulsetur   Prelatus dicat "Pax vobis", sacerdos, "Dominus vobiscum ', sed non dicatur, "Flectamus genua," nec "Gloria in excelsis," nec "Credo," nec "Agnus Dei," nec "Ite, missa est," nisi in matrici ecclesia ubi penitentium fit reconciliatio et crismatis consecratio [*York Missal,* 1 96] The reservation of the Blessed Eucharist for the morrow is thus prescribed · Et communicent maiores ecclesie Sanguis penitus sumatur   De corpore Domini in crastinum servetur, et a prelato ubi servandum erit, reverenter reponatur —[*Ibid*, 98] For the washing of feet, or the "maundy," and the washing of the altars with wine and water and a bunch of hyssop, or of savin, we have these rubrics   Post refectionem, circa horam vespertinarum, conveniant prelatus et clerici omnes ecclesie ad ecclesiam, Et facto prius mandato pauperum, postea fiat mandatum fratrum ubi prelatus et decanus et maiores ecclesie nudis pedibus accincti lintheis lavent fratrum circumsedentium pedes, et cantetur interim antiphona, "Dominus Jesus postquam," cum reliquis antiphonis quæ ad hoc institute sunt in antiphonario Post hec, diaconus in albis, et subdiaconus, et ceroferarii in medium procedant, ubi diaconus legat in modum lectionis Evangelium secundum Johannem, "Ante diem festum Pasche," &c Interim a ministris ecclesie ponantur coram prelato et ceteris consedentibus mappe, et nebulo cum vino quasi ad cenandum Finita vero lectione post mandatum completum, statim prelatus dicat hanc orationem, "Adesto, Domine," &c

His peractis, statim sacerdos cum ministris et crucifero et ceroferariis scilicet in albis, comitante clero, ad altaria lavanda procedant, ubi prius aqua benedicta superinfundatur, laventque sacerdos et diaconus altaria cum ysopo et savina scilicet mixta, et deinde vinum superinfundatur   Dum hec fiunt canatur *R*, "Circumdederunt me," cum versiculo   Postea vero dicitur antiphona de Sancto cuiuscunque altare erit, et sacerdos subiungat versiculum cum oratione de eodem, &c   Hoc ordine fiat per singula altaria   Post hec vero bini et bini dicant completotorium privatim —[*York Missal,* 1 101]

Good Friday,

by the priest who celebrated what is still called
the Mass of the Presanctified ; the second he shut
up in its pix, and put along with the cross that
had just been kissed, within

The Sepulchre,

which always stood on the north side of the
chancel. This holy week sepulchre was almost
always a slight and temporary erection of wood,
hung with the best and richest palls of gold and
silver cloth, or costly silks, which could be found,
or had been bequeathed for the purpose. Usually
there stood within it a winged angel watching, as
it were, its little door ; and tapers burned, and
people prayed about it, day and night, from Good
Friday till early morn at Easter.[74] Sometimes, however, this tomb was made to be lasting, and built
of stone. Thus, as a work of art, and crowded
with sculptured watching angels and guarding
soldiers, it often lent no small beauty to the
(241) church wherein it stood, as may be witnessed

---

[74] Of this sepulchre, the following notices are found among the
accompts of St Nicholas' church, Great Yarmouth "A.D 1465.
Paid for setting up the sepulchre, drying the sepulchre's cloth ;
bearing the whip, for two pullies over the sepulchre, in the
chancel roof ; for taking down the sepulchre, for mending the
sepulchre, for mending an angel standing at the sepulchre ; for
dressing and watching the sepulchre, for tending the sepulchre's
lights."—Swinden, *Hist of Great Yarmouth*. 811

EASTER SEPULCHRE AT HAWTON

f om the examples which yet
a Hav n a, and other places,
vhisperings, wh t was the belie
of gone-by ages. H s the no
sought, in olden ti s
o that upon the a
of our Lord might
shown the reade[r]

The Kissing of t

n, as it was more g

The Creep

was done with pre
we have already d
Saxons. The way
used to go through
order touching th
nge of the cramp
nge to the Cros
documents[?]

On this sclem
that the people
a kind of pub
them by then
little bundl
to come and

from the examples which yet remain at Heckington, Hawton, and other places, and tell us, in low
whisperings, what was the belief, what the ritual
of gone-by ages. How the nobility of this land
sought, in olden times, to be buried at this spot,
so that, upon the slab over their graves, the body
of our Lord might rest at Easter, we have already
shown the reader.[75]

The Kissing of the Cross on Good Friday ·

or, as it was more generally called,

The Creeping to the Cross,

was done with precisely the same ceremonial as
we have already described among the Anglo-
Saxons. The way in which our Catholic kings
used to go through this day's ceremonies, or, "The
order touchinge their cominge to service, hallow-
inge of the crampe rings, and offeringe, and creep-
inge to the Crosse," is shown us in several existing
documents.[76]

On this solemn day of sadness, it would seem
that the people of their own free will underwent
a kind of public penance which was inflicted on
them by their parish priest, who smote with a
little bundle of rods the hands of those who chose
to come and outstretch them to him for that pur-

---

[75] Vol III. pp 76, 77
[76] *Northumberland Household Book,* 436

pose. To such a rite Sir Thomas More refers when he says :—"Tindall is as lothe, good tender pernell, to take a lyttle penaunce of the prieste, as the ladye was to come anye more to dyspelying that wepte even for tender heart twoo dayes after when she talked of it, that the priest had on good friday with the dyspelying rodde beaten her hard uppon her lylye white hands."

The purchase of these rods (242) for Good Friday, is noticed in some old church expenses thus :—For disseplynyng roddis, and nayles for the sepulchre, 2d.[77]

The service for Good Friday was, in fact, almost exactly such as had been followed among the Anglo-Saxons. The cross was crept to on bended knees, and kissed ; the Mass of the presanctified was celebrated ; and after even-song, which was said at the end of Mass, the celebrant put off his red chasuble, and along with another priest—both barefoot—carried the third reserved particle of the Blessed Eucharist from Maundy Thursday's con-secration, enclosed in a pix, and the cross that had just been kissed, to the sepulchre wherein he left them with lights burning around till Easter Sunday morning. The ceremonies in the York Missal are almost the very same as those we have described.[78]

---

[77] *Churchwarden's Accounts of St. Mary Hill, London,* A D 1510, in Nichols, *Illustrations, &c ,* 105.

[78] At the reading of the Passion, the altar-cloth was thus taken from off the altar. Non scindamus illam ; sed sortiamur de illa

(243) The Sarum rites for

(244) *Holy Saturday*

vary not a tittle from the olden ones : the new
fire, the paschal candle, the baptismal font, were

---

cuius sit   Ut scriptura impleretur   ¶ Hic distrahantur lin-
theamina super altare connexa —[*York Missal*, 1 102.]

The ceremony for kissing the cross was thus ordered. Orationibus completis, prelatus et ministri in revestiario discalceati
in albis tantum procedant super tapeta strata et in australi parte
chori sedeant super scannum substrato illis tapeto, et lintheo
super pulvinaria iniecto   Deinde vicarii duo in albis a dextra
parte altaris stolas suas coram se in modum crucis habentes nudis
pedibus super tapeta ab altari usque in chorum expansa proce-
dentes , et crucem coopertam cum cervicali superposito baiulantes
canant antiphonam "Popule meus "

Duo diaconi in albis, nudis pedibus, in medio ante ostium occidentale chori respondeant, ter genua flectendo, " Agyos o theos "

Chorus similiter ter genua flectendo, dicat antiphonam, " Sanctus Deus "

Postea dicti duo vicarii cum cruce aliquantulum progressi dicant
antiphonam, " Quia eduxi te," &c

Tandem duo vicarii intra ianuas australes chori super gradus
altiores stantes discooperta cruce dicant hanc antiphonam, " Ecce
lignum Crucis," &c

Chorus flexis genibus dicat " Ecce lignum Crucis," &c

Interim prelatus, et ministri, et decanus, cum reliquo clero
adorent crucem, alia antiphona interim canenda, " Tuam Crucem
adoramus, Domine," &c

Item dum chorus adorat, canatur hymnus,—

> " Crux fidelis inter omnes
> Arbor una nobilis," &c

¶ Dum populus adorat, canatur antiphona cum versu, " Dum
fabricator mundi," &c

Tandem adorata cruce baiulent eam duo vicarii usque ad locum
sepulchri , ubi prelatus eam accipiens incipiat has antiphonas, et
chorus finiat, " Super omnia ligna cedrorum," &c

Postea prelatus ponat flexis genibus crucem in sepulchro et
duos cereos accensos cum duobus urceis   Postea thurificet eam,

each, as they had heretofore been, hallowed. This may be seen from the monuments of our old and ever to be beloved ritual.

[The Church and clergy began to assume their festal appearance : the Mass was postponed till late : for at Eastertide it was not forgotten that the Vigil services belong properly to the night and not to the preceding day. The white albs and festive array are the precursors of what is to follow, and the best vestments are to be worn unless baptisms are to be held, in which case prudence dictates the wearing of second best.

The procession goes through the West door of the choir to a column on the south side of the nave for the blessing of the new fire : there is no cross, the censers have no burning coals, the candles are not lighted : a boy in a surplice,

---

et tunc erectus incipiat antiphonam, " Sepulto Domino signatum est monumentum," &c Chorus canendo finiat.

Deinde prelatus casulatus, et ministri in albis in revestiario calciati accedant ad gradus ante altare, dictisque " Confiteor " et " Misereatur," et absolutione, cum precibus, et oratione " Aufer a nobis," more solito prelatus accipiat in armariolo calicem cum corpore Domini quod a pridie servabatur ; et precedentibus duobus torchiis accensis usque ad altare baiulet Sacrificioque super altare collocato, vinum aqua mixtum non sanctificatum in calicem ponat et thurificet, ablutisque manibus redeat ad altare pretermissisque, " In spiritu humilitatis,' &c , et facta conversione ad populum, dicat statim mediocri voce, " Per omnia sæcula," &c.; " Pater noster," &c , " Libera nos, quæsumus," &c. In qua oratione dividat corpus Domini, sicut fieri solet aliis diebus.

Hac enim die sacrificium non offertur sacramentaliter sed sumitur altera die oblatum, prelato autem cum silentio communicato, ut premittitur, cum ceteris qui communicare voluerint —[York Missal, i. 105-108]

carrying a candle fastened upon a pole [see illustra-
tion], follows the Holy Water, and the rest
follow. The new fire is struck out of flint
and steel, and is blessed : from it are lighted
the candle upon the pole and a second candle
in case of accident, and the coals of the
censer are kindled. The choir returns to
the chancel singing the hymn *Inventor rutili*,
and the blessing of the Paschal Candle
follows : the incense is fastened in it, and
the candle is censed, and from it are lighted
all the candles in the Church.] [79]

In many of our larger churches for the

Paschal Candle,

blessed with so much form this day, the candlestick was seven-branched, made of laton or brass,
so that it could be easily set up or taken to pieces
again, and of itself a beautiful work of art, spreading out its six limb-like arms with their tapers
over a wide space of the presbytery. It was so
fashioned that the candle reached almost to the
vaulting of the roof : from the seventh or upright
branch in the middle, arose a tall thick piece of
wood, sometimes round sometimes square, but
always, as it would seem, painted to look like
wax. This wooden imitation of a candle, which
rested on the socket of the middle branch, was

---

[79] [*Use of Sarum*, xix. vol. i. p. 144, printed in full here by Dr.
Rock (pp. 245–248) since it was not in his text of the Consuetudinary.]

called—it is not known why—the "Judas of the paschal," at the top of which was let in the true wax candle, which was often not round but (245) square.[60] To light it, as well as, no doubt, to carry off the smoke, they contrived at Durham Cathedral an opening in that part of the ceiling just above it.[81]

[Then follow the reading of the lessons and the singing of the Tracts with their collects, and then the septiform Litany, and the quinqueform Litany already mentioned (p. 100), and so the Blessing of the font is reached and the baptisms, if any one is present to be baptized. The metrical Litany *Rex sanctorum* links this to the Vigil Mass :[82] after the *Kyrie*, on this day as well as]

---

[60] Item, paid for twelve *Judicis*, to stand with the tapers, 2s.—*Illustrations*, 9

Mem., that the *Judas* of the pastal, i e the tymbre, that the wax of the pastel is driven upon, weigheth 7 lb —*Ibid*, 107

[81] *Ancient Monuments and Rites*, &c , 9

[82] As at Salisbury, so did they at York for all these ceremonies. In Sabbato sancto Pasche, ignis de berillo vel de cilice exceptus in occidentali parte ecclesie accendatur. Prelatus vero post nonam decantatam sacris vestibus capa alba serica indutus, precedentibus ministris in albis cum textu et cum cruce appenso et thurifero cum thuribulo vacuo, et cum cerco haste affixo qui ab aliquo maiori debet ferri et ceroferariis cum cereis non accensis et puero cum aqua benedicta ad ignem benedicendum procedat maioribus ecclesie proximo prelatum sequentibus et inferioribus subsequentibus Stanteque in ordine clero, prelatus cum ministris stans iuxta ignem dicat legendo · "Dominus vobiscum," &c ; "Deus qui filium tuum angularem scilicet lapidem," &c , "Domine sancte pater omnipotens eterne Deus benedi✠cere et sanctifi✠care digneris istum ignem," &c.

Benedictio incensi

. "Oremus. Veniat, omnipotens Deus, super hoc incensum larga tue benedi✠ctionis infusio," &c

(249) upon Whitsun eve, at the moment the officiating priest sang the first words of the *Gloria in excelsis Deo*, the bells (250) rang out a full peal, and all the canons and clerks who were chanting in the choir, knelt down for a second, took off the black choir-copes and arose clad in their surplices ; and vested thus white came to church and performed the choir duty, all through the Easter

---

Deinde aspergatur ignis a prelato aqua benedicta, et impleto thuribulo de igne benedicto, et incenso benedicto a prelato imposito thurificetur ignis a prelato   Postea accensis cereis videlicet tam cereis a ceroferariis deportatis quam cereo haste affixo de igne benedicto, redeat in chorum processio ex parte boriali, et prelatus cum ministris et maioribus ecclesie processionem sequatur, ceroferariis canentibus hunc hymnum, "Inventor rutili dux bone luminis," &c   Sequitur benedictio cerei Paschalis a diacono dalmaticato facienda, prelato capato interim in sede sua residente. "Exultet iam angelica turba," &c —[*York Missal*, 1 109]

Postea septem pueri in suppelliciis vel in albis in choro letaniam hanc cantent, choro eis alterna respondente

Deinde quinque diaconi vel subdiaconi in suppelliciis hanc continuo subiungant letaniam, et cum dicitur "Sancta Dei genitrix," procedat processio ad fontes benedicendos precedentibus puero cum aqua benedicta et ceroferariis et crucifero, et duobus diaconibus in suppelliciis cum crismate et oleo, et subdiacono cum textu et diacono in albis, et his qui letaniam canunt in medio processionis subsequentibus· prelatus vero capatus cum capellano et baiulo suo crucis et duobus ceroferariis sequatur processionem —[*Ibid*, 119]

Deinde rector chori incipiat "Kyrie leyson," &c

Deinde prelatus cum vii vel v diaconibus dalmaticatis et totidem subdiaconibus tunica festive paratis precedentibus ceroferariis et ij thuribulis introeat ad altare, factaque confessione et dictis "Kyrieleyson," ut supra, prelatus incipiat "Gloria in excelsis Deo," quod dum canitur, classicum pulsetur. Oratio, "Deus qui hanc sanctissimam noctem," &c   ¶ Ad Colossen , "Fratres, si consurrexistis," &c.

Duo vicarii in albis cantant "Alleluia"   Quo incepto, chorus nigras cappas exuant et missam in suppelliciis expleant —[*Ibid*, 123]

holidays till Low Sunday. This casting aside of the black cope, was meant to teach them, not merely to drop the livery of sorrow, but to put on the new man.

Connected with this change of dress by the clergy, was a domestic custom thus described in the Liber Festivalis :—

In die pasche.

Good friends ye shall know well that this day is called in many places God's Sunday. Know well that it is the manner in every place of worship at this day to do the fire out of the hall, and the black winter brands, and all thing that is foul with smoke shall be done away, and there the fire was shall be gaily arrayed with fair flowers, and strewed with green rushes all about, showing a great ensample to all Christian people, like as they make clean their houses to the sight of the people, in the same wise ye should cleanse your souls, doing away the foul brenning (burning) sin of lechery, put all these away, and cast out all thy smoke, dust, and strew in your souls flowers of faith and charity, and thus make your souls able to receive your Lord God at the feast of Easter— (*Deponentes omnem maliciam*) and put away all malice and all sorrow, for right as ye will suffer nothing in your house that stinketh and savoureth evil wherewith ye may be deceived, right so Christ, when he cometh into your house of your souls, and he find there any stink of wrath, envy, or any other (251) deadly sin, he will not abide there, and anon he goeth his way. And then cometh the fiend in and bideth there.[83]

Just before the first streak of dawn upon

Easter Morning,

the church was lighted up, and thither every body hastened ere one toll had been given on the bells. Two of the upper priests, accompanied by the acolytes and the thurifer, and followed by the whole clergy, walked to the sepulchre, and having fumed it with incense on their bended knees, most reverently took out the pix which held the body of our Lord, and carried it to the high altar, where they hung it up within the cup or dove beneath the canopy. All the bells then rang out a gladsome peal at once. Going back again with the same attendants, these two priests next took out of the sepulchre the crucifix which had been kissed, and buried there on Good Friday. Holding this cross between them in both their arms, they entoned the anthem *Christus resurgens ex mortuis*, and then began the procession to some small altar, at the foot of which they laid the crucifix down upon a cushion ; and the clergy and people came or 'crept,' as they did on Good Friday, and kissed it. This was an act of devotion

---

[83] Fol xxxviii.

which our Catholic countrymen well understood,
and warmly loved ; and our old writers often
spoke of it.   Langland sketches what once was
an English Easter morn thus :—

"Men rang to þe resurreccioun · and with þat ich awakede,
And kallyd kytte my wyf · and kalote my doughter,
A-rys, and go reuerence · godes resurreccioun, (252)
And creop on kneos to þe cryos · and cusse hit for a Iuwel,   .
For godes blesside body hit bar for oure bote,
And hit a-fereþ þe feonde · for such is þe myghte,
May no gryshche gost · glyde þer hit shadeweþ ! " [84]

By the cross, as on Good Friday, there was a
basin into which each one dropped his offering ;
from the *Northumberland Household Book*, we
find that " My Lords offeringe accustomede yerely
upon Ester day in the morning when his Lord-
shippe crepith the Cros after the Resurrection,"
was iiij [85]

In some large churches, however, this ceremony
was done after another way.   Instead of a pix
in the usual shape, they had, for the occasion,
a beautiful golden image of our Lord, standing
upright and holding the flag of the cross in his
left hand.   The breast of this figure was so
hallowed, that the blessed Eucharist could be
shut up inside by a rock-crystal door through
which the sacrament was seen ; and this image,
enclosing the body of our Lord, was put, together

---

[84] *Piers Ploughman*, Passus xxi., 472–479 [ed Skeat, 395]
[85] *Ut s* 335.

with the cross, on Good Friday, into the sepulchre.
"There was in the abbye church of Duresme a
verye solemne service uppon Easter day, be-
tweene three and four of the clocke in the
morninge, in honour of the Resurrection, where
two of the oldest monkes came to the sepulchre,
beinge sett upp upon Good Friday, after the passion,
all covered with red velvett and embrodered with
gold, and then did sence it, either monke with
a pair of silver sencers sitting on theire knees
before the sepulchre   Then they both rising came
to the sepulchre, out of the (253) which, with
great devotion and reverence, they tooke a marvelous beautifull image of our Saviour, representing the resurrection, with a crosse in his hand, in
the breast whereof was enclosed in bright christall
the holy Sacrament of the altar, through the which
christall the Blessed host was conspicuous to the
beholders.   Then, after the elevation of the said
picture, carryed by the said two monkes uppon
a faire velvett cushion, all embrodered, singinge
the anthem of *Christus resurgens*, they brought
it to the high altar, settinge that on the midst
thereof, whereon it stood, the two monkes kneel-
inge on theire knees before the altar and senceing
it all the time that the rest of the whole quire
was in singinge the aforesaid anthem of *Christus
resurgens*. The which anthem beinge ended, the
two monkes took up the cushions and the picture
from the altar, supportinge it betwixt them,

proceeding, in procession, from the high altar
to the south quire dore, where there was four
antient gentlemen belonginge to the prior, appointed to attend theire cominge, holdinge upp
a most rich canopye of purple velvett, tached
round about with redd silke and gold fringe;
and at everye corner did stand one of these gentlemen to beare it over the said image, with the Holy
Sacrament, carried by two monkes round about
the church, the whole quire waitinge uppon it
with goodly torches and great store of other lights
. . . till they came to the high altar againe, whereon they did place the said image, there to remaine
untill the Ascension day." [86]   One of such images
was bequeathed by cardinal Beaufort to Wells
cathedral.[87]   The cathedral of Lincoln possessed
" an image of our Saviour silver and gilt, standing upon six lions, void in the breast, for the
sacrament for Easter-day, having a beral before
and a diadem behind, with a cross in hand, weigh-
ing thirty-seven ounces." [88]

From Easter morning, till the Ascension,

A Cross of Crystal,

or beril, was carried in all processions ; just as
the blood-red wooden cross had been borne

---

[86] *Ancient Monuments, Rites, &c , of Durham*, 10

[87] Unam ymaginem argenteam deauratam resurrectionis Dominicæ stantem super viride terragium amilasatum, habentem
birillum in pectore pro corpore Dominico imponendo, ponderis
trojani octuaginta et (254) quindecim unc' —*Mon Angl*, ii 280

[88] *Ibid*, viii 1279

throughout Lent. [89] This 'cross of christall,'
is noticed in the Easter morning's procession,
at Durham; [90] and others of the kind are often
found mentioned in old church-plate inventories:
Lincoln cathedral had its 'cross of chrystal with
a crucifix, silver and gilt—with a lamb in the
back,' &c, and a 'cross of berall and copper
with a pike of iron;' [91] and among cardinal
Wolsey's plate, was 'oone parte crystall gainy-
shid,' with silvar and gilte waying clerly beside
the cristall cxxviij oz. [92]

Every day through Easter week, a solemn procession led by no less than four rulers of the
choir and (255) accompanied by the holy oils,
walked, after even song, to the newly hallowed
baptismal font, to fume it with incense and make
a station at its side. All, but the boy who carried
the book, were vested in albs. In these as well
as in all other processions on high festivals, the

---

[89] ¶ De cruce sine vexillo

In ecclesia Sarum et secundum Ordinale Sarum, nunquam ad
processionem portatur crux cum vexillo, sicut habetur in multis
ecclesiis

Sed in tempore paschali portatur crux de [var cum] berillo vsque
ad Ascensionem Domini —*Crede Michi* [Wordsworth, *Tracts of C
Maydeston* (H.B.S.), p 53]

[90] *Ancient Monuments*, &c., 11.   [91] *Mon Angl.*, viii 1280

[92] Gutch, *Collect. Curiosa*, ii. 323   York minster had Una crux
de rubeo jaspide ornata cum argento deaurato, cum petris infixis
in pede ligneo depicto .   Item una crux de christallo cum
pulchro pede bene sculpta, &c (*Mon Angl*, viii 1204). These
were short crosses to stand upon the altar it is likely the red
jasper one served for Lent , the one of crystal, for Paschal
time.

year through, a number of banners, each with
its own device, were borne.   On

Ascension Day,

however, the one of the Lion went first; after it

came all the smaller banners, and, last of all, the
image of the dragon, as is shown in this woodcut
from the scarce (256) illustrated edition of the
Sarum Processional, printed A.D. 1528. This was

meant to say how Christ our Lord, the lion of the tribe of Juda, had, by his uprising into heaven, won his last fight with the devil the mighty dragon.[93] On

Whitsunday,

at undern song tide or tierce—that hour of the day when the Holy Ghost came visibly down upon the first believers at Jerusalem—and before the High Mass, a band of priests, with burning thuribles in their hands, went and stood at the altar's foot, to begin the hymn *Veni Creator Spiritus.* After kneeling lowly down and kissing the ground, they arose, and going up all together to the altar, fumed it with incense.[94]

Another peculiarity of the Salisbury ritual, was the way in which, upon All Saints' day, or

---

[93] See Wordsworth, *Salisbury Ceremonies and Processions*, p 193 In the Windsor inventory (A.D. 1385) mention is made of Unus draco, et unus leo pro processione in Rogationibus cum sex hastis et quatuor vexilla nova, cum imaginibus poncionatis —*Mon Angl*, viii 1367

[94] In die Penthecostes incipiat executor officij horam terciam ad gradum chori, et tunc procedant cum ceteris sacerdotibus thuribulis precedentibus ad gradum altaris Et ibi omnes simul incipiant hymnum *Veni Creator Spiritus*, genu flectendo, et postquam inceperint terram osculando et genu flectendo, cum surgentes thurificent altare

℣ Chorus vero cum genu flexione respondeat osculando formulas, et ex vtraque parte simul totum versum stando prosequatur

¶ Nota *stando* Postquam sacerdotes thurificauerint altare omnes simul osculentur illud. Et sic faciendum est in quolibet versu Crede Michi [Wordsworth, *Tracts of C Maydeston* (H B S), p 60]

(257) *All Hallows,*

the eighth response at matins used to be sung.
Five boys—emblematic of those five wise maidens
in the parable—robed in surplices, and each with
an amice, veil-like, drawn over his head, and
holding a lighted taper in his hand, came forth,
and, standing at the steps between the choir
and the presbytery, sang that response—*Audivi
vocem de cœlo dicentem: Venite omnes virgines
sapientissimæ, &c.*[95]

Such, reader, are the chief though not all the
beauties of our dear old Sarum rite, which, after
all, was so very Anglo-Saxon in its leading features.
To love those olden ways in which our fathers
for ages trod, is what has been told us and taught
us by some of the highest holiest men who have
lived at different times and various places in
God's one catholic everlasting Church. How St.
Charles Borromeo strove and wrought successfully
to keep up the liturgy and ritual as they were
left by his predecessor, the great St. Ambrose;
how Cardinal Ximenes preserved, at Toledo, the
Mozarabic service—are facts well known. Benedict XIII., while Abp. of Benevento, among other
revivals of forgotten or neglected rites, and other
services rendered to the liturgy, brought back into
use at his cathedral the ceremony of washing the
altar with water and wine, on Maundy Thursday,

---

[95] [*Use of Sarum,* lm. (55), vol 1. p 125]

for which he is much praised by Cardinal Borgia.[96] The Holy See, nay the Church herself, has always acknowledged the lawfulness of keeping up local rites and praiseworthy customs in different countries. The council of Trent, *Sess. XXIV.*, in its *Decretum de Reformatione Matrimonii, cap.* i., says:—Si quae provinciae aliis, ultra praedictas, laudabilibus (258) consuetudinibus et cæremoniis hac in re utuntur, eas omnino retineri sancta Synodus vehementer optat. For the holy See, and the Roman Congregation of Rites, Gavanti, than whom a more trustworthy witness could not be found, assures us that:—Proprios mores unaquæque habet ecclesia et laudabiles consuetudines, quas non tolli a cæremoniali Romano, neque a rubricis Breviarii, sæpius declaravit Sacra rituum Congregatio.

That a difference in her ritual could nowise hurt the Church's oneness of belief and teaching, has been ably shown by Father De Azevedo, one of the brightest lights which shone in that learned Association for liturgical studies, formed and often presided over in person by Benedict XIV.[97]

---

[96] *De Cruce Vatic*, 74

[97] This intimate friend of that Roman pontiff says —

Tantum abest, ut veteri assentiamur quærelæ, in Ecclesia, quæ unicam fidem profitetur, tot officii recitandi institutiones nequaquam esse ferendas, ut ipsam iis varietatibus, tanquam variis gemmis, et monilibus exornatam, variaque supellectili divitem confidenter prædicemus Christi sponsa est, adeoque pretiosum exposcit indumentum multiformi colorum nitore distinctum. Quid autem vestes multicolores nisi varietas sacrorum rituum quibus ecclesiastici viri Deo laudes persolvunt ? Unam quidem Ecclesiam

(259) Between the Anglo-Saxon and the Sarum rite there was but small difference: this latter bore about it a strong sister likeness to the first, so that, while looking upon the one, we, after a way, behold both. In its features and its whole stature, we gaze, as it were, upon our fathers in their religious life; we read their ghostly annals, through a thousand years and more, as a Catholic people. It tells us what men and women, old and young, high and low, then did and must have done to have got for this land of England that sweet name, among the nations, of "the island of Saints." When we take a remembrance of this liturgy with us into the tall cathedral and the lowly parish church, those dear old walls that catholic hands built are again quickened into ritual life; we see the lighted tapers round the shrine, or circling about the Blessed Sacrament hung above the altar; we catch the chant, we witness the procession as it halts to kneel and pray beneath the rood-loft; to the inward eye, the bishop with his seven deacons and as many subdeacons, is standing at the altar sacrificing, and as he uplifts our divine Lord in the Eucharist, for the worship of the kneeling throng,

---

universalem et orthodoxam confitemur, sed unius corporis plura membra diversa obire munia in unum finem tendentia quis nescit? Praeterea, uti gentium, ac nationum mores diversi sunt, ita ad actus religionis, cultumque Divinum diversis utuntur institutis, quæ, salva Christianæ fidei integritate, vix possent ab eis vel omitti, vel auferri —De Azevedo, *De Divin. Off et Missæ Sacrif. Exercitationes*, Venetiis, 1783, 1 38, Exercise x

we hear the bell toll forth slowly, majestically.
From the southern porch-door, to the brackets on
the eastern chancel wall for the B. V. Mary's and
the patron saint's images, every thing has its own
meaning and speaks its especial purpose, as intended by the use of Sarum. Can these rites
never again be witnessed in England? They
may. Let us hope then—let us pray for their
restoration, so that England may once more gaze
upon her olden liturgy ; let us hope and pray
that her children, in looking upon, may all ac-
knowledge their true mother, and love and heed
the teaching the while they study the ritual of
the Church of our Fathers

FINIS

POSTSCRIPT

SINCE Dr. Rock began this work in 1849 much
has happened in the liturgical world, and the aim
of this brief postscript is to add some notes bearing
upon the development of his subject since his
time. A great deal has been done by the editors
in revising his notes and giving more modern
references without changing anything but minute
details, and every page of the new edition contains alterations of this sort, which do not alter
Dr. Rock's work, but make it more serviceable to
its new generation of readers. Since his time
many MS. texts have become available in print,
and many rare incunabula have been reprinted;
for example, the whole set of Sarum Service-
books is now available, the Leofric Missal has
been finely edited, the Henry Bradshaw Society
has supplied editions of the Winchester Troper,
the Maydeston Tracts, &c., the Surtees Society has
re-issued York Service-books, and so on: thus
many of the rare sources, on which Rock was the
first to draw, are now accessible to an increasing
public.

To a certain extent this means that more

accurate information is now to be had: thus
Rock's account of the Sarum Consuetudinary is
now superseded (vol. i. p. 3), his edition of Beroldus has given place to Magistretti's new edition
(vol. 1. p. 433), his remarks about the Penitential
of Theodore need to be corrected by more modern
researches of Stubbs in *Councils and Ecclesiastical Documents*, Schmitz in his *Bussbucher* and
others (vol. iii. p. 190, a note which is chiefly
omitted in the new edition as being misleading).
Again, his reference to the Codex of Ceolfrid
needs now to be completed by a mention of the
identification of this MS. with the celebrated
Codex Amiatinus now at Florence (vol. i. pp. 285,
286): his treatment of the Guilds must be supple-
mented by such books as those of Toulmin Smith,
Gross, Brentano, &c., and the kindred subject of
the Mystery plays has been illuminated by the
publishing of the Townley series of religious
dramas, and of the plays represented at York,
Coventry, Chester, to which Rock makes a passing
reference (vol. 11. p. 425).

Again, much of the controversial matter has
become out of date: indeed in vol. 1. parts of a
voluminous dispute with Mr. Maskell conducted
in the notes have been omitted in this edition;
but there remain scattered up and down the
volumes more isolated remarks which have been
left standing though they are no longer appropriate; such as that upon the cut of the shrine

of St. Edward the Confessor in vol. iii. p. 383, and others as to the practice of the English Church.

If the learned author were alive now and wished to find examples of the old English ways which

Modern English Chasuble

were so dear to him he would have to go to the Churches of the Establishment rather than to those of the Roman Catholic body. There at any rate he would find that his eloquent plea for the revival of " our old majestic chasuble, with its beautiful symbolism, the apparelled alb, the full

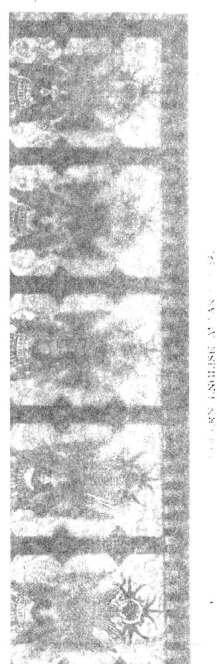

GOLDEN ENGLISH ALTAR - 153.

of St. Edward the Confessor in vol. iii. p. 383, and others as to the practice of the English Church.

If the learned author were alive now and wished to find examples of the old English ways which

Modern English Chasuble

were so dear to him he would have to go to the Churches of the Establishment rather than to those of the Roman Catholic body. There at any rate he would find that his eloquent plea for the revival of "our old majestic chasuble, with its beautiful symbolism, the apparelled alb, the full

MODERN ENGLISH ALTAR CLOTH

flowing surplice" (vol. i. p. 343), has not been
without fruit. If he desired to find the successors
of the English nuns whose embroidery was famous
throughout Europe (vol. ii. pp. 274, 275), he would

Modern English Cope

have to look in Anglican convents; the chasuble,
cope and altar cloth here figured give some idea
of their work, while the mitre is an excellent
proof of the rivalry in zeal and skill which is kept

up by many ladies living busy lives in the world
but none the less eager to bear their part in the
adornment of the House and worship of Almighty
God.   These illustrations of modern vestments,

Modern English Mitre

and again the picture of a modern pastoral staff,
which represents another class of the ecclesiastical
ornaments of to-day, show a tangible result of
Rock's labours and influence; and they are but

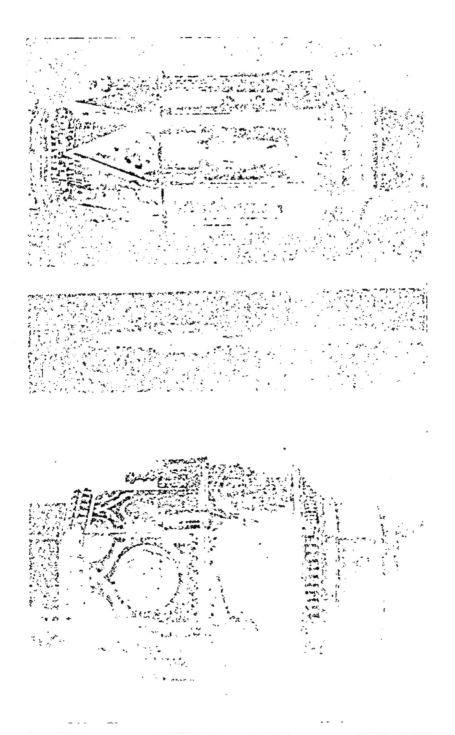

up by many ladies living busy lives in the world but none the less eager to bear their part in the adornment of the House and worship of Almighty God. These illustrations of modern vestments,

Modern English Mitre

and again the picture of a modern pastoral staff, which represents another class of the ecclesiastical ornaments of to-day, show a tangible result of Rock's labours and influence; and they are but

HIGH ALTAR IN LENT ARRAY

page 303

a few specimens of a mass of work done on the
old English lines which was taken up later,
under the influence of his book. The same
may be said to a large extent of the modern

revivals of ancient ... the arrangement of
churches. The ancient array can now be
seen revived in a great number of English
churches, if not ...
obscuring the wh... ...

ALTAR IN LENT ARK.

a few specimens of a mass of work done on the
old English lines, which was taken up largely
under the influence of his book. The same
may be said to a large extent of the modern

Egmanton Church

revivals of ancient ways in the arrangement of
churches. The ancient Lent array can now be
seen revived in a growing number of English
churches, if not in its full form with the Lent veil
obscuring the whole of the sanctuary, yet at least

in a degree which produces the sad and almost dreary effect that reigned in the churches in the old days through the early weeks of Lent until Passiontide came in with its red glory of triumph and its ruddy anticipation of the Passion. The ancient pyx can be seen hung up where the reservation of the Blessed Sacrament is conceded, the ancient screens are not only restored but are made the models of new rood-lofts, where the sign of our Redemption stands as of old, and the crucifix is the middle point between the faithful in the nave and the living presence of their Lord vouchsafed to them at the altar.

The researches which Dr. Rock instituted have not only proved fruitful in these ways: they have led to more developed inquiry, which has to a certain extent carried things past the point reached by him. As to ornaments, for example, many new inventories have been published, notably those of Canterbury by Legg and Hope, those of Salisbury by Wordsworth and others not cited by Rock from other cathedral, monastic, collegiate, and parochial churches; and these publications, which are widely scattered, have now been indexed, and thus made more readily accessible to students.[1]

The question of the English liturgical colours has been elaborately investigated, and the results are summarised in Mr Hope's paper in the Trans-

[1] *Bibliographie générale des Inventaires imprimés* MM. de Mély and E Bishop (1892)

actions of the St. Paul's Ecclesiological Society.
The pre-reformation ornaments have been handled
in a similar summary—Mr. Micklethwaite's Alcuin
Tract on " The Ornaments of the Rubric." With
regard to the history and development of the
vestments, more serious corrections have been
made, and more modern works need to be con-
sulted by the student; such as those of Braun,[2]
Magistretti,[3] Grisar,[4] Wilpert,[5] or the summary in
Lowrie's *Christian Art and Archæology* (ch. vi.),
or Duchesne's *Early Christian Worship* (ch. xi.).
In particular the section with regard to the pallium
(vol. ii. p. 126) needs much correction in view of
recent research.

There are many points which show that Dr.
Rock was more familiar with the customs of the
later middle ages than with those of the earlier:
for example, he says (vol. i p. 101) that an
illumination of the crucifix " always preceded the
Canon of the Mass in all old MSS " : this is true
in a sense of later mediæval books—though even
in their case there would be many exceptions—but
not at all true of the earliest MSS. In them the
Canon begins at the versicles before the Preface ;[6]

---

[2] *Die Priesterlichen Gewänder* (Freiburg, 1897), *Die Pontificalen Gewänder* (Freiburg, 1898)

[3] *Delle vesti ecclesiastiche in Milano* (Milan, 1897)

[4] *Analecta Romana*, ch. xii (Rome, 1899).

[5] *Un capitolo di storia del vestiario* (Rome, 1898, 1899).

[6] See *Gelasian Sacr*, 695, *Missale Francorum*, 692 ; and even the *Leofric Missal*, p 60

and rightly so, for this is the true opening of the *Anaphora*, and it was a liturgical blunder to alter it. For these reasons the earliest ornament to the Canon was given at this point: for any such decoration we must go down to the Carolingian days when, with the advent of the new "Gregorian" Sacramentary a new custom came in: the *Anaphora* was now placed in a prominent position in the volume, and soon attracted to it the attention of the miniaturists, who, up till then, seemed to have confined it either to special ornamental pages or else to the title-pages of the various books of the Gelasian Sacramentary.[7] They now developed the glorification of initials, and principally of the V or V D occurring at *Vere Dignum*, the beginning of the Pieface: more rarely it is the P of the *Per omnia secula* before the Preface that is glorified, or an independent miniature is inserted At a later date, and to a less degree at first, attention was given to the T of *Te igitur*, which now began to be reckoned the opening words of the Canon, and the T is converted into a crucifix in the eighth century MS. at Paris known as the Sacramentary of Gellone.

From that time onward the custom spread, but for a long time yet the T in many MSS. was little —if at all—adorned, or was far less decorated

---

[7] See the facsimiles of Delisle, *Memoire sur d'Anciens Sacramentaires*, and Ebner, *Quellen*, p 430, &c.

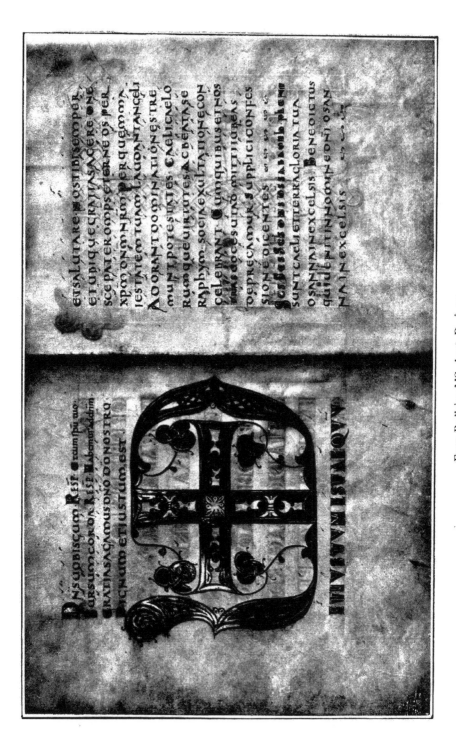

From Bodleian MS. Auct. D., i. 20

than the V D while an elaboration of the letters
was a far more common method of adornment
than the transformation of the T into a crucifix,
which is rare till the end of the tenth century.
So the appearance of this sign here belongs to
the later middle ages, and synchronises with the

Beginning of the Canon, Fourteenth Century

development of the doctrinal fashion of setting
the Sacrifice of the Eucharist in connexion with
the Passion to the exclusion of the Resurrection,
Ascension and heavenly priesthood of Christ.
The illustration on the opposite page from a
Sacramentary of the ninth century shows one
of the transitional stages: the V D is set in

than the V D ; while an elaboration of the letters
was a far more common method of adornment
than the transformation of the T into a crucifix,
which is rare until the end of the tenth century.
So the appearance of this sign here belongs to
the later middle ages, and synchronises with the

The Beginning of the Canon, Fourteenth Century

development of the doctrinal fashion of setting
the Sacrifice of the Eucharist in connexion with
the Passion, to the exclusion of the Resurrection,
Ascension, and heavenly priesthood of Christ.
The illustration on the opposite page from a
Sacramentary of the ninth century shows one
of the transitional stages: the V D is still the

chief illumination, but the T has begun to be glorified, for it may be seen showing through the vellum
of the right-hand page of the two reproduced.

At a later stage still the crucifix became independent of the T of *Te igitur* and was relegated
to the page facing it, and the T began to de-
velop afresh, and such adornments were given to
it as that reproduced on p. 307. It is with these
later stages that Dr. Rock shows himself to have
been more familiar than with the earlier

Again, a more modern writer would be too
cautious to speak of the Mozarabic Liturgy as
having been framed by St. Isidore (vol. i. p. 105);
he would probably give as author of the *Micrologus* not Ivo of Chartres (vol. i. p. 102), but
Bernold of Constance:[8] he would have pointed
to the use of the *Ave Maria* text as the Offertory
for Wednesday in the December Embertide according to the Gregorian arrangement, not at the
fourth Sunday in Advent, for that Sunday was
destitute of a solemn service of its own till a much
later date than that of St. Gregory (vol. iii. pp.
315, 316)· he would not have committed himself to the statement that the cross always stood
upon the altar (vol. i. p. 267), for mediæval altars
comparatively rarely had crosses set on them, and
the custom of placing one there has come from
the processional cross being set at the back of the

---

[8] *Revue Benedictine*, xii. (1895), p 395.

altar after the procession before Mass. It was far more common to have the crucifixion represented on the reredos or superfrontal.[9]

In other cases Dr. Rock knows the Roman Missal better than the old English rite. else he would not have spoken as he did of the *Lavabo* (vol. iii p. 129); for the verses *Lavabo inter innocentes* were not said at that point in the English rite, as he points out (vol iv. p. 150), but the prayer *Munda me domine;* and the ceremony was known in England as the " Lavatory," not the *Lavabo* Nor would he have spoken so confidently of a shelf being set upon English altars at the end of the fifteenth century to carry not only the candlesticks, but crucifix and even flower-vases (vol. i. p. 238, n. 58). The existence of the last at such a date is so far unsupported, the crucifix was rare, and the shelf is a matter of the keenest controversy among experts.[10] In the same note his statement that frontals should be of the same colour as the vestments is certainly not always borne out by the pictures, and the demand for similar identity between frontal and frontlet is not always supported by the ancient inventories.[11] The identification of the " Jesus Mass " (vol. iii. p. 113) with the Mass of the Five Wounds is another

---

[9] See the altars in *Alcuin Club Collections*, vols 1 and 11.

[10] *Alcuin Club Tracts*, 1 "The Ornaments of the Rubric," by J. T. Micklethwaite, 23, 63

[11] See for example the Lincoln inventory of 1536 in Dugdal *Monasticon*, vi. 1286.

case in point: the term properly denotes the *Missa de nomine Jesu*, which was a common votive Mass before the festival of " The most sweet name of Jesus " began in England in the latter half of the fifteenth century.

Sometimes, on the contrary, Dr. Rock makes a distinction between English and foreign custom which is not legitimate : thus he says, speaking of the Gabriel, or Ave, bell, that " the midday bell was never rung in England " (vol. iii. p. 339).

Prayers, however, are prescribed in the Primers to be said " at the tolling of the Ave bell at none for a memory and remembrance of the passion and death of Christ," some Responds, the Passion Collect *Domine Jesu Christe, fili Dei vivi, qui pro salute mundi*, and the Lord's Prayer. These were no doubt to be added to the usual devotions of that hour, and the ordinary custom is there thus laid down :—

" Every day in the morning after iij tollings of the Ave bell say iij times the whole salutation of our Lady, Ave Maria : that is to say, at vi the klock in the morning iij Ave Maria, at xij the klock at none iij Ave Maria, and at vj the klock at even."

The devotions are thus prescribed .—

" This prayer shall be said at the tolling of the Ave Bell. *Suscipe verbum virgo Maria* . . . *Ave:* say this iij times. And afterward say this collect following : ℣ *Dilexisti justitiam*. . . .

R̸ *Propterea unxit. . .   Or. Deus qui de beatæ Mariæ virginis utero. . . . Pater Noster. Ave."* [12]

The indulgences attached were great, and these were made the excuse for the prohibition of "the knolling of the Aves after service and at other times" by the Injunctions of A.D. 1538 [13]

Various subjects less technically liturgical are also so handled as to make a word of caution necessary. Ecclesiology has had much to say since Dr. Rock's time on the subject of Leper Windows, Ankret's cells, and Low Side windows (vol. iii. p. 118).[14] Antiquarians have disputed much as to the relics of St. Cuthbert (vols. i. p. 415, ii. p. 303), about which Dr. Rock himself does not seem to have had a consistent opinion. Anglo-Saxon scholars have discussed at length the meaning of Alfred's Æstel (vol. i. p. 292) since Dr. Rock's time as well as before, and equally without coming to a decisive conclusion : a clearer point, and one in which it seems clear that Rock is in error, is in reference to the Belts of Pater-nosters of which he speaks (vol. iii. pp. 5, 7). The word Beltidum was explained by Spelman as meaning a rosary; but the latest editors of the Acts of the Council have much more

---

[12] Hoskins, *Primers*, 126.

[13] Burnet, *Hist. Reform.*, Record No. xi of Part 1 Book 3

[14] Valuable papers are to be found in *St Paul's Eccles Soc Trans.*, and in *Archæologia Aeliana*, parts 56, 57 (Newcastle-on-Tyne).

probability on their side in referring it to the
seven tunes of bell-ringing, *i.e.* Bel-tidum.[15]

Attention has already been called to the curious
mistake (vol. i. p. 47) by which the opening woodcut
of the Gradual was taken to represent a miracle of

Ad te levavi animam meam

the Holy Sacrament instead of being a symbolical
representation of the opening words *Ad te levavi
animam meam.* The miniature here reproduced
shows the same idea, less magnificently executed,
but more unmistakeable since there is no altar
represented, and the figure is not that of a priest

---

[15] Haddan and Stubbs, *Councils,* iii. 585.

saying Mass; and moreover, the pictuie adorns the A of the *Ad te levavi* Introit of the First Sunday in Advent.

Enough of this ungenerous task of picking holes in a book which in its day was a fine monument of erudition, and of so solid a structure that it is of great value still. It might easily have been enlarged and supplied with further notes, references, and illustrations, both literary and pictorial: but this was not the scope of the new edition; the task of the editors has been the less onerous one of reproducing Dr. Rock's work with some greater fulness in references, some additional illustiations, &c., to which (in nearly all cases) he called attention; and their best tribute to the scholarship of their author lies in the fact that this postscript of typical emendanda and corrigenda can be as short as it is.

INDEX

ABDINGHOFF Abbey, I. 340
Abingdon Register, IV. 52, 65
Abingdon, *Survey of Worcester Cathedral*, II 164
Ablutions, IV. 192 and *ff.*
Absolution at burial, II 385
Acca, St., I 197
Acta Sanctorum, *see* Bolland
Adamnan, *Vita S. Columbæ*, I 220, 235, 237
Adela, II. 310, 311
Advent, IV. 215
Ælfled, I. 338-340; ii p. XII, 78, 131, 204; III 148; IV 43, 45, 147
Ælfred, I. 232, 236-240 *See* Asser
Ælfric, Homilies of, i 20, 21, 22, 88, 120; II. 244, 365, 366; III. 120, 121, 134, 135, 146-148, 153, 298, 300, 400, IV 67, 71, 99
Ælfric's Canons, I 134, 135, 140-142, 251, 309, 312; III 259, 260; IV. 106 *See* Thorpe
Ælfric's Gloss, II 80
Ælfswid, II 225
Aelred, I 49; II 160-162; III 133, 344, 393
Æstel, I 236-240, IV 311
Æthelbald, II. 267
Æthelstan, I 354, II 265, 269
Æthelwulf, II. 265-268
Agnes, St, Church at Rome, II. 123
Aimo, I. 19
Aix, University Statutes, ii. 58
Aix-la-Chapelle, I. 167, 287, 340, 341; II 58
Alan of Tewkesbury, II 189, IV. 190

Alb, I. 307-314, 347-374
Alban's Abbey, St, I. 199; II. 170, 177. *See* Matthew Paris
Alcuin, i. 18, 19, 20, 39, 63, 64, 119, 226; II 51, 146, 147, 239, 244; III 16, 17, 120, 125-137, 151-154, IV 22-27, 127, 128
Alcuin Club Collections, II. 403
Aldborough Church, III 2
Aldhelm, St, I 109, 162, 178, 183, 249, II 227, III 139, 140, 143-145, 151, 300; IV. 5, 15, 38, 51, 82, 147
Aldred, I. 224
Aldric, II 132
Alemann, *De Lateranensibus Parietinis*, II 115
Alet Pontifical (in *Archæologia XXV*), I. p XV, 24, 34, 90, 99, 240, 250, 374, 378, ii. p. XI., 20, 24, 367; III 142
Almuce, II 43-50, 70-75
All Saints' Day, IV 294
Altar, i. 152-165, 178-217, 243; II 234, IV. 234-245. *See* Consecration, Frontal, Riddel
—— stripped, I 188, IV 273
Amalarius, I. 66, 67, 70, 71, 72, 81, 94, 117, 165, 168, 175, 310, 314, 325, 326, 331, 372, 377, 396; II 12, 79, 152, 200, 201, 204, 205; IV 5-13, 19, 20, 34, 39, 40, 42, 47, 82, 83, 99
Ambo, I 166-171, IV 35-37, 244
Ambrose, St, I 27, 28, 56, 99; II 259, 260

Ambrose Church at Milan, St , 1. 184, 232. *See* Ferrario
Ambrosian rite, 1 26, 81, 102, 103, 273, 353 ; iv. 112, 113 *See* Beroldus, Casola
Ames, *Typographical Antiquities*, iii 223, 224, 233, 238, 265
Amice, 1 376-399
Analecta Hymnica, iv. 30
Analecta Liturgica, iv 31
Analecta Romana, iv. 305
Analogium, 1 169, 170
Anastasius, 1 131
Angels, cult of, iii 133-137
—— Guardian, iii 170-174
Angelus, iii 280 , iv 311
Angers, 1 271, 352, 390 , ii 61
Anglia, iv 6, 7
Anglo-Saxon Chronicle, 1 13, 222, iii 292, 293, 298, 400
Anglo - Saxon Liturgical Customs, iv 1-130
Ankret, iii. 93-101
Annales Ælfredi, 1 236
Anne, Alexander, brass, 1 264, 265
Ansegisus, 1 227, 316 ; ii 22
Anselm, St , 1 55, 58, 61, 123, 209 , ii. 125, 126, 186; iii 243; iv 148. *See* Vita
Antiphoner, iv 19, 245
Antiq. Soc MS , ii 252
Antiquarian Repertory, ii 330, 347 , iii 111
Antony, Bp of Durham, *see* Beck
Antwerp, ii 56
Apparels, 1. 358-373
Archæologia, 1 p xv , 234; ii 255 , iii 232, 249-251. See also *Alet Pontifical, Ethelwold Benedictional*
Archæological Institute, iii 99
Archæological Journal, 1 191, 194, 199, 200, 356 ; ii 148, 253, 255, 262 , iii 14, 46, 99, 202, 363
Aregius, 1 308
Arles, ii 112, 113
Arsenius, 1 49, 50
Arthur, King of Cornwall, 1 42, 43

Arundel Church, 1. 191
Ascension Day, iv 292
Ashbourne Church, 1 p xiv , 179
Ashby de la Zouch, iii 361, 362
Ash Wednesday, iv 72-74
Ashwell, *Gestus Eccles* , 1 100
Asser, *De Rebus Gestis Ælf* , iii. 294, 298 , iv 17
Astel Church, 1 191
Augustine of Canterbury, St , 1 14, 29, 56, 244 *See* Vita
Aurelius *Rule*, ii 286
Austin of Hippo St , 1 66, 67, 100 , ii 76, 286
Autun, 1 311, 315
Ave, iii 258-279 , iv 155
Avowries, ii. 394 and *ff*, 252, 334

Baines, Bp , 1 340
Baker, Geoffrey, de Swinbroke, *Chron* , iii 251
Baldricus (Baudre), ii 312
Bale, 1 248 , ii 44
Balteum, *see* Girdle
Balther, St , iii. 19
Baluze, *Capitularia*, 1 71, 72, 259 , ii 153 , iii 16 Cp 1 340
Bangor, 1 218
Barnes, Bp , *Ecclesiastical Proceedings*, iv 179
Bartholomew of Farne, St , iv. 171
Bassingbourne, ii 347
Bastard, 1 364, 391
Battle Abbey, *Historia Fund*, 1 198, 295 , iii 296
Bawdekin, ii 230
Bayeux, 1 261-263
—— Tapestry, ii 252, 320
Beadsmen, iii 107, 108
Beam, iii 388 , iv 242, 243
Beauchamp Chapel, iii p vii , 54, 73, 74
Beauties of England, ii 262 ; iii 31, 43
Beck, Anthony, Bp of Durham, 1. 186, 357 , ii 179, 180, 190
Becon, Thos , ii 261, 295-298, 376, 377 , iii 97
Bedale Church, 1 191

Bede, *Hist. Eccl*, 1 12, 15, 16,
30, 108, 120, 145, 162, 178,
181, 182, 198, 213, 218, 244,
11 113, 128, 184, 238, 239,
240, 242, 243, 244, 245, 246,
250, 253, 254, 255, 264, 266,
272, 278, 111 3, 11, 12, 119,
123, 124, 128. 288, 289, 290,
293, 295, 299, 400, 1v 74,
49, 128

Bede, other works, 1 16, 17, 18,
32, 57, 65, 66, 118, 119, 120,
136, 149, 161, 166, 168, 201,
206, 207, 208, 213, 245, 253,
324, 11 64, 77, 81, 185, 195,
214, 226, 238, 241, 249, 253,
278, 389, 111. 4, 117, 121,
128, 129, 134, 135, 150, 201,
205 206, 259, 290, 292, 299,
302, 332, 401-403, 1v 4,
12-16, 40, 49, 50, 67, 89, 90,
109, 113, 119-127

Bede-roll, 11 280 and *ff*, 330
and *ff*

Begu, 11 245

Bell for the hours, 1v 167

—— hand-, 11 372-373 378, 379;
111 81, 365, 366, 1v 179,
182

—— on vestments, 1 327, 340,
341, 11 23, 31, 85, 106

—— sacring, 1 60, 1v 178, 182

—— sanctus, 1v 178

Bellman, 111 80, 81

Bellotte, *Observationes ad Ritus
Ecclesiæ Laudunensis* 1 173,
269, 277, 11 61, 217

Belt of Pater Nosters, 111 4, 6,
7, 1v 311

Benedict of Peterborough, *De
Miraculis S Thomæ.* 111 313,
340, 349-351, 379, 384, 412

Benedict, St, 1v. 5

Benedict XIV, *De Sacro Missæ
Sacrificio,* 1 85, 102, 370

—— *De Servorum dei Beatif,* 111
409

Benediction by bishop at Mass,
1 24, 1v 42-46, 225-227

—— at the end of Mass, 1 116

—— of ornaments, 1 32, 250,
11 218-221

Benedictional, 1v 247 *See* Ethelwold

Benet Biscop, St, *see* Vita

Bennet, *Hist Teukesb*, 1. 360

Benoit, *Histoire de Toul,* 1 296

Berdewell Brass, 111 281, 282

Berengarius, 1 51-53

Bernard, St, 11 98

Beroldus, *Eccl Amb Mediol
Kalendarium et Ordines,* 1
353, 1v 299

Bertrand, 11 279

Besthorp, 111 42

Betham, *Irish Antiquarian Researches,* 1 222, 233, 234

Beverley Minster, 1 396

Bewforest brass, 11 170, 171

Bianchini, 11 109

Bibliotheca, 1 229-231

Bidding the bedes, 11 286-305,
330

Biel, 1 75, 268

Bier, 11 378

Bilfrid, 1 224

Birchington, Stephen, 11 189,
190, 111 272, 273, 392

Birinus, St, *see* Vita

Birmingham, St Martin's
Church, 11 17

Bishop's throne, 1 164, 165

Black Prince, 111 54

Bleys, W de, *see* William

Blomefield, *Norfolk,* 11 215, 303,
323, 325, 327, 333, 335, 337,
343, 344, 351, 352, 353, 397,
400, 403, 111 32, 35, 41, 43,
50, 51, 66, 70, 73, 76, 79,
80, 82, 93, 104-107, 166,
218, 221, 222, 226, 234, 238,
280, 282, 1v 168, 169, 188,
195, 266

Blount, *Tenures,* 111 30, 42

Bodleian MSS, 1 10, 11 232, 289
Auct D 1 20, 1. 72, 73
Auct. D inf. 2, 11, 11 p.
x111, 399
Auct D sup 120, 3, 111. 296
Douce 30, 1 354
Gough Liturg 3, 11 p x111,
394
Hatton 93, 1 16, 17, 58, 59,
170

Boexken van der Missen, Dat, i p xiii, xvi, 45, 46, 335, 336, 392 , iv. 188, 189, 194, 196

Boke of Curtasye, iii. 232 ; iv 27, 143

Boke of Presydentes, iii 103

Bolland, Acta SS , i 19, 49, 50, 107, 112, 121, 144, 219, 220, 241, 248, 249, 253, 258, 259, 296, 308, 326, 348, 381, 399; ii 19, 22, 23, 55, 58, 79, 82, 94, 111, 127, 150, 169, 223, 225, 250, 274, 275, 347 , iii 119, 123, 126, 128, 145, 146, 149, 179, 190–196, 253, 292–295, 304, 309, 315, 322, 324, 336, 339, 370, 382–385, 396, 400, 406, 414, 415 , iv. 16, 34, 37, 38, 43, 51, 52, 65, 128, 129, 148, 162, 171, 173, 207, 225

Bona, Cardinal, i 133, 134, 269, 383, 406

Bonanni, *La Gerarchia Ecclesiastica*, i p xv , 351, 363, 370, 388 , ii. 14, 80

Boniface, St , i. 66, 130, 162, 230, 295 , ii 237, 238, 241, 242, 259, 280, 281, 307, 308, 309 , iii 10, 11, 14, 121, 402 ; iv 109

Bonitus, St , *see* Vita

Book of Common Prayer, i 382

Bordon, ii 163

Borew, John, ii 55

Borgia, Cardinal, ii. 181

Borromeo, *see* St Charles

Bosham, Herbert of, iv. 232

Bottari, *Roma Sotterranea*, i. 270, 271, 384, 385

Bourdon, iii 357

Boy-bishop, iv 250–256

Boys, *History of Sandwich*, i 187, 367, 398 , ii. 7, 277, 293, 303–306, 335, 341, 342, 372 ; iii 226; iv 252

Bracelets, i 354–357

Brachialia, ii 136

Branch-light, ii 391 and *ff*

Brandon, St , iv 166

Brayley, *Graphic Illustr* , iii. 388

Bray's Funeral, Lord, ii 391, 407, 408, 414

Bread, Holy, *see* Eulogia

Brescia, ii. 62

Bridge-building, iii 41, 164

Bridport, Giles de, ii 372, 379

Brigid, St , i 222

British Museum MSS —

Add 22,285, ii 158 ; iii. 39, 40, 75

Add 28,962, iv 161

Add 30,337, iv 112

Claudius A. iii , i. p. xiv , 296 , ii 82, 105

Claudius A. viii , ii 52 ; iii 75, 82, 84

Claudius B vi , 52

Claudius C vi , ii 311

Domitian A. xvii., i 357; ii p xi , 44 ; iv. 157

Domitian vii 2, i 168 , ii. 278, 280

Egerton 613, iii 284

Galba A. xiv , ii 287, 288

Harl 2342, iii. 178

   2382, iii 199

   2908, i 310

   2966, ii 248

   2978, ii. 248

   4866, iii 270

   2278, iv. 239

Julius A vi., i. 110, iii. 141, 145

Lansd 403, ii. 276

Nero C. iv., ii. 83, 130, ii 83

Nero D. i , iii p vii , 406

Nero D iv, i 217, 223 , iv. 36

Nero D vii., ii 274, 275

Otho B. ix , iii 130

Tiberius A iii , iv 6

Tiberius B viii , ii p. xi , 18, 203

Tiberius C i , i 16, 17, 153

Titus A i., i 297, 345, 349, 408 , ii 23, 24

Titus D. xviii , iii. 245

Titus D xxvii , iii 136, 188 , iv. 103, 104

Vesp. A. i , iv 102, 103

Vesp. B xii., iii. 141

Vesp D i , ii 136

British Museum MSS (*cont*)—
  1 A. xviii , iii 15, 16
  2 A xxii , ii 192
  2 B. vii , 1 292; ii 100, 180, 210
  1 D. ix , ii 270
Bromton, *see* John
Bromyard, John, *Summa Predi-cantium*, 1 343, 344, 375
Bronescomb, Bp , effigy, ii. 174–176; iii 158, 170, 171
Brotherhood, Monastic, ii 270 and *ff*, 306 and *ff*
—— of Holy Trinity, ii 328, 329, 330, 332, 333, 344
Broughton Castle Church, 1 191, 192
Brower, *Annales Trevir*, iii 289
Bruno Signiensis (d'Asti), 1 267, 268, 396, 406 , ii. 87, 99, 116, 117, 119, 120, 121
Bruns, *Canones*, 1 92, 115, 342
Bugga, *see* Alcuin
Burchard, St , *see* Vita
Burg, John de, *see* de Burg
Burgess, Bp of Sarum, 1 3
Burnet Bp , iii 121
Burse, iv 236, 237
Bury St Edmunds, *Wills*, iii 214, 215, 219, 222, 223, 237, 266, 269, 330, 331 , iv 174,
—— Abbey, iii 341 *See* Joscelin of Brakelond
Byssus, ii 86

Cabasilas, N , *see* Nicholas
Caerimoniale Episcop , ii 93, 122, 173 , iii 409
Cæsarius of Arles, St , 1 29, 56, 81, 104, 115, 116, ii 286, iv. 45, 46. *See* Vita
Caius Coll , Camb , MSS . 1 181
Caligæ, ii 204
Calixtus II , iii 364, 365
Cambridge Univ Libr MSS , iii 320, 324, 339, 340, 344
Cambutta, ii 151
Camden, *Britannia*, 1 158 , iii 15, 61, 69, 235
Camelacium, ii 101
Campagi, ii 204

Cancellieri, *Descrizione della Setti-mana Santa*, ii 35
Candlemas, iv 67–69
Candles, i 211 , iv. 168
Candlestick, seven-branched, iv. 243
Canon of the Mass, ii. 58, 59, 65 and *ff* ; iv. 179–192, 305–308
—— Crosses in, 1 66–95
Canonisation, iii. 407–409
Canopy of altar, 1 153–161 ; iv. 234 and *ff*
Cantatorium, 1 170 , iv. 20
Canterbury, *see* Dart, Gervase, *Inventories*
Cantilupe, Bp , ii 373, 374 ; iv. 165, 182
Cantor, *see* Ruler
Cantuar, Hist. Prior. Eccl., ii. 23 ; iii 219
Canynges, W , 1 286 , ii 8, 48
Cap, ii , 47, 51–59
Capgrave, ii 52, 359; iii. 243, 244, 312, 316, 322, 347, 354, 393, 412 , iv 186
Cardwell, *Prayer Book of Edw. VI* , ii 370, 371
Care-cloth, iv 201
Carpentier, ii 58
Carpet, 1 213, 214
Carter, John, *Specimens*, ii. 175, 176, 318
Casola, *Rationale*, 1 378
Cassock, ii 16–19
Catalani, *De Codice S. Evang.*, 1 370
—— *Pontificale Romanum*, ii 97
—— *Rituale Romanum*, ii 62, 381, 382
Catherine's Day, St., iv 255
Cava, *see* La Cava
Caxton, *Handbill*, 1 10
—— *Liber Festivalis*, 1. 145, 146 ; ii 52, 298, 299
Cecilia, St , iii 205
—— Church at Rome, ii 118
Ceillier, *Histoire des Auteurs Sacrés*, 1 54
Celsius, *Hist Bibl. Reg Stockh* , 1 216
Celtic Art, 1 219–225

Ceolfrid, St., *see* Vita
Cerne Abbey, iii 30
Certain, iii 103–107
Chained Books, iii. 43, 44
Chalice, i 33, 115, 130, 215–217, 329–332
—— Mixed, i 120
Chambre, W. de, *see* William
Chamillard, *De Corona*, i. 386, 387
Chanter, *see* Ruler
Chantry, iii. 84–113
Chapter house, iv. 144, 145
Charlemagne, i 225–228 ; iii 16, iv 136
Charles Borromeo, St, i 273, 368, 369, 372, 373, ii 173
Chasuble, i 257–301, 313, 314, iv 74, 215, 300
Chaucer, ii 60, 69, 70, 198, 335, 379, 380, 381, iii 199, 205, 225, 228, 231, 269, 276, 284, 346, 361, iv. 167
Chichele, Abp, effigy, ii 134, 139, 177
—— Statutes, iii 187
Choir, i 165
Chrism, iv 89–94
Chrismal, i 108, 109, 157
Christmas, iv 248
Chrodegang, ii 66
Chron. Centul, i 63, 111, 130, 157, 166, 167, 316, 403, ii 22, 23, 81, 154, 247, iv 230
Chronicle of Dunstable, iii 38
Chron Fontan, i 227, 316 ; ii. 22
Chron of Monte Casino, i. 233
Churchwardens' Accounts—
St Helen's, Abingdon, ii 418
St Margaret's, Westminster, ii 324, 332
St. Martin Outwich, ii 60
St. Mary Hill, i 186, 400 ; ii. 45, 60, 199, 294
St Michael's, York, ii. 219
Stanford-in-the-Vale, i. 111, 358
Walberswick, ii 219
See also i 393
See Illustrations
Ciampini, *Vet. Mon.*, ii. 80

Ciborium, *see* Canopy
Ciclatown, ii. 230
Cicognara, *Memorie della Calcographia*, i 42, 203, 205
Cirencester Church, ii 17
Cistercian Statutes, i. 187, 188 ; iii 179, 180
City Companies, ii 358 and *ff*
Clarke, Dr. Adam, i. 97, 98
Clemente San, Church at Rome, i. p xiii, xiv., 151, 169
Clericatus, *Decisiones Sacramentales*, i 130
Cluny, i 131
Cobham College, Indent de Vestim, i. 336, 367
Coif, ii 54
Coin bent for a vow, iii. 190, 384
Cole, Arthur, brass, i. 384 ; ii 48
Coleshill, iii 30
Collar, i 382–389, of Esses, iii 52, 53, 361
Collectaneum, iv. 20
Cologne, *see* Council, Crombach, Hartzheim, Synod
Colours, ii 213–218, iv 304
Columba, St, *see* Vita
Comb, ii 101–104
Communion, in one kind, i 133–135, iv 190–199, 203
See Viaticum
Compline, iv 11, 153
Confession, iii 300, iv. 260–262
Conrad of Woltelsbach, *Chron. Moyunt*, i 163, 302
Consecration of Church or Altar, i 23, 24, 34–37, 89, 90, 193, iii 289, 306–309
Constitutiones artis geometricæ, i 59
Cooper's Report, ii, 270, 271
Cope, i 295 ; ii 20–43, 69–71
Corona, i 156–161, iii 120, iv. 235–240, 243
Coronation Service, i. 227, 228
Corporal, i 32–34, 210–214, iv. 174, 175
Corpus Christi College, Cambridge, MSS, i 181 ; iii. 16, 17, 159, 296
Corpus Christi College, Oxford, MSS., ii. 17

Corpus Christi College, Oxford, Staff, ii. 156
—— Statutes, *see* Foxe
Cotman, *Sepulchral Brasses*, ii. p. xi, 13
Councils—
Agde, i 116
Aix-la-Chapelle, ii. 66, 152
Ancyra, i. 114
Braga, i. 342
Cambrai, i. 338, 376, 386 (A D 1586)
Chalchuth, i. 35, 36, 128, 143, 179; ii 66, 246, iii. 6, 400, iv 20, 132, 133
Cloveshoo, i. 14, 136, 137, 138, 205, iii. 20, 133, 259, 399, iv 1, 2, 31, 120, 121
Cologne, ii. 19
Exeter, ii 372, 378, 379, iii 219, iv. 179
Hatfield, iii 150
Jerusalem (Bethlehem), i 78, 79, 99, 105, 106
Lateran, iii. 58, 62
London, i. 146, ii 201
Lyons, ii 286
Nantes, i. 110
Nicæa, i 115
Orleans, i. 116; ii. 286; iv 46
Oxford, i 55, 127; ii. 383; iv. 70, 181, 193
Paris, iii. 278
Quercy, i 94
Rheims, ii 160
Rome, ii 66, iii 274
Rouen, ii. 3
Toledo, iv. 42
Westminster, ii 19
Worcester, ii. 52
York, i. 145
See also Synod
Cowl, i. 395-399
Coxe, Rev. H O, ii 330
Crombach, *Hist SS. trium Regum*, i 169, 178, 190; ii 57, 61
Cross, customs connected with, iv. 126-134
—— creeping to, iv. 99-104, 279, 280, 287
—— in cemetery, &c., ii. 250; iii. 11-16; iv. 266-268

Cross, of ashes to die on, ii 375
—— signed at the Canon, i. 66-95, on a deed, iv. 130-134
—— on altars, i. 192, 213, 240; iv. 308
—— method of signing, iv 155
—— pectoral, ii. 143-149
—— processional, iv. 263, 264, 290, 291
Crown of Bishops, ii 76-80
Croylandensis Hist Cont, ii 398; and *see* Ingulph
Crozier, ii. 178-193
Cruche-head, ii 158
Crucifix, i 248-255
Cruet, i 125, 126, 216
Crumena, i 408
Crusade, iii 367-376
Crystal, i 234-240
Cullum, Sir J., *Hist of Hawsted*, ii 249; iv. 182
Cumean, i 109
Cumhdach, i 233, 234
Cuthbert, i 162, ii. 238, 242, 246, 247
Cuthbert, St, ii 171. *See* Vita
Cynehard, ii. 280, 281, 308
Cyprian, St, i 49, 136
Cyril, St, *Mystag*, i 100, 101

D'Achery, *Spicilegium*, i 227, 316, 398, 400, 404, ii 6, 22, 102, 247, 283, 311
D'Agincourt, *Histoire de l'Art*, i 166, 233; ii. 80, 182; iv 112
D'Azevedo, iv. 296
Dalmatic, i 307-315, 318-327
Dar(l)ington Church, i. 191
Dart, *Canterbury Cathedral*, i. 179, iii 54
—— *Westminster*, i p xiv, iii. 318, 323
Dead, prayer and services of, ii. 237-419, iv. 204
Death-bill, ii 308 and *ff*.
De Brahon, *Pallium Archiepiscopale*, ii. 105, 124
De Burg, John, *Pupilla Oculi*, i 122, 123, 127, 128, 194, 343, ii. 219, 278; iii 99, 358
De Dene, Wm, ii 127

Dedication stone, I 179
De Moléon, *Voyages Liturgiques*, I 53, 131, 168, 263, 271, 272, 300, 328, 334, 343, 346, 351, 371, 390; II 24, 71, 94, 168, 216, IV 14, 149
Denys, St, I 130, 131, 242 *See* Félibien
De Plove, N, IV 177
De Vert, *Explication*, I p XIV., 259, 270, 296, 346, 348, 371, 390
De Wanda, I 4, 5
Dibdin, *Typog Antiq*, I. 396; II 165; III. 238
Diceto, Ralph de, III 400
Dies iræ, IV 205
Dionigi, *Vatic Basil Crypt Monum*, I. 275, 366, 384, 402; II 121, 123, 134, 197, III 371
Dionysius, St, *see* Vita
Diptychs, I 167. 168, II. 108. *See* Bede-roll, Gori
Directorium, I 10, IV 172 *See* Wordsworth
Dirige, II 404; IV. 140
Dives and Pauper, I 364, 365, 392, II 232, III 164, 171, 175, 200, 201, 285, 286, IV. 162, 168, 202
Doctrynal of Dethe, III 253
Dodsley, *Collection of Old Plays*, II 349
Dole, II 331; III 4-9, 26-33
Domi, *De utraque pænula*, I. 273
Doom, III 157-166
Dorchester Church, Oxon, I 407; II 54, 142, 147, 170, 250
Dover, St Martin's, *see* Inventory
Dowsing, W., III 220
Drythelm, II 239, 266
Dublin, Trin Coll MSS, I 222
Du Bouchet, *Histoire generale de la Maison de Courtenay*, I 307
Du Cange, II 58, 104, 138
Dugdale, *Hist. St Paul's*, I 125, 132, 157, 201, 242, 296, 300, 302 323, 328, 333, 341, 359, 363, 382, 400, 401; II 15, 16, 25, 26, 27, 30, 32, 35, 44,

45, 70, 85, 92, 103, 133, 135, 157, 165, 166, 197, 199, 207, 212, 215, 216, 218, 230, 231, 387; III 32, 71, 72, 83, 88-90, 102, 105, 121, 224, 315, IV. 233, 252
Dugdale, *Monasticon Anglic.*, I 124, 126, 158, 187, 188, 189, 198, 199, 200, 201, 241, 242, 302, 328, 334, 351, 352, 358, 360, 362, 383, 393, 398, 401; II 4, 6, 7, 18, 33, 40, 44, 45, 46, 52, 70, 88, 89, 90, 92, 100, 101, 103, 123, 135, 156, 157, 158, 165, 166, 167, 171, 181, 212, 215, 216, 217, 229, 231, 313, 318, III 25, 40, 44, 62, 76, 107, 110, 111, 214, 220, 221, 225, 230, 237, 245, 305, 315, 331, 332, 335, 336, 341, 378, 386, 393, 397, IV 6, 7, 10, 52, 65, 160-162, 180, 204, 218, 233, 236, 238, 252, 254, 260, 290, 291, 309
—— *Warwickshire*, II 350, III. 28, 31, 32, 41, 46, 47, 55, 57, 72, 74, 83, 222, 258
Dunstable, *see* Chronicle
Dunstan, St, I 296
—— *Pontifical*, I 34, 36; II 117, 118. 142, 150, 152
—— *Regularis Concordia*, I p. XIV, 134, 135, 177, 314, II 20, 251, 252, 258, 259, 272, 274, 309, 310, 345, IV 6, 7, 10, 65, 74, 75, 80-89, 98, 100, 101, 104, 114-119
—— *See* Vita
Durandus, *Rationale*, I 75, 83, 315, 317, 342, 409, II 104, 144, 201, 381, IV 176, 232
Durham, *Hist Dunelm Script Tres*, I 186, 351; II. 88, 97, 141, 180, 191, 211, 314, 315, III 42, 320, 335, 341, 375, 397, IV 185 *See also* Beck, Liber Vitæ, Simeon
Durham Abbey, I 197; III 183, 275, IV 190, 222, 240, 284, 290, 291
—— *Antiquities and Rites*, I 124; II 26, 280; III 94, 315, 320,

333, 337, 338, 378, 379, 396, 397

Durham MSS, ii 313, 314; iii 109

—— Ritual, ii. 284, 285; iii 119, 124-127, 130, 131, 133, 135, 141, 146, 156; iv. 125, 126

Dying, rites for the, ii. 365 and ff

EADBURGA, i. 231

Eadfrid, Bp, i. 224

Eadmer, i 157, 165, 171, 177, 178, 180, 182; ii 125, 126, 224; iii 292, iv 148, 200

Easter Day, iv. 116-119, 287-292

—— Even, iv 106-116, 281-287

—— Sepulchre, iii 76-79, iv. 103, 116, iv. 278

Ecclesiological Soc, St. Paul's, Transactions, iv 242

Ecclesius, Bp of Ravenna, i 259, 322

Ecgwin, St, i 248

Eddius, see Vita, St Wilfrid

Edgar, Canons under, i 107, 108, 120, 181, 213, 374; ii 13, 254, 386, iii 7, 143, 300, 306, 358

Edmund of Canterbury, St, ii 371

Edward, Confessor, St, Laws, ii 3, 389

—— Life, ii 250　See Vita

Edward the First, Lib Quot. Garderobæ.　See Wardrobe

Edward VI, Injunctions, iii 166, 194, 387

Effigies at funerals, ii 395; iii 48, at shrines, iii 384

Egbert, Confessionale, i. 112, 113; iii 300

—— Dialogus, i. 135, 136; iv 1

—— Excerptiones, i 15, 108, 144, 165, 182; ii 66, 365, iii 259, 294; iv. 2, 3, 21, 37

—— Pœnitentiale, i. 107, 251; ii 366

Egbert Pontifical, i 25, 34, 36, 153, 309, 311, 312, 318, 374; ii. 142, 150, 218; iii 1, 12,

124, 125, 131, 141, 144, 145, 182, 289; iv 18, 44, 45, 53-64, 68, 71, 79, 80, 86, 87, 92, 95, 102, 103, 113, 118, 126

Eichstadt, i. 296

Eldefonso, i 92, 119

Eleanor, Queen, iii 36-38, 48, 58, 71, 83

Eleutherius, St., i. 12

Elevation of the host, i 60; iv. 180-183

Elfsin, Abp, ii 124, 125

Elizabeth of York, Privy Purse exp, ii 330, iii 234

Ellis, Introd. to Domesday Book, iii 319

Elphege, St, see Vita

Elsin, i 248

Ely, i 296, 297

—— History of, i 210, 243, 297; ii 23

—— Thomas of, i 210, 243, 249, 297, 381; ii 23; iii 149, 194, 292-295

Emancipation, i 159

Endightment against Mother Messe, i 55

England, a Relation of, ii 232

English Founders and Founderies, i 10

Ennodius, ii. 77

Enstone Church, i 191

Ephræm Syrus, St., ii 259

Epiphanius, St., ii. 260

Epiphany, iv. 256

Epitaph, iii 44-70

Erasmus, iii 328

Erkenwald, St, iii 312, 315, 322, 347

Ernulf, i 121, ii 31

Esteney brass, ii 170, 174, 178

Ethelbert, King of Kent, i 13

Etheldreda, St, see Vita

Ethelred, laws of King, i. 111, ii 261

Ethelwold, St., Benedictional, i p xiv, 24, 152, 153, 174, 182, 210, 217, 229, 256, 298, 349　See Vita

Ethelwolf, Carmen de Abbat. Lindisf, i 155, 156, 161, 163, 215, 225, 247; iii. 122, 127

Ethilwald, Bp , 1 224
Eton College Statutes, 111 267 ,
    1v 154
Eucharist, *see* Host
Eulogia, or Holy Loaf, 1 110-
    113 , 1v 189, 214
Evagrius, 1. 50
Eveillon, *De Process Eccles* , 11
    61
Evensong, 1v 10, 11, 149-153
Eresham, Revelations of a Monk,
    111 223
Exchequer, Kal and Invent ,
    111 52, 222, 230, 232
Exeter, 11 174-175 , 111 10, 123,
    139 *See also* Council, Leo-
    fric, Synod
Exeter Cathedral, Some Account of,
    11 295
Exeter Pontifical, *see* Lacy
Expositio Brevis Liturgia Gal-
    licana, 1 30, 80, 356 , 11 106
Exultet, 1v 111, 112

FABYAN, *Chronicle*, 11 248, 334 ,
    111 35, 71, 73, 106, 180
Faldstool, 11 209-213
Fan, 1v 225, 229-233
Fanon, *see* Maniple, Amice
Fasting, 1 61, 138 , 1v 50, 164
Felibien, *Histoire de l'Abbaye de*
    S Denys, 1 130 , 11 165
Feretory, 111 336 and *ff*
Ferrario, *Basilica Ambrogiana*, 1
    184, 232, 233
Festival, The, 111 200, 201, 203,
    236-239, 273, 274 , 1v 167,
    271, 273, 286
Finchale, *see* Priory of Finchale
Fisher, Bp of Sarum, 1 3
—— Cardinal, 11 418
Fitz-stephen, *Vita S Thomæ*
    Cant, see Vita
Florentius, St , Hist Monast
    of, 1 408
Flower, 1 295-301, 322
Fontinel, *see* Chron
Forannan, St , 1 340
Formale, 11 35
Fountains Abbey, 11 89
Foxe, Bp , *Statutes,* 11 202 , 111
    227

Foxe, *Acts and Monuments,* 1 112,
    11 39, 40 , 111 365
Fraction of the host, 1 101-106
Fraternity, *see* Brotherhood
Freculf, *Chronicle,* 1 12
Frere, *Use of Sarum,* 1 5, 9, 125,
    313, 315, 327, 332, 333 , 11 5,
    37, 38, 42, 70, 345, 378 , 111
    233, 391, 396 , 1v 144-146,
    152, 158, 159, 224, 249, 270,
    273, 283, 294
—— *Winchester Troper,* 1v 28-34,
    66, 298
Frigyth, 11 245
Frithestan, Bp , 1 338-340
Frithstool, 111 302-305
Froissart, *Chronicle,* 111 173, 185,
    186, 247, 252, 368
Frontal, 1 183-190
Froude, *Remains,* 1 25
Fulcuinus, *Gesta Lobiensium,* 11
    283
Fuller, *Hist Waltham Abbey,*
    1 393
Funeral rites, 11 248-261, 377-
    419 , 111 21-114

GABRIEL Bell, 111 279
Gall, St , Monachus Sangallensis,
    11 153
Gallican Rite, 1 27-30, 227 *See*
    Expositio, Missale, Sacra-
    mentary
Gang-Days, *see* Rogation
Garampi, *Illustrazione di un*
    Sigillo, 1 341 , 11 85, 120,
    121, 211, 228
Garland, 11 59-63, 340, 341
Gavanti, *Thesaurus,* 1 273, 274,
    275 , 11 10, 11, 173
Geddington, 111 37
Gelasian Sacramentary, 1 128
Genealogy, 1v 141
Geoffrey of Coldingham, 11 211
Georgi, *Lit. Rom Pont* , 1 70, 71,
    72, 126, 132, 301, 330, 404,
    405, 409 , 11 9, 122, 1v
    40, 47
Gerald, Bp of Toul, 1 347
Gerbert, *Mon Vet Liturg Ale-*
    mann , 1 70, 79, 83, 84, 182 ,
    11 194

Gerbert, *De Cantu et Musica sacra*, ii 100
—— *Iter Alemann*, ii 194
Gervase of Canterbury, i 157, 165, 171, 177, 180, 181; ii 102, 120, 125, 126, 129, 133, 187, 188, 193; iii. 99
Gesem or Gesina, iii. 220
Geste of King Horn, iii 357
Giffard, Godfrey, Bp. of Worcester, i 306, 323, 360; ii 85, 171, 199, 200
Gilbert of Hoyland, i 54
Gilbert, Bp of Limerick, i. 121, 125, 315, 402
Gilbert of Sempringham, i. 398; ii 18, 312, 313, 318, iii 245
Gild, ii 275, 276, 319 and *ff.*; iv 299
Gild-hall, ii 351, 352
Gildas, i, 211
Giraldus Cambrensis, ii 263; iii 366-368
Girdle, i 399
Giunta Pontifical, i p xiv, xv, 274, 360, 361, 362, 391, 392, ii p xi, xii, 8, 72, 73
Gloucester Cathedral, i 191
Gloves, ii 28, 132-134
Goar, *Rituale*, i 356
Godiva, iii 7
Godric, St, *see* Vita
Golden Legend, *see* Wynkyn de Worde
Good Friday, iv 99-106, 278-280
Gori, *Thesaurus Veterum Diptychorum*, ii 108
Goslin, St, Invent Corp, ii. 79
Gospel-book, *see* Text
Gospel at Mass, i 60
Gotselin, i 202, ii 228
Gough, R, *Sepulchral Effigies*, i p xvi
Grabe, i 98
Gradual (book), i 170, iv. 246
—— (Chant), i 170
Grancolas, i 133; iv 14
Grandison, Bp, *Statuta*, i 335, 345, ii 6, 9, 12, 13, 53, iii 246
—— *Ordinal*, ii 42
Green, *Hist of Worcester*, ii. 17, 33, 92

Gregory the Great, St, i 13, 14, 21, 43-48, 80, 97, 247, 309, 318, ii 105, 113, 114, 145, 260; iii 61, 120
—— Sacramentary (Menard), i. 228, 327, 404; ii 103, 116, 205, 206, 220, 259, 282, 285; iii 205, iv 97
Gregory of Tours, St, i 50, 69, 211, 247, 258, ii. 145, 214
Gremiale, *see* Lap-cloth
Grimaldi, *Liber Instrum*, i. 275, 366, 402; ii 118, 134
Grimold's Sacramentary, i 315. *See* Autun
Grindal, *Injunctions*, iii. 274, 275, 298
Grossetete, iv 201
Guala, *see* Walo
Guitmond, i 104, 105
Gundulf, iv. 193
Gunton, *Hist of Peterborough*, i. 349, 351, 352, 353, ii 53, 278, iii. 76
Gutch, iv 212, 215, 260, 291
Gutensohn and Knapp, *Die Basiliken*, i 150
Guthlac, St, *see* Vita
Gyr v. Hist Abbat (Auct anon), i 230

Hackney Church, ii. 72
Haddan and Stubbs, *Councils*, ii. 258
Hadrian II, iv 25, 26
Hales, Alexander, i 208
Halliwell, *History of Freemasonry*, i 59, 60
Hardress Church, ii. 53
Harduin, *Conc*, i 79, 94, 99, 106; ii 3, 19, 57, 152, 286; iii 58, 62
Hardyng, *Chronicle*, iii. 22, 70
Harold, King, *see* Vita
Harpsfield, N, iii 382
Hartzheim, *Catalogus*, i. 169, 227
Harvey, Eliz, brass, ii. 159, 160
Hatcher, Mr, i 2-4
Hawkins, *Origin of the English Drama*, ii 350
Hearne, *History of Glastonbury*,

ii 302, 303 , iii 39, 40, 103, 105 , iv. 247

Hearne, *Liber Niger*, iv 188. *See* Langtoft

—— *Pref Leland*, ii 316, 317

Hearse, ii 328, 361, 399 and *ff.*, 410 , iii 75 , iv. 270

Heckington Church, iii 78

Hengrave, iii 27

Herbert, *Livery Companies of London*, ii 359, 360, 361, 362, 363, 365 , iii 86

Hereford Cathedral, i 193 , iii. 357

—— Missal, i 102

Hewald, i 198

Hexham, i 149, 180

Heyworth, Bp Lichfield, *Statuta*, ii 44, 70

Hickes, *Thesaurus*, i 17; ii 320, 321, 322 , iii 9, 10, 291

Hilda, St., ii 245

Hildebert, ii 196 , iii 329 , iv. 232

Hildephonsus, *see* Eldefonso

Hilton, *Scale of Perfection*, ii 302

Hist. Nem , ii 52

Histories, iv. 142

Hittorp, i 348, 349 *et passim*

Hollis, *Monumental Effigies*, i p. xv., ii p xi., xii, 48, 55

Holsten, *Codex Regularum*, ii 66, 286 , iii 373 , iv 5

Hone, *Anc Myst*, ii 328, 329, 330, 332, 333, 344, 355, 356, 391, 392

Honorius of Autun, *Gemma Animæ*, i 75, 82, 83, 87, 88, 117, 118, 121, 122, 170, 171, 268, 269, 303, 314, 348, 389, 406 , ii 5, 87, 152, 155, 172, 173, 381 , iii 120

Hood, ii 74 75

Horæ Beatissimæ Virginis Mariæ, ii 248

Horman, *Vulgaria*, i 125 , iv 148

Horn, i 158

Horn-books, iv 247

Hospitaler, iii 371, 372

Host, i 33-37, 118-126 , iv. 180-195 *See* Fraction, Reserved, Singing Bread

Host, miracles of, i. 49-51

—— elevation, i. 60 , iv 180

Hours of prayer, iv. 1-18 , 138-169

Housel, *see* Communion

Hoveden, R do, *see* Roger

Hubert, Abp , iii 126, 133, 187

Hucbald, i 63, 64

Hugh of St Victor, St , i 406

—— of Cluny, *see* Vita

—— of Lincoln, *see* Vita

—— of Rouen, iii 157, 177

Hure, ii 52

Hussey, Prof , on Bede, i 30

Hymns, iv 13-15

Hymns of A.-S Church, iv. 15, 70, 97

Illustrations, &c , ii 7, 12, 135, 324, 332, 348. 418 , iii 336

Illyricus, Mat. Flaccus, *Ordo*, i 326, 327, 403 , ii. 132

Iltut, St , i 218

Image of Pity, iii 63

Images, i 244-255 , iii 79

Imma, ii 243

Incense, i 161-164 , iv 36 and *ff*, 121, 144, 150-153, 216, 220, 223, 224

Indulgence, iii 57 and *ff*

Ingulph, i 159, 188, 214, 215, 252 , ii 23 , iii. 13, 303, iv. 133, 134

Innocent III , *De sacro altaris, mysterio*, i 75, 83, 88, 166, 168, 169, 193, 268, 330, 342, 365, 379, 405 , ii 87, 98, 99, 117, 118, 119, 143, 144, 168, 196. iii 361, 369

Innocents' Day, iv 250-256

Intention at Mass, i 61-65

Intercession of Saints, iii 128

L'Interpretation de la Messe, see Boexken

Inventories of Christ Church, Canterbury, i. 125, 157, 164, 171, 177, 191, 222, 235, 241, 242, 303, 323, 333, 350, 358, 382, 401 , ii 26, 28, 29, 31, 32, 88, 103, 120, 121, 133, 134, 140, 156, 167, 177, 191, 192, 231 , iii 390, iv. 148

Inventory, Lincoln Cathedral,
1. 242, 302, 393 , 11 135, 166,
215, 217, 231 , 111 220
—— St Martin's, Dover, 1 352
—— Winchester Cathedral, 1
241, 351, 360, 383 , 11. 33, 88,
156, 165
—— York Minster, 1. 158, 200,
242. 328, 11 89, 92, 135, 215,
216, 111 386
Invitatory, 1v 4, 12, 13
Invocation of Saints, 111 118–285
Isidore of Seville, St , 1 90, 91,
143, 259 ; 11 142, 149
Islip, Abp , 1v. 162
Islip roll, 11 315, 392, 393, 402,
416, 417
Ivo of Chartres, *Micrologus*, 1
74, 82, 87, 208
—— *Decretale*, 11 286

JARROW, 1 200
Jerome, St., 1 317 , 11 76
Jerusalem Cross, 11 183
Jesus Mass, 111 92
John of Avranches, *De officiis
ecclesiæ*, 1 125, 324, 332 , 11
274, 345 ; 1v 149, 181
John of Beverley, St , 11 254,
347 *See* Vita
John of Cornwall, *De Canone*,
1 54
John of Glastonbury, *Chronicle*,
1 43, 201, 359, 383, 402 , 11
25, 26 , 111 62, 63, 214, 223,
395
John of Hexham, 1v 186
John of Hoveden, 111 245
John, Bp of Liège, 1 337, 338,
376
John of Salisbury, *Policraticus*,
1 159
—— *Epist*, i 405
John the Deacon, *see* Gregory
John Bromton, *Chronicle*, 1 10 ;
ii 4. 111. 75, 94, 95, 361, 362 ,
1v. 172
John Chrysostom, St , 1 57, 58,
100
John Garland, *Dictionarius*, 1.
303, 304, 393, 400 , 1v.
232

John Garland, *Commentarius*, ii.
4, 5 ; 111. 211–213
—— *De Ornat Altaris*, 1 311
—— *De Vestimentis Sacerdotali-
bus*, 1 367
John, St. Lateran Church, 1.
169 , 11 80, 115
John's Day, St , 1v 249
Joscelin of Brakelond, *Chronicle*,
11 98, 99, 158, 325 ; 111 314,
315, 321–323, 389
Joscelin of Furness, 111. 311 ; 1v.
148
Judgment, Day of, *see* Doom
Judicia Civitatis Lundoniæ, ii.
323
Juliana of Norwich, 111 158, 198,
219, 283
Juliana, St , *see* Vita
Justin Martyr, St , 1 97
Justinian, Emperor, 1 259

KECELL, W , 111 179
Kemble, *Cod Dipl Anglo-Saxo-
num*, 1 65, 132, 158, 159, 161,
197, 214, 316, 318, 331 , 11.
22, 147, 167, 225, 252, 265,
266, 267, 268, 269, 271, 273,
274, 289, 290, 320, 321, 322 ,
111 2–4, 8, 9, 11, 14, 132, 140,
146, 292 , 1v 18, 19, 38, 131,
132
Kemp, Abp , 111 38
King's College, Camb , Statutes,
1v 154
Kiss of Peace, *see* Pax
Knight, *Life of Colet*, 1v. 254
Knyghton, *see* Twysden
Krazer, *De Apost nec non Antiq.
Eccl Occident Liturgiis*, 1.
372

LABBE, *Bib Noviss MSS*, 1 130
La Cava, Cavensis Cœnob De-
dic , 11 169
Lacy, *Pontifical*, 1 17, 153, 162,
193, 312, 342 ; 11 142, 148,
159, 209, 210, 212, 111 307,
308
—— *Register*, 111 44
Lady Chapel, 111 216

Lambeth MS, No 209, 1 p xv, 311
—— Gospel Book, 1 222
Lancaster Cross, 11 255, 111 14
Lanfranc, 11 125, 227
—— De Corpore et Sanguine, 1 51, 52, 53
—— Decreta, 1 121, 11. 247, 310, 311
Lantern, 11 374
Langtoft, Chronicle, 1v 166, 167
Langton, Constit, 111 21
Laon, see Bellotte
Lap-cloth, 1 334-336
Lateran Basilica, see John
Latimer, Sermons, 11 319
Lauds, 1v 6, 7, 143, 144
Lavatory, 111 106; 1v 192-195, 309
Lawson MS, 1 373, 11 p x11, 85
Lebeuf, 1v 25, 26
Le Brun, Explication de la Messe, 1. 76, 272, 390
Lebwin, St, see Vita
Lectern, 11 165, 166, 1v 244
Legend, 1v 245
Legendes of the Sayntes, 11 359
Legg and Hope, see Inventories
Legh, Roger, brass, 111 60, 61
Leland, Collectanea, 1 200, 317, 355, 395, 11. 6, 39, 45, 46, 102, 3:5, 395, 396, 402, 403, 405, 406, 407, 409-411, 412, 413, 414, 111 23, 38, 39, 275, 366
—— Itinerary, 1 189, 191, 236, 11 317, 352, 354, 355, 356, 357, 386, 111 4, 14, 15, 34-36, 69, 164-166, 233, 235, 336, 1v 166, 202, 203, 257, 259
Leman, brass, 11 13, 14
Lenauderius, De privil doct, 11 58
Lent, 1v 75-78, 257-287, 303
Leo, Bp of Ostia, Chron S Mon. Casin, 1 233
Leo IV, Homil, 1 110
Leofline, Abbot of Ely, 1. 297
Leofric, Bp, 11. 167
Leofric Missal, 1 30, 32, 61, 62, 88, 109, 134, 143, 153, 162; 11 220, 246-248, 249, 252,

256, 257, 259, 268, 271, 289, 310, 311, 111 2, 125, 145, 152, 401, 1v 19, 41, 48, 68, 69, 73, 80, 86, 87, 93-96, 101, 104, 105, 113, 114, 207, 298, 305
Leper, 111 99
Lessons at Matins, 1v. 139-142
Liber Pontificalis, 1 154, 155, 162, 167, 196, 197, 211, 232, 348; 111 404, 1v 25, 26
Liber Vitæ (Durham), 11 278-280, 283, 285, 311
Lichfield, 1 222; 11 171, 111 398
Lidgate, 11 190, 111 245, 248
Lights at an altar, 1v. 243
—— at a grave, 111 70 and ff
—— at a shrine, 111 294, 340-343
—— at Mass, 1v 32
—— at other times, 1v. 121-124
Lily, 111 202-206
Lincoln Cathedral, 111. 335, 336. See Inventory
Lindanus, Panoplia Evang, 1. 131, 276
Lindisfarne, 1 217, 223-225
Lioba, St, see Vita
Litany, 111 181-185
Livery, 11 333 and ff.
Londin. Historiola, 11 341 See also Judicia
Longchamps, W de, 1 350
Louterell Psalter, 11 170
Loving Cup, 11 273-277
Lucius, King of Britain, i 12
Luitprand, 11 169
Lull, 11 280, 307, 308
Lupus, St, Vita S. Wigberti, 1. 20
Lyndwood, Provinciale, 1 36, 134, 146, 11 2, 15, 49, 54, 219, 374, 111 2, 59-62; 1v. 162
Lyons, 1. 346 See Missale

MABILLON, Annales Ordin. S. Bened, 11 82
—— Acta Sanct Bened, 1.16, 149, 210, 295, 340; 11. 77, 78, 124, 128, 151, 152, 154, 184, 214, 247, 368, 390, 111. 16-

19, 152, 188, 260, 280, 292, 299, iv. 51, 52
Mabillon, *De Liturg Gall.*, i. 28, 29, 92, ii 151, 152, 282
—— *Iter. Italic*, i 231
—— *Museum Ital*, i 70, 71, 129, 130, 170, 175, 326, 331, 407, ii 11, 79, 92, 103, 104, 119, 120, 122, 123, 136, 144, 145 191, 215, 216, 247, iv. 40, 41, 231, 232
—— *Vetera Analecta*, ii 133, 158, 166, 200, 279, 285, iii 144, 329
Macclesfield, iii 61
Machyn, *Diary*, ii 291, 335, 341, 342, 357, 358, 359, 360, 379, 392, 394, 395, 396, 397, 399, 400, 401, 404, 405, 414, 417, 418, 419, iii. 82, 181, 182; iv 256
Maffei, i. 31
Magdalen Coll, Oxford, ii 204, 206, 207; iii 81, 214, 226, 267
—— Statutes, *see* Waneflete
—— MS, i 265
—— brass, i 384
Magni Speculi Exempl, iii 203
Magri, *Hierolexicon*, i 277, 369; ii 168, 169; iii 371
Mai, iii 144
Maidstone Church, ii. 93
Mainz, *see* Conrad
Majesty, ii 400, 401, iv. 175–178
Maldonatus, i 84, 85
Mallius P, ii 117
Malmesbury, W. de, *see* William
Maniple, i 318–320, 338, 343–346
Manners and Household Expenses, iii 37, 48, 58, 82, 83, 329
Manual, iv. 247
Manuale Ecclesiast, ii. 208, 209
Manumission, iii. 9, 10
Manuscripts, i 217–242
Marbodus, i. 201, 202
Margaret of Scotland, St, ii. 124, 125, 274, 275
—— *See* Vita
Marlot, *Metropolis Remensis Historia*, i, 306, 307

Martene, *De Antiq. Eccl Rit*, i. 24, 25, 34, 36, 90, 99, 122, 142, 143, 182, 319, 320, 327, 404, ii 20, 61, 118, 132, 142, 144, 150, 152, 368, iv 80, 196
—— *De Antiq. Monach Rit*, i 352
—— *Thesaur. Anecd*, i. 30, 80, 131, 188, 212, 309, 338, 356, 376; ii 6, 19; iii 179, 180, 369, 372
—— *Vet Script*, i 109, 338, 376, 408, iii 95, 301, 310; iv. 160, 267
—— *Voyage Littéraire*, i. p. xv., 119, 178, 199, 271, 307, 311, 340; ii 63, 90, 153, 163, 167, iii 100, iv. 230, 231
Martin, St, *see* Vita
Martyrology, iv 9, 10, 145, 245
Mary, B V, Cult of, iii. 142–156, 196–286
—— Anthem, iii. 224–231, iv. 153, 154
—— Image, iii 218–231, 240–246, iv 151, 154
—— Mass of, iii 213–216
—— *See* Vita
Maskell, *Ancient Liturgy*, i 67, 68, 96, 97, 123, 127, 133, 135, 137
——*Monum Ritual. Eccl Anglic.*, i 90, 100, 318, 319, 320, 367, 394, 395, 396, ii 138, 170, 177; iii 308
Masonry, Poem on the Constitution of, i 59
Mass, Doctrine of, i. 14–106
—— Description of, iv 31–50, 170–228
—— Penny, ii 405 and *ff* ; iii. 23 and *ff*
—— Posture at, i 58–61
—— *See Boerken*, Canon
Matins, iv 4–6, 138–143
Matthew of Westminster, i. 160; iii 345, 346
Matthew Paris, *Gesta Abbatum*, i. 186, 189, 301, 303; ii 18, 28, 52, 94, 141, 159, 164, 177, 212, 213, 228, 229, 339, 347,

349, 350, 401, 402 ; 111. 213, 214, 224, 229, 314, 323, 324, 327–329 , 1V 179, 180, 235, 265

Matthew Paris, *Hist Anglorum*, 1 195 , 11 19, 31, 42, 54, 59, 60, 126, 127, 218, 228 , 111 39, 214, 328. 368, 392

Maundy Thursday, 1V 85–99, 273–277

Mawley Vestment, 1 286, 303

Maximianus, Bp of Ravenna, 1 259

Maxstock, 111 32

Maydeston, C , *Crede Mihi*, 11 216, 217 , 1V 145, 146, 269, 273, 291 , 1V 145, 146, 206, 263, 269, 273, 291, 293, 298

Mayhew, Bp , 1 398

Mazer, 11 276–278

Meaux, 1 259

Mediolanensis, Acta Eccl , 1. 273, 368, 369, 373 , 11 173

Mellium, 1 336

Memories, 1V 143

Menard, 1 228, 327, 404, 11 103, 116, 132, 205, 206, 220, 259, 282, 285 , 111 204, 205 , 1V 97

Menas, St , 1 50

Menev Ann Eccl , 111 311

Merton College, Oxford, 11 58

Messe, see *L'Interpretation*

Metaphrastes, 111 240–242

Methonensis, N , *see* Nicholas

Middleton, 111 24

Middle Claydon Church, 1 264

Milan, *see* Ambrose, Ambrosian, St Charles, *Mediolanensis*, Synod

Minster Church, 1 401

Missa, the Dismissal, 1 117

Missæ, De Ordine, 1 170 , 111 149, 150, 401 , 1V 18

Missal, 1V 246

Missal Sherborne, 111 49

Missale Francorum, 1 81 , 11 282

Missale Gallicanum, 1 29 , 11 283

Missale Gothicum, 1 27, 28 , 11 282

Missale Lugd (Lyons), 1 378

Missale Mozarabum, 1 90, 91

Missale Praedicatorum, 1 335

Missale Romanum, 1 80, 102, 172

Missale Sarisbur , 1 87, 101, 102, 103, 313, 330, 367, 394 , 11 216, 261 , 111 172, 207, 208 , 1V 194, 201–204

—— *See also* Hereford, Leofric

Mitre, 11 75–98

Molanus, *Natales Sanctorum Belgii*, 1 340

—— *De imaginibus*, 11 58

Molinet, *Chanoines Réguliers*, 11. 14, 71

Monte Cassino, 1 131, 233

Month's mind, 11 258, 417

More, Sir Thomas, 1 60 , 11 232, 406 , 111 263, 395, 413, 414 , 1V 105, 263

Morin, *De Sacris Eccl ordinationibus*, 1 25 , 1V 229

Morley Church, 111 105, 106

Morrow Mass, 1V 9

Morse, 11 23, 31–35

Mortar, 111 72

Mortes, 11 396, 400

Mortuary, 111 21–30

—— roll, 11 308 and *ff*

Mozarabic Rite, 1 90–93 , 1V. 308

Munich MS Gospel-book, 11 81

Muratori, *Liturg Rom Vet* , 1 27

Myrroure of our Lady, 111 260, 261 ; 1V 138, 139, 155, 156

Mystery-plays, 11. 344 and *ff* ; 1V 299

NASMITH, *Catalogue*, 1 143, 248 , 111 159, 1V 147

Nauclerus, 1 248

New College, Oxford, brasses, 11 53, 54, 192

—— vestments, 11 90, 134, 156

Nicetius, St , 1 258

Nicholas Cabasilas, 1 77, 78

Nicholas, St , *see* Vita

—— Day, 1V 250–255

Nicholas Methonensis, 1 77

Nichols, 1 186, 400, 11 45, 60, 199, 219, 294, 418; 111. 74, 215, 280; 1V 202, 280

Nicolas, Sir H , *Battle of Agincourt*, iii 220, 251, 255
—— Seo *Test Vet*
Nimbus, iii. 120
Ninian, St , i 38, 39, 218
Noche, ii 33
Nocturn, iv. 139
Nonant, Bp , Lichfield, *Satutes*, i 8, ii 345
Noncommunicating attendance, i 114-117
Norbert, St , *see* Vita
Northumberland Household Book, ii 7, 333, 349, iii 215, 234, 238, iv 275, 279, 288
Northumbrian Priests, Law of, i 181
Norwich Consuetudinary, iii 73
Notes and Queries, iii 100, 235, 236
Numeral, iv 18, 21
Nuremberge Chronicle, ii 174

Obit, ii 268, iii 80-114; iv 145
Obley or oflete, *see* Host
Odericus, *Ordo Senensis*, i 268, 312, 328, 346
Odo of Bayeux, ii 257
Odo, St , *see* Vita
Offa, iii 16
Offertory (ceremony), i 114, iii 21 and *ff.*, iv 38, 39, 173
—— (Chalice veil), *see* Veil
Oils, hallowed, iv 89-94
Oldham, Bp , *see* Register
Oliver, *Monast Dioc Exon*, i 335, 345, ii 6, 9, 13, 42, iii 44, 215
Orey, ii. 321
Ordericus Vitalis, i 295, 366, ii 64, 162, 285, 286, iii 217, iv. 161, 162
Ordinal, i 9-11, iv 247
Ordination, i 24, 25, 140-146, iv 53-64
Ordo Romanus, i 129, 130, 170, 174, 175, 349, 407, ii 11, 12, 79, 91, 92, 103, 104, 119, 120, 122, 123, 136, 144, 191, 215, 216, 247, iv. 40, 41, 43, 114, 205
Ordo Senensis, *see* Odericus

Ordynarye of Crusten Men, i 396
Organ, iv. 50-52
Orientation, i 171-178
Ornaments of altar to be clean, i 58
Orphrey, i 300, 359, 365, ii. 26-30
Orval Abbey, i 271
Osbern, i 19, 47, ii 82, 147, iii 188, iv 34, 65
Osculatorium, iv 187
Osmund, St , *Treatise*, i 6-11; ii. 378, iv 181
—— *See* Register, Sarum
Oswald, St , *see* Vita
Oswin, St , *see* Vita
Othery Church, iii 98
Ottery, S Mary, *see* Grandison, Oliver
Ottoboni, *Constitutions*, i 327
Oxford Cathedral, ii 259, iii. 91
—— University Statutes. iii 39

Paderborn, i 199
Painted Chamber, Westminster, ii 20, 91
Palgrave, *Ancient Kalendars*, iv. 228
Pall for the altar, i 210-214, 243
—— for shrine, iii 293
Pallium, ii 104-130, iv 305
Palm Sunday, iv 78-82, 264-270
Palmer, iii 360
Pamelius, *Liturgicon*, i p xv, 70, 81, 103, 315, iv 27, 113
Papal supremacy, iii 400-403
Papebroche, *Conatus*, i 348, 368, 383
Paris, i 334
Paris, M , *see* Matthew
Paschal candle, iv 111-113, 281-284
Paschasius Radbertus, i 39, 45
Passional, iii 4, iv 245
Paste, iv 202
Paten, i 32, 328-333, iv 225
Pateshull, Bp of Lichfield, i 8; iv 181
Patrick, St , i 219
Paul's Cathedral, London, St., i. 132, 201. *See* Dugdale, Sparrow-Simpson

Paul the Deacon, *Vita S Gregorii*, i 43, 45

Pavia, i 130

Pax, i 113, iv 46 and *ff*, 185-190, 227, 228

Paxbrede, ii 34, iv 187-190

Peckham, Abp, ii 371, 373, iii. 58, 59 ; iv 182, 237

Pectoral, ii 33

Pelagius, Pope, ii 113

Pellicia, *De Christianæ Eccl. politeia*, i. 370

Pellicea, ii 2, 3, 16-19

Penance, iv 213

Penitential, iv 21, 72

Pera, i 408

Perch, iii 388

Perpetuæ et Felicitatis Passio, i 307, 308

Perpetuus, St, i 258

Pertsch, *Tract de origine, &c, pallii*, ii 119, 124

Peter of Blois, *Serm*, i 54

Peter's, St, Church at Rome, i 131, 211

Peterborough, ii 171 ; iii 24 *See* Sparke, Whytleseye

Petrus Damianus, *Tractatus*, i 50, 51

Pew, i 60

Pfaff, i 101

Pharus, iv 123

Piazza, *L'Iride Sacra*, ii 17

Piers Plouhman, ii 274, iii 163, 164, 172, 229, 283, 361, 363, 364, iv 164, 167, 197, 264, 288

Pilgrims, iii 356-380

Pilgrymage of Perfection, iii 216

Piscina, iv 153, 154

Pistolesi, *Vaticano descritto*, i 196. iii 332

Pius VII, *Apost Instit*, ii 208, 209

Pix, i 108, 125, 156, 157 ; ii 371 and *ff*, iv 235-241

Placebo, ii 404

Plecgils, i 37-47

Poderis, i 374, 375 ; ii 218

Pointel, iv 148

Poitiers, W de, *see* William

Political Songs of England, ii 52 ; iii 167

Pome, ii 134, 135

Ponser, ii 137, 138

Pontefract, iii 35

Pontificale Romanum, i 193, ii 97 *See also* Alet, Dunstan, Egbert, Exeter, Giunta, Giorgi, Reims, Robert of Jumièges

Pontif Eboracen. Hist, i 158, 178, 215, 216, 226, 243, iii 19

Portiforium, iii 43

—— of Salisbury, *see* Sarum Breviary

Portous, iv 246

Poulson, *Beverlac*, ii 357

—— *History of Holderness*, iii 2

Povyard, *Dissertatione*, i 168, ii 196

Pownall, General, i 234, 235

Præp Sacerd Celebraturi, ii 13

Praxedis, St, Church at Rome, ii 118

Precinctorium, i 404

Presanctified, Mass of the, i 109, 134, 135, iv 104-106, 280

Presbytery, iv 217

Pricksong, iii 214, 215

Prime, iv 8, 144

Priory of Finchale, ii 172, 348 ; iii 58

Processional, iv 246, 247

Processions, ii 337 and *ff*, iii. 181, 391-398, iv 210, 262-268, 291

Proses, iv 23, 172

Psalter in Rock's possession, iii. 4, 5, 209, 210, 211, 356

Pseudo-Alcuin, ii 51

Pudsey, Hugh, Bp of Durham, i 301

Pugin, A W, i 285

Pulleyne, Robert, i 53, iii 169, 171

Pulpitum, iv. 244

Pupilla Oculi, see Do Burg

Purgatory, ii 241, &c ; iii 2-80

Pye, i 10 *See* Directorium, Wordsworth

Pytchley, ii. 251

Quæstiones Vet. et. Nori Testam., i 308

Quatford Church, iii. 61
Quatuor Sermons, i 145
Quintilian, i 30

RABANUS MAURUS, i. 267 , ii. 118
Radbert, see Paschasius
Radulphus Tungrensis, i 118
—— of Coggeshall, iii 95, 301, 310 , iv 160
—— of Fulda, iii 18, 19, 152
—— of Rochester, i 350
—— of Shrewsbury, iii 275
Raine, St Cuthbert, i 182, 197, 338, 340, 354, 355, 399, 400; ii. 102, 103, 147, 222, 234, 318, 348, 349 , iii 149, 177, 191, 195, 332, 340, 341, 379, 380 See also Wills and Inventories
Rask, Anglo-Saxon Grammar, i 216
Rational, i 302-306 , ii 106, 131
Ratisbon, St Emmeram, i 72
Ravenna, i. 259, 260, 322 , ii 106, 118
Raynald, Annales, ii 53
Raynaud, De puleo, ii 58
Raynold, Archbp , Constitutiones, i. 58 , ii. 8
Records, Description of Public, ii 223
Reculver, i 236
Reed, eucharistic, i 128-132
Reginald of Durham, i 223, 224, 322, 338, 376, 377 , ii 4, 18, 52, 78, 102, 147, 195, 214, 222, 249, 294, iii. 94, 166, 173-176, 190-197, 227, 228, 260, 268, 306, 319, 321, 329, 339, 342-346, 355, 377, 379, 385, 389, 390, 397, 398, 410; iv 163, 166, 167, 170, 172, 177, 226
Regino of Prum, i 110, 128 , ii 206, 286, 287
Register of Hugh Oldham (Bp. Exeter), ii 45
—— of St Osmund, i 5, 194 , ii 15, iv 237
Regnobert, St , i 261-263
Regnum, ii. 98

Regularis Concordia, see St. Dunstan
Reims, i 259, 346, ii. 82
—— Pontifical, i. 227 See also Marlot
Relics, i 35 , iii. 287-356, 381-414
Reliquary, iii 295-302,394 and ff
Reliquiæ antiquæ, iii 170, 283, 284
Remigius of Auxerre, i 169
—— of Rheims, St., i 258, ii. 213
Renaudot, Liturg Orient Collectio, ii 286
Repa, iii 336 and ff
Requiem, ii. 404
Reredos, i 186
Reserved Sacrament, i 34, 108, 128, 134, 135, 157 , ii. 371 and ff , iv 234-241, 265, 273, 277-279, 286-289
Rete, ii 94
Revue Benedictine, iv 308
Reyner, Apostolatus Benedictinorum, see St Dunstan, Regularis Concordia, and Lanfranc, Decreta
Richard I , iv 159, 160
Richard, St , of Chichester, see Vita
Richard of Hexham, i 180 , iii. 304, 305
Rich Man's Duty, iii 220
Riculf's Will, i 316, 340, 345, 377, 399 , ii 23, 102, 206
Riddels, i 186
Riguet, ii 93, 94
Ring, ii 140-142
Ripon, iii 14
Riquier, St , see Chron. Centul.
Rishanger, Chronicle, iii 190, 191, 193, 384, 385
Rites of Durham, see Durham
Ritson, Collection of Metrical Romances, ii 38 , iii 357, 373
Rituale Rothomagense, i 276
Rituale, see also Catalani, Durham
Roach Smith, Collectanea Ant, iii 363

Robert of Jumièges, *Pontifical*, 1. 250
Robson, *Three Early English Romances*, 11. 417
Roc, 1. 316–318
Rocca, *Scholia*, 1. 79
—— *Opera*, 1 p xiii, 131
Rochester, *see* Thorpe, Sheppy
Rochet, 1 375, 11 14–16
Rock, *Early Church in Ireland*, 1 219
—— *Hierurgia*, 1 133, 135, 167, 173, 281, 310, 11 8, 111 327, 328
Rogation Days, 111 181, 182, 297, 298, 1v 120
Roger de Hoveden, 1 132, 395, 11 42, 129, 375, 111 36, 37, 230, 233, 309, 310, 368, 1v. 235
—— de Wendover, 1 49, 160; 111 96, 158, 160, 161, 166, 193, 247, 260
—— of Pontigny, 111 243
Rokewode, *see* Archæologia, Painted Chamber, Westminster; Vet Monum
Rome, *see* Giunta, Lateran, Missale, Ordines, Pontificale, Rituale, Sacerdotale, Sacramentary, *Sacr Cærim*
Rood, 1 59, 1v 242–245
Rosario della gloriosa B. V. M., 111 268
Rosary, 111. 262–275
Rosweyd, *De vitis patrum*, 1 50
Rouen, 1 272–276, 11 71, 1v 149 *See* John of Avranches, Rituale, Sacerdotale
Rubricæ Generales Missalis, 1 60, 61, 189, 376
Rud, Thomas, 11 313, 314
Rudborne, T, 111 166
Rue, Abbé de la, 11 227
Ruft, 1 383, 384
Ruinart, Dom, *Ouvrages Posthumes*, 1 346, 347, 11. 124
Rulers of the choir, 11 165–167, 1v 156–160
Rupert of Duyts, 1 74, 75, 184, 268, 389, 11 6, 1v 84, 110
Rutland Papers, 1 124, 395, 11 213, 1v 227

SABELLIS, Cencio de, i 407, 408
Sacerdotale seu Manuale Rothomagense, 1 387
Sacerdotale Romanæ ecclesiæ, 1. 352, 11 p xi, 10, 11
Sacramentary, 1v 19
Sacramentary of Gellone, 11 172
Sacrament. *Gallican*, 11 285
Sacrament *Gelas*, 1 128
Sacram Rom Eccl, 1 34 *See also* Gregory, Grimold, Menard
Sacrar Cærem Rom Eccl, 11 72
Sacrarium, 1v 193, 194
Salisbury Cathedral, 11 36, 174, 111 220 *See* Sarum
Salve Regina, 111 209, 225, 227, 256, 257
Salvius, St., *see* Vita
Salzburg, *Catalogus Episc*, 1 188
Samson, St, *see* Vita
Sandals, 1 327, 11 194–208
Sandini, *Vitæ Pont Rom*, 11. 57
Sandwich, *see* Boys
Sarnelli, *Antica Basilicographia*, 1 150, 167, 11 11, 56, 57, 60
Sarum Breviary, 1 10, 11. 404; 111 113, 207, 208
—— Gradual, 1 p xiii, 48
—— Horæ, 111 114, 209, 240, 261, 264, 265
—— Manual, 11 136, 369, 370, 375, 378, 380, 382, 383, 384, 385, 386, 387, 388, 390, 111 112, 113, 172, 208, 346, 376, 377, 1v 176, 177, 180, 192
—— Missal, *see Missale*, Throckmorton
—— Consuetudinary, 1 1–11; 1v 299
—— Processional, 1 331, 367, 11 5, 30, 37, 292, 293, 378; 111 53, 182, 183, 209
—— Statutes, 1v 255
—— Use, 1v 135–297 *See also* Frere, Maydeston, St. Osmund
Sassi, 1 102
Saussay, du, *Panoplia Sacerdotalis*, 1 269, 276, 277, 371
Scappus *Die Birihis Rubis*, 11. 58
Scollop shell, 111 361, 368

Seal, ıı 141

Sebbı, ıı 255

Sedılıa, i 335; ıı. 104

Selsey, ııı 3

Sens, ı. 263, ii 102

Septuagesıma, ıv. 69, 70

Serarıus, *Opusc.*, ıı 60, 61, ıv 108

Service-books, ıv. 18–30

Sevılle, ı. 328

Shaw, *Dresses and Decoratıons*, ı 110, 263, 341, ıı. 57, 58, 91, 190, 192

Shelf of altar, ı 186, iv. 309

Sheppy, Bıshop, effıgy, ıı 134, 174

Sherborne Abbey Cartularıum, ı. 350, ıı 135

Sherburn Hospıtal, ııı 25, 26

Sherıngton, ııı 103, 105

Shrınes, ııı 292–312, 378–399; ıv 264

Shrove-tıde, ıv. 70–74

Sıcardus, *Mıtrale*, ıı 86, 200

Sıdonıus, Apollınarıs, ı 173

Sıena, *see* Oderıcus

Sıgebald, ıı. 280

Sılvestre, *Paléog Unıverselle*, ıı. 82, 172

Sımeon of Durham, ı 197, 254, 355, ıı. 157, 160, ııı 291, 374

Sımon, Bp of Exeter, ı. 298

—— of Ghent, *Ancıen Rıwle*, ıv 234

Sıngıng Bread, ı 124, 125

Sıxtus IV., ıı 50

Sıxtus V, ı 386

Slındon, Sussex, ıı. 35

Socrates, *Hıst Eccl*, ı. 115

Sod, ı. 158, 159

Sommerard, De, ı. 185

Soul-shot, ııı 2, 21–33

Sozomen, *Hıst. Eccl*, ı 115

Sparke, *Hıst Anglıc Scrıpt*, ı. 203, 301, 334, 341, 350, 352, 359

Sparrow-Sımpson, *Regıstrum*, ı 375; ıı 38, 42, 44, 55, 70, 369, 370, 391; ııı 388, ıv 153

Spelman, *Concılıa*, ı 374; ııı 303

Spoon, ı. 126

Sporley, ııı. 75, 81, 82, 84

Staff of bıshops, ıı. 149–178

—— of Rulers, ıı 23, 40, 164–167

Stanbury, Bp, ı. 397, 398

Stanford-ın-the-Vale, *see* Inventory

Steeple Aston, i 185

Stephen, St, Day, ıv 66, 249

—— of Autun, *De Sacr Altarıs*, ı 75, 96, 268.

—— of Orleans, ıı 9

—— of Tournay, *Epıst.*, ıı 154

—— Pope, ı 51

Stıll days, ıv 98

Stockıng, ıı. 204–208

Stodely brass, ı 401

Stoke by Clare, ıı 46, 52

Stole, ı 311, 312, 337–343

Stowe, *Survey of London*, ıı 59, 323, 325, 326, 327, 328, 333, 334, 340, 356, 357, 379, 391, 417, ııı 27, 34, 110, 231

—— *Annals*, ııı 90, 328

Stratford, Abp, effıgy, ıı. 121

Strete brass, ıı. 53

Strutt, J, ıı 203

Stubbs, Th, *Actus Pontıf*, ıı. 129, 222, ıv 274

Subcıngulum, ı 380, 402–409

Subtıle, ı 316, 327

Subucula, ı 374, 375; ıı 13, 14

Sudarıum, ı 336

Super altar, ı 181, 194–209

Superhumerale, ıı 131 *See* Amıce

Surıus, *Vıtæ Patrum*, ı 34, 49; ıı. 142, 147, 250; ııı 242

Surplıce, ı 285, 357, 375, ıı 1–14

Sursum Corda, ı 136

Sutton Coldfield Church, ı 266

Swallowclıffe Church, ı. 194

Swapham, R, *Cœnob Burg Hıst*, ı 203, 301, 350, 352

Swınbroke, *see* Baker

Swındon, *Hıst. of Gt Yarmouth*, ıı 323, 372, 416; ııı. 80, 81, 110; ıv 278

Swınfield, John de, ıı 55

Swıthın, St, *see* Wınchester

Symmachus, Pope, ı 308

Synodus Castellana, i 387
—— Collensis, 1 386, 387
—— Coloniensis, 1 387
—— Exoniensis, 1 55; 11 201;
  111 21, 1v 160, 187, 188
—— Florentina, 1 387
—— Imolensis, 1 378
—— Leodiensis, 1 337, 338, 376
—— Mediolanensis, 1. 273, 368,
  373, 386
—— Mertonensis, 1v 165, 188
—— Placentina, 1 386
—— Sodorensis, 1 122, 127
—— Torcellana, 1 387
—— Veneta, 1 386
—— Venusina, 1 387
—— Wormiens, 11 60
Syon cope, 11. 26, 35, 229, now
  at the South Kensington
  Museum
—— Martiloge, 111 39, 40, 75
—— Monastery, 11 258

TABERNACLE, 1v 238, 241, 242
Tabula, see Frontal, Waxbrede
Tailors' Gild, Salisbury, MS
  Register, 11 339
Tassell, 1 323, 11 24-29
Tau, 1 88
Te Deum, 1v 142
Templars, 11 27, 111 369-373
Tena, 11 54
Tenebræ, 1v 82-84, 99, 144, 270-
  272
Tertullian, Adıers Prax, 1 27
Testamenta Eborac, 1 126, 187,
  202, 11 302; 111 21, 22, 26,
  27, 30, 35, 36, 44, 50, 52,
  80, 87, 89, 93, 172, 237, 253,
  254, 268, 1v 145, 166
Testamenta Vetera, 1 126, 203,
  11 10, 138, 141, 215, 111 21,
  22, 26-28, 41-43. 48, 49, 51,
  57, 70-76. 79, 106-110, 221,
  229, 242, 243. 252, 272, 323,
  324, 336
Text, 1 222-224, 236, 241, 242,
  249, 265, 11 81, 1v. 35-37,
  190, 220-223
Theodore, Cap, 1 107, 11 281
—— Liber Pœnit, 1 15, 25, 33, 109,
  112, 118, 119, 164, 171, 212,

314, 11 258; 111 156, 294,
  300, 1v 52, 72, 73, 77, 122,
  125, 130, 208, 299
Theodoret, 111 381, 382
Theodoric, Vita S Margaretæ, see
  Vita
Theodulf, Capit, 1 138
—— Carmina, 1 310; 11. 77, 205
Thomas Aquinas, St, 1 405; 11
  143, 144
Thomas of Canterbury, St, 1 5,
  6, 263, 264, 271, 11 91, 120
  129, 140, 188-190, 111 348-
  354 See Vita
Thomas, Bp Lincoln, Holsome
  and Catholyke Doctrine, 1
  368, 393
Thomasius, Sacram Rom Ecc., i.
  34, 79, 1v 26
Thorn, W, Chron, ii 53; 111 48
Thornton Romances, 111 282
Thorpe, Ancient Laus, 1 15, 20,
  21, 22, 25, 61, 107, 108, 109,
  111, 112, 113, 118, 119, 120,
  121, 124, 134, 135, 136, 138,
  139, 142, 144, 165, 171, 181,
  182, 212, 213, 251, 309, 314,
  374, 11 3, 66, 244, 254, 258,
  261, 281, 319, 320, 323, 365,
  366, 386, 389, 111 1, 7, 120,
  121, 134, 135. 143, 154, 227,
  259, 260, 294, 298, 300, 302,
  306, 358, 1v 1, 2, 3, 6, 7, 17,
  18, 21, 33, 37, 38, 49, 50, 52,
  71-77, 91, 120-126, 130,
  208, 217, 219
—— Registrum Roffense, 1 187,
  189, 336, 351, 355, 357, 367,
  381, 382, 401, 11 27, 29, 36,
  87, 165, 111 50, 58, 66, 1v
  134, 233, 238
—— Works, see Ælfric
Throckmorton cope, 11 29, 30,
  35
—— Missal, 1 344; 11 17, 75
Thurible, hanging, 1 162
Tiara, 1 393, 11 99-101
Tideswell Church, 111 31
Tierce, 1v 8, 9
Tiraboschi, Storia della Lett Ital,
  1 31, 231
Toga, 11 107-111

Tombs, iii 44–57
Tonge Church, iii 40, 214
Tonsure, i 144–146; ii 76
Topogr Hiberniœ, ii 263
Torel, W., iii 37, 330, 331
Toul, i 296
Toulmin Smith, *York Mystery
    Plays*, ii 347
Tours, iv 149
Transubstantiation, i   18–56,
    76–106
Trental, ii 259–261
Treves, i 199
Triangles, ii 36–38
Trindle, iii 194, 342–344
Trinity Coll, Camb, MSS, iii
    282, 283
—— Hall, Camb, MS, iii 316
Troper, iv. 22–31, 246
Tunicle, i 315–328
Tunna, ii 243
Turketul, i 251, 252
Twysden, *Hist Anglic Script*, i
    10, 180, 197, ii 4, 8, 129,
    221, iii 48, 75, 95, 96, 99,
    138, 246, 305, 360, 361, iv
    186, 217, 242–245

Udalric, St., i 121, ii 6, iv
    110, 111
Ughelli, *Italia Sacra*, ii 63, 191
Ultan, i 225
Unction of the dying, ii 365–370
Upcheriny of the messe, the, i 56
Urswick, Christopher, brass, ii
    55, 72
Utterson, *Early Popular Poetry*,
    iii 169, 358, 359, 375

Vallicella, i 231
Valor Eccl, iii 24, 30–33, 40, 71,
    82–85, 92, 105, 108, 111,
    112, 213, 223, 232, 341
Vandrille, St, *see* Vita
Vasor, i 307
Vatar, *Des Processions de l'Eglise*,
    ii 61, 62
Veil in Church, i 36, iii 81;
    iv 50, 257–262
—— Chalice, i 333, iv 225
—— Humeral, i 329–334, iv
    218, 225

Venantius, St, *see* Vita
Venice, ii 56
Venitare, iv 207
Vercelli, i p xiii, i 110, 231
Verger, ii 39
Vergil, Polydore, ii 59, 347;
    iii 264, 268, 270
Vernicle, iii 361
Vesey, Bp, brass, i 266
Vesting prayers, i 403–405
Vetusta Monumenta, ii 82, 91,
    315, 320, 394, 416, 417
Viaticum, i 107–109, ii 368
    and *ff*
Vigil of a knight, i 159
Vigilius, Pope, ii 113
Vita—
  Benedict III, i 211, 348
  Gaufrid, ii 28
  Harold, i 163, 199, 297
  St Anselm, iii 292
  St Augustine, Cant, i 202;
    ii 228
  St Benedict Biscop, i 149,
    247, iv 15, 16
  St Birinus, i 34, 407, 408,
    ii 142, 147, 250
  St Bonitus, i 259
  St Brandon, iv 166
  St Burchard, ii 154
  St Cœsarius Arelat, i 116,
    258, 308, ii 111, 150, 184,
    214
  St Ceolfrid (Bede), i 230, ii.
    185, 389, iv. 299
  St. Columba (Adamnan), i.
    220, 235, 237
  St Cuthbert, i. 65, 112, 136,
    144, 253, 373, ii 77, 195,
    241, 242, 243, 249, 253, 278;
    iii 94, 166, 176, 196, 197,
    227, 299, 306, 319, 321, 339,
    343, 346, 355, 356, 378, 385,
    389, 390, 398, 410, iv 40,
    49, 163, 166, 167, 311
  St Dionysius, ii 151; iii. 293
  St Dunstan, i 19, 49, 107,
    296, ii 223, iii 119, 126,
    145, 146, 344, iv 16, 37,
    43, 65, 172, 220
  St Edward Confessor (Aelred),
    ii. 160–162, iii 344

Vita (*continued*)—
St. Elphege, ii. 82, 147 ; iii. 292 ; iv. 34
St. Etheldreda, i. 248, 249, 381 ; ii. 250, 251, 254 ; iii. 149, 194, 196, 292, 293, 295, 382, 383 ; iv. 52
St. Ethelwold, ii. 368, 390
St. Gall, ii. 152
St. Godric, i. 49 ; iii. 173, 174, 190, 192, 193, 196, 227, 228, 260, 268, 342, 345, 377 ; iv. 170, 172, 177, 243
St. Guthlac, i. 16 ; iii. 123, 128, 292, 337, 406, 414, 415 ; iv. 128, 129
St. Hugh of Lincoln, i. 49 ; iv. 186
St. Hugh, Abbot of Cluny, ii. 23, 223
St. John of Beverley, iii. 179, 304, 383, 396
St. Juliana, iii. 138, 139
St. Lebwin (Hucbald), i. 64
St. Lioba, iii. 18, 19, 152
St. Livin, i. 295
St. Margaret of Scotland, i. 241, 249, 253 ; ii. 22, 225, 274, 275 ; iv. 162, 173
St. Martin of Tours, ii. 152
St. Mary, iii. 240, 242
St. Nicetius, i. 258
St. Nicholas, iii. 369, 370
St. Norbert, ii. 18, 19
St. Odo, i. 47
St. Oswald, i. 49 ; iii. 11, 295
St. Oswin, iii. 324, 339, 342, 383, 394, 405, 410
St. Patrick, i. 219
St. Richard of Chichester, iii. 190, 192, 253, 384, 412
St. Salvius, i. 399
St. Samson, ii. 77, 78, 184
St. Swithin, iv. 51, 52. *See* Winchester
St. Thomas of Canterbury, ii. 126, 127, 188, 189, 190, 344, 346 ; iii. 195, 243, 313, 330, 349, 350–352, 375, 384, 411, 412 ; iv. 190, 248
St. Vandrille, i. 121
St. Venantius, i. 69, 173

Vita (*continued*)—
St. Walthen, iii. 311
St. Waltheof, i. 49, 201 ; iv. 148
St. Werburg, iii. 205
St. Wigbert, i. 20
St. Wilfric, ii. 96
St. Wilfrid (Eddius), i. 149, 210, 216 ; ii. 146 ; iii. 4, 5, 122, 129, 295, 400
St. William of York, ii. 54, 55 ; iii. 195, 196, 309, 315, 322, 331, 385
St. Willibrord, i. 199 ; ii. 146
St. Wulstan, i. 402 ; ii. 2, 160–162 ; iv. 16
Vitalis, St., Church at Ravenna, i. 259, 260, 322
Vitriaco, J. de, iii. 369, 371, 372
Voragine, J. de, *Golden Legend*, ii. 188
Votive Masses, i. 62–65 ; iii. 154

Wakefield, iii. 35
Walafridus Strabo, i. 85, 116, 117, 326 ; ii. 152
Waldeby, Abp., i. 287
Walden, T., iii. 409
Walhere, St., i. 326
Waller, *Monumental Brasses*, i. p. xv., xvi. ; ii. p. xi., xii., 47, 54, 160, 171
Walo, Cardinal, i. 110, 231
Walsingham, iii. 37, 48, 52, 185, 242, 310, 311, 333, 334
Waltham Abbey, i. 297. *See* Fuller
Walthen, St., *see* Vita
Waltheof, St., *see* Vita
Walton, *Treatise on Tithes*, ii. 323, 391, 417
Walwin, i. 232
Waneflete, Bp., ii. 202, 206
Wanley, *Librorum vet. Catal.* in Hickes' *Thesaurus*, i. 17, 235 ; ii. 288 ; iii. 9, 130, 139, 143 ; iv. 102, 147
Wardrobe, *Liber Quot. Garderobæ*, ii. 140, 399 ; iii. 192, 232, 334, 388 ; iv. 250, 251, 256, 274
Warren, *see* Leofric Missal

Warton, *Hist Anc Poetry*, III
199, 205
Water, Holy, I 59, IV 125, 126,
208–210
Watson, *see* Thomas, Bp of
Lincoln
Waverley Annals, III 390, 404
Wax image (*see* Effigies) offered,
III 191, 195
—— brede, IV 146–149
—— taper offering, III 191–196
Way, *Promtorium Parvul*, I 185
Wazor, I. 340
Weber, *Metrical Romances*, II 408,
415
Wedding, IV 200–204
Weever, *Funeral Monuments*, II
294, 351; III 29, 46, 47, 51,
53–57, 67–69, 80, 261
Wells Cathedral, I 396, II 36
Wendover, R de, *see* Roger
Wensley brass, I 266, 300, 357,
360
Werburg, St., *see* Vita
Westminster Abbey, I 185, 192,
287, II 174, 390, III 71,
317–320, 324–328, 333, 334
See Painted Chamber, Este-
ney, Eleanor, Sporley
—— M of, *see* Matthew
Wharton, *Anglia Sacra*, I 49, 126,
350; II 2, 23, 31, 127, 189,
190, 191, III 62, 166, 219,
244, 273, 311, 390, IV 243,
275
—— *Hist de Ep et Dec Lond*, II
341, III 34
Whitsunday, IV 293
Whittington Coll Statutes, IV
162, 251
Whytlescye, Walter de, *Cænob
Burg Hist*, I 334, 341, 350,
359
Wigbert, St, *see* Vita
Wikes, *Chron*, III 309
Wilfric, St, *see* Vita
Wilfrid, St, *see* Vita
Wilkins, *Concilia*, I 14, 36, 55,
58, 112, 122, 124, 125, 126,
127, 129, 136, 137, 138, 143,
145, 146, 179, 188, 195, 327,
374, II 8, 19, 49, 50, 52, 54,

67, 96, 97, 99, 163, 164, 199,
201, 205, 246, 291, 292, 345,
371, 372, 373, 374, 378, 379,
383; III 6, 20, 21, 40, 58, 97,
133, 150, 166, 180, 183, 187,
194, 215, 219, 259, 260, 275,
277, 279, 298, 387, 399, 400,
IV 1, 2, 121, 131, 160, 165,
168, 170, 179–189, 193, 198,
202, 213, 214. 226, 235–238,
254, 256, 260, 270
William I, I 296, 297
—— de Bleys, I 124, 126, 179;
II 372
—— de Chambre, II 16, 398,
III 42
—— Bp of Norwich, II 45
—— of Malmesbury, *De Antiq
Glaston Ecc*, I 189, 201, 249,
250, 349
—— *De Vita S Wulstani*, II 2
—— *Gest. Pontif Anglorum*, II
125, 227; III 7, 15, 344, IV
16, 38, 51, 73, 163, 172
—— *Gesta Regum Anglorum*, I 13,
355; II 67, 68, III 138, 291,
301, 311
—— of Poitiers, II 227, 228
—— St, of York, *see* Vita
Willibald, St, I 199
Willibrord, St, *see* Vita
*Wills and Inventories of the Nor-
thern Counties*, I 186, 187,
301, 352, 353, 357, 359, II
25, 139, 141, 180, 210, 230,
231, 397, 398, 404, 407, III
21, 22, 25, 26, 42, 55, 75, 76,
86, 102, 112, 202, IV. 249, 260
Winchelsey, Abp, IV 165
Winchendon, I 401
Winchester Cathedral, Bidding
Prayer, II 288
—— I. 217, 228–230, II 83, 88,
174, 215 *See* Frere, Inven-
tory
—— School, Chapel Exp, II 339,
IV. 148 *See* Woodloke
Windsor, Register, I 126, 201,
360, 362, 383, 401, II. 6, 7,
33, 40, 165, 167, 215
—— Register of St George's
Chapel, III 221

Windsor Chapel, III 43
Wine, Eucharistic, 1. 125-128
Winwaloe, St, 1 348
Wolstan (monk of Winchester),
   1 156, 173, 180, II 368, 390,
   IV 51, 52
Woltelsbach, Conrad of, *Chron
   Mogunt*, 1 163, 202
Woodloke, Bp, II 373, 374
Worcester Cathedral, II 96, 97,
   163, 164 *See* Giffard, Green
—— Abbey, *Privilegia Concessa*,
   II 96, 97, 163, 164
Wordsworth, *Chr Direct Sac*,
   1 10
—— *Linc Cath Stat*, 1 10
—— *Salisbury Processions and
   Ceremonies*, 1 3, 125, 203,
   241, 302, 333, 350, 382, 400;
   II 30, 35, 40, 103, 135, 156,
   167, 197, 206, 212, 345, III
   50, 332, IV 233, 236, 260,
   293
Wulstan St, *see* Vita
Wynkyn de Worde, 1 396, II
   188, 395

Wynkyn de Worde, *Golden Legend*, III 161, 167-169, 171,
   183, 184, 186, 242, 283, 313,
   IV 252

YEPEZ, *Coronica General*, II 283
Yew trees, II. 261
York Bidding Prayer, II. 299–
   301
—— Manual, II. 299-302, 378,
   III 113, 172, 209, 346, 376,
   377
—— Memoirs of, II 276, 277
—— Minster, 1 200, 217, 225-
   228, II 36, 174, III 331,
   332. *See* Pontif Ebor.,
   Toulmin Smith, Stubbs,
   Vita, William
—— Minster, MS Gospels, II
   289, 290 *See also* Inventory
—— Missal, IV. 184, 196, 204,
   262, 270, 277, 281, 282,
   285

ZACCARIA, *Biblioth Ritualis*, 1. 85
Zacharias, Pope, 1. 66

THE END

Printed by BALLANTYNE, HANSON & Co
Edinburgh & London

Ingram Content Group UK Ltd.
Milton Keynes UK
UKHW021054300323
419409UK00005B/219